CONTROL TOWERS

The development of the Control Tower
on RAF Stations in the U.K.

by Paul Francis

Published 1993 by
Airfield Research Publishing
9 Milton Road
Ware, Herts SG12 0QA

ISBN No. 0 9521847 0 2

Cover Photograph: Control Tower built
above General Service Shed annexe,
Kenley. Photo: Graham Crisp

Typesetting and design by:
West 4 Printers Ltd.,
8 Essex Place, London W4 5UT

Printed by:
Russell Press
Radford Mill, Norton Street
Nottingham NG7 3HN

LIST OF CONTENTS

The subject of airfield architecture has attracted a great deal of interest particularly the control tower, which is probably the most interesting building for the airfield historian.

Growth in membership of the Airfield Research Group shows that there is a wide general interest in the subject and a lot of enthusiasm for the study of surviving buildings. With this in mind I began in 1990 to collect material for a book on airfield architecture. Through collating this information on buildings, it soon became apparent that there was enough material on control towers alone. The preparation of this book was the result.

The first part briefly describes the function and procedure of the control tower, the development of air traffic control, including pre-war civilian air traffic control, air traffic signals and personal experiences of people who were stationed in the control tower.

The main part is devoted to the identification of the various types, beginning with the watch office of the early 1920s to the modern control towers built in the late 1950s and 1960s. There are details of modifications carried out on watch offices and control towers over the period of their use and a description of each type supplemented by photographs, scale plans and line drawings showing the front elevation. All drawings of buildings including plans and elevations are to a scale of two millimeters to one foot (2mm = 1ft). Where known, the original drawing numbers are used in table form with a brief description of each drawing. The title "watch office" is given to those buildings that were designed before 1944 and were known as such on the original drawings. References to left and right are correct when viewing from the rear (i.e. inside with your back to the rear wall).

The last part describes landing aids and equipment and finally the development of airfield lighting.

It must be appreciated that a book such as this owes much to original drawings and site plans, the main source of which is the RAF Museum. Anyone who has studied airfield site plans in any detail will know that quite often the drawing numbers given are incorrect; two examples that spring to mind concerning the watch office are Bardney and Westhampnett. Furthermore, sometimes only one drawing number is given for a particular building and this may not be the original but a modification carried out late in the war when the site plan was drawn. It can be seen therefore that an unsuspecting researcher may think he has discovered a rare or unusual building type, when in fact all he has found is a deviation drawing. Of course the reverse can also be true. For example, the watch office with operations room, etc., is a building that was continually modified over the course of the war. The site plan (assuming the building has been demolished) may only show the original drawing number which could be a 1940 drawing for a type "A" building. Does this mean that the building was never modified, or is it a simple case of not all the relevant drawing numbers being listed – and if so which ones?

The only way to be sure, unless it is possible to get access to all the relevant drawings is to carry out field work in the hope that this will establish the correct identity of the building. Of course it is not always possible to do this if the building is on MoD property, or worse – demolished. In situations like this photographs are the only answer, assuming that you can find one.

These are just a few of the problems of writing about airfield architecture and until the missing building drawings and photographs are all located and understood some of the facts contained within this book cannot be proven.

Acknowledgements.

A book such as this inevitably owes a large debt to friends and colleagues of the Airfield Research Group and I have been overwhelmed by the generous help given by many people; in particular I would like to thank Des Cook, Denis Corley, Graham Crisp, Fred Cubberley, Peter Davis, Aldon Ferguson, Mick Fisher, Guy Jefferson, Brian Martin, Norman Parker, Ian Reid, Gordon Samuels, Ian Shaw, Julian Temple, John Hamlin for proof-reading the manuscript, the staff at RAF Swinderby, RAF West Raynham, Major Jonathan Borthwick, Ken Hunter of the RAF Museum Hendon, Rover Group, and British Aerospace Warton.

To everyone who has helped and encouraged me, I owe a great deal of thanks and my apologies go to anyone who I have omitted.

Finally, nothing would have been possible if was not for Joan Scrivener of West 4 Printers who produced all the art work and typing. For her hours of patient work I am indebted.

Paul Francis, May 1993.

When commercial air transport became a reality shortly after the 1914-18 war, services were very few and air speeds were low. Under these conditions, the risk of collision between two aircraft was virtually non-existent.

As public confidence in air transport increased so did the number of services, until it became apparent that some sort of air traffic control was necessary. In 1927 the Government sponsored a Marconi transmitter at Mitcham Common, about two miles from Croydon airport (London Airport).

In September 1931, to assist pilots flying in the UK, the Automobile Association established a wireless station at Heston. Comprehensive weather reports were broadcast with equipment supplied by Standard Telephones and Cables Ltd. Transmission was just below the Croydon wavelength (900m) at 833m and the station broadcast at 30 minutes past the hour, seven days a week.

In 1932, a wireless school was set up by Air Service Training Ltd at Hamble for future ground and air wireless operators. The course lasted six months, and students were taught to read Morse code at 20 words per minute, commercial wireless procedure and the "Q" code, of which 50 of the signals were to be known by heart. At the end of the course the student gained his wireless licence.

On 19th November 1933 the Croydon Controlled Zone came into being, one of several zones surrounding certain airports having Air Ministry Control (Area Stations) throughout the UK. Aircraft were not permitted to enter the Controlled Zone during conditions of poor visibility (QBI) without first obtaining permission from the control tower. The object was to ensure that only one aircraft at a time would be in the Controlled Zone, thus eliminating any possibility of a collision.

Parliament set up the Maybury Committee in July 1935, chaired by Brigadier General Sir Henry P. Maybury, which stated:

i) We recommend freedom of flight for aircraft without radio facilities. A meteorological organisation and a comprehensive air traffic control organisation adequate to secure the safety and regularity of air communications should be provided, maintained and operated by the Government.

ii) We recommend that aerodrome proprietors should be responsible for providing the necessary equipment, other than radio, to enable their aerodromes to be used in safety under conditions of poor visibility.

The country was divided into Communications Areas, each with its central control, and these were further reduced into Controlled Zones to control aircraft and maintain wireless communication. There were four main areas, those of Croydon, Portsmouth, Heston and Manchester West with Ronaldsway. Any aeroplane in a Communications Area used the appropriate wavelength adopted for the area. For Croydon Control the wavelength of 333 Kc/s was used for wireless telegraphy or 363 Kc/s for wireless telephony. Heston and Portsmouth used 348 Kc/s and Manchester Control 348 Kc/s and 363 Kc/s. By May 1936 there were three separate Marconi radio

Communication areas and Controlled Zones (shaded) as at January 1937. Croydon was mainly concerned with continental traffic. Gatwick was under Heston's control.

sets at Croydon, all with their radio transmitters at Mitcham, one of which was used exclusively for dealing with each aircraft as it was given permission to approach the airport in QBI conditions. A pilot could, due to poor visibility, check on his dead-reckoning and by request bearings could be taken.

A chart was used to plot bearings and "fixes" with the help of lengths of thread which emerged from the position occupied by the Pulham, Lympne and Croydon D/F stations. Both Pulham and Lympne, on request, obtained a bearing of an aircraft and transmitted it to Croydon, where its position was plotted as the point of bearing intersection which was quite often in the shape of a triangle known as a "cocked hat". This only took two minutes to complete and could be obtained at regular intervals in order to bring the aircraft to the airport.

In the main control room at Croydon there was a large map of the London-Continent area on which the officer in charge kept track of all aircraft within the Croydon area by means of pins with identification flags, the direction of the flag showing that the aircraft was either out-bound or in-bound. The positions of the flags were simply up-dated with each communication with the pilot.

Teleprinters and telephones were used for inter-departmental and messages to other airports. Pneumatic tubes (Lamson tubes) were used for messages within different rooms of the tower on either written or teleprinted slips.

A pilot wishing to depart obtained the latest meteorological information and gave details of his intended route and destination. In a Controlled Zone such as Croydon he reported to the Control Officer and received flying directions. When his aircraft was ready for take-off, he waited outside the landing area until he was given permission to taxi. Permission was granted at Croydon by displaying a green panel showing an appropriate letter belonging to the airline company or an X for other aircraft. At Heston an intermittent white light was flashed from the tower. When the pilot reached the take-off point he waited for a further signal and permission was granted to take off by a steady white light from a fixed Aldis lamp on the control tower gallery, the "lookout" man having checked that the airfield was clear.

Several more D/F stations came on-line in 1936 so that, for example, a pilot flying between Jersey and Southampton would, after entering the Portsmouth area, obtain bearings from and report to the Portsmouth Station until told to communicate with Southampton.

The international "Q" code was devised for communication between ground wireless stations and aircraft. Each item in the code has three letters, commencing with the letter "Q" from which it derives its name. The object was to keep communication between ground and air to a minimum.

A Selection of the "Q" Code (AP1529) 1937

QAA(5)	–	Estimated arrival (5 minutes)
QAL	–	Going to land
QAZ	–	Flying in a storm
QBE	–	Winding in my trailing aerial
QBF	–	Flying in cloud
QBG	–	Flying above cloud
QBH	–	Flying below cloud
QDM	–	What is my bearing?
QDT	–	Flying in clear visibility
QDV	–	Bad visibility
QFM	–	Fly at .... height
QFX	–	I intend to work on my fixed aerial only
QGK	–	I have left the Controlled Zone
QGL	–	You can enter the Controlled Zone
QGM	–	You cannot enter the Controlled Zone
QGN	–	May I land?
QGO	–	You cannot land
QGP	–	What is my turn for landing?
QGQ	–	Wait for my instructions
QRD	–	I am flying from ....
QRN	–	I am troubled by atmospherics
QTF	–	What is my position?
QTH	–	My position is ....
QTI	–	Track

Call Signs at Ground Stations 1937

In conjunction with the Q code, ground stations (airports) were known by a three letter code beginning with the letter "G". They were as follows:

Station	Call Sign	Description
Birmingham	GEX	Subsidiary Station
Belfast Harbour	GEV	Area Station
Bristol	GJB	Area Station
Croydon	GED	Area Station
Doncaster	GJI	Subsidiary Station
Guernsey	GVE	Subsidiary Station
Heston	GEU	Area Station
Hull	GEB	Area Station
Inverness	GJH	Area Station
Jersey	GVC	Area Station
Kirkwall	GJC	Area Station
Lympne	GEG	Collaborating with Croydon Area
Manchester (Barton)	GEM	Area Station
Ringway	GFR	Subsidiary Station
Newcastle	GJK	Area Station
Newtonards	GET	Subsidiary Station
Perth	GJJ	Collaborating with Renfrew Area
Portsmouth	GEN	Area Station
Pulham (D/F station)	GEP	Collaborating with Croydon Area
Renfrew	GER	Area Station
Ronaldsway	GJE	Collaborating with Manchester West
Shoreham	GFH	Subsidiary Station
Sollas	GJM	Area Station
Southampton	GJD	Subsidiary Station
Sumburgh	GJF	Area Station
Yeadon	GJG	Subsidiary Station

Markings on Civil Aerodromes in the 1930s

Licensed airfields were usually marked with a white circle in the centre of the landing area. The circle was flush with the aerodrome surface and had an overall diameter of 100ft with a band width of 5ft. If displayed, the name of the aerodrome was shown due south of the circle and 100ft distant from it, in bold letters, 20ft long, 16ft wide and each letter spaced 16ft apart. The line of the lettering would run from east to west so that it could be read by an observer looking northwards, and the circle and letters were of either chalk or concrete painted white to show up well against the natural colouring of the aerodrome surface.

Two types of boundary markers were used:

1. An elevated type, triangular in section, seven feet long, standing up to 3ft from the ground, usually painted white with a red band in the centre.

2. A type flush with the ground, 20ft long and three feet wide, painted white.

Blind Approach: The Lorenz system

The greatest difficulty a pilot had to contend with when approaching an aerodrome was landing in fog. Navigational skill and D/F bearings could bring him over the top of the airfield but if fog obscured the ground his most difficult task was still ahead.

To help with landings under these conditions a system of directional wireless was developed by Lorenz AG of Stuttgart, Germany and was known as the Lorenz system. The first installation was at Tempelhof, Berlin, in 1934/5 and the first UK airfield to use the system was Heston in 1936.

The Lorenz system was based on the phenomenon associated with ultra short waves following a straight line. Ground equipment consisted of three ultra short-wave transmitters, while the aircraft carried two extra ultra short-wave receivers in addition to the standard wireless set for direct communication with the control tower.

In principle, when an aircraft was on the best line of approach, a continuous note was heard by the pilot in his headphones, but a deviation from his path was indicated by the signals changing to either dots or dashes depending on which side of the path he wandered. The zones of dots and dashes were spread progressively from the beacon at an angle of 60 degrees from the correct approach line and could be heard up to 15 miles away at 1,500ft. About eight minutes were needed for the approach, which would begin about 12 miles out on entering the zone of dots and dashes. The final glide was started when the aircraft arrived over the first marker beacon at about 1,000ft and roughly two miles from the airfield.

As an additional aid to the pilot a visual indicator instrument was provided in the cockpit. When the aircraft was approaching the airfield on the correct landing path, a continuous line of dots and dashes was indicated; if the pilot strayed either side the continuous line was replaced with either dots or dashes.

Main Beacon Aerial

The aerial of the main beacon took the form of two vertical rods, each only a few feet in length and mounted vertically end to end. On either side of this aerial, at a distance of ten feet was a dummy aerial (reflectors), a very important feature of this system. They enabled the ultra short-wave field to be deformed to an accurate and controlled extent, resulting in a series of signals indicating to the pilot whether his flight path was correct.

Marker Beacons

The outer and inner marker beacons were necessary to assist the pilot approaching the airfield and indicated to him his exact position so that when the outer marker was passed, low pitch signals at the rate of two per second were superimposed upon the signals of the main beacon. When the inner marker beacon was passed, signals of a high pitch at the rate of six per second were heard.

Beacons were located well away from any other buildings or obstructions and were therefore a considerable distance from the control tower. As a result, the beacons were operated by remote control. If the beacons failed an alarm was sounded warning the Control Officer of a fault. One of the difficulties when installing a Lorenz system was to eliminate any interference from external objects. Both Croydon and Heston experienced considerable interference. At Croydon for example, it was the spire on Wallington church which had the effect of producing a distinct kink in the beam, while at Heston a large hangar badly affected it.

Standard Telephones and Cables had the British rights and the system became known at RAF Stations as Standard Beam Approach (SBA) and in Germany it was further developed as Knickebein (Bent Leg), an aid to blind bombing used during the Battle of Britain.

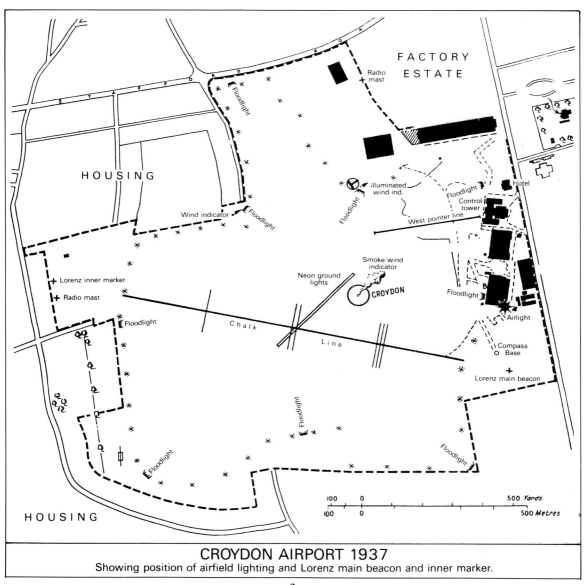

CROYDON AIRPORT 1937
Showing position of airfield lighting and Lorenz main beacon and inner marker.

Despite civil traffic control being developed between the wars, on military airfields air traffic control was practically non-existent. It was limited to the Duty Pilot, whose essential equipment consisted of only a note-book, a quantity of pyrotechnics and, on occasion, an exceptional refinement in the form of a radio. A report issued by Air Commodore Leckie in 1937 recommended that the "Watch Hut" be redesigned and enlarged, manned by an officer with the authority to direct aircraft in the air, prevent departure if weather became unfavourable and to redirect an aircraft if an airfield became congested.

In December 1937 the AOC-in-C Bomber Command suggested the opening of Military Area Control Centres to control en-route traffic and in January 1938 the responsibility for organisation and administration was vested in Bomber Command. The RAF selected 12 officers for air traffic control duties and they were posted to Uxbridge for a short training course and then to Croydon airport for practical experience. Having completed their training the officers, now called Flying Control Officers, were paired off to set up Regional Control Organizations and posted to six airfields selected for their strategic importance: Abingdon, Boscombe Down, Leuchars, Linton-on-Ouse, Mildenhall and Waddington.

During the early part of the war it became necessary to expand control over aircraft at RAF stations and this became even more apparent as the bomber offensive gathered momentum. As pilots could not be spared, large numbers of civil Controllers were drafted. This was recognised by the Air Ministry as being a specialist job and selected officers in the Special Duties branch of the service were posted in May 1941 to form the new Regional Control School at Brasenose College, Oxford. Some 40 Controllers a month graduated from the school, which transferred to Watchfield at the end of 1941 and became known as the Flying Control School. It was administered by the RAF, but manned by civilian staff of Air Service Training Ltd. In 1946 the school's name was changed to School of Air Traffic Control and remained so until the unit was combined with the Central Navigation School at Shawbury in February 1950 to form the Central Navigation and Control School. At this time the station was under the command of Group Captain B.T.R. Roberts with Sq/Ldr. J.A. Jarvis in charge of the School.

Mainly ex-RAF aircrew pilots and navigators made up the bulk of the RAF intake, but there were also candidates from overseas countries. The course for Flying Control Officers at Shawbury in 1951 took 12 weeks to complete, and normally there were two courses of 33 students at any one time. For the first two weeks the students gained knowledge in the lecture rooms and the following three weeks were spent in synthetic control exercises in mock control rooms. In the next five weeks the pupils carried out real and synthetic exercises and the remaining two weeks were taken up with revision and examination.

Synthetic and "Live" Training

The second phase of the course, the Synthetic Control exercise, enabled the pupil to sit at the control desk in a mock control room. The desk was an exact working replica of a typical control desk found in any control tower of the period. The pupil could, for example, call Group HQ, speak to the Airfield Controller, talk to and receive messages from pilots of aircraft within the circuit, give taxi-ing instructions to aircraft on the ground and receive phone messages - all made possible by instructors in a sound proof room. Each session was very intense and lasted up to four hours.

In a duplicated control room inside the control tower (at the top of the tower in the Chief Instructor's Block) QGH (Controlled Descent Through Cloud) exercises were practiced "live" with Anson Mk T.21s and Wellington T.10s, provided by the Blind Flying School. The pilot carried out the Controller's instructions to bring the aircraft down through cloud so that he was in line with the centre of the runway ahead by means of D/F bearings and VHF homings. GCA and ILS were included in the curriculum when the Ground Controlled Approach (GCA) School moved from Wyton on March 15th 1953. Special facilities were provided to cover the numerous and complex flying procedures with which a Flying Control Officer could be faced. The primary objective was to enable him to take a solo watch at RAF or civil airfields within a month of completing his training.

As part of the special equipment available in 1951 there were two synthetic control rooms, an R/T practice room, an equipment demonstration room complete with a model of an airfield used for practice in flare path layout, and a radar demonstration section. Link trainers manned by pupils provided practice in let-down, homing and stacking procedures and in the use of BABS. Voice-recording equipment was used to improve the pupils' style of speech over the R/T. In addition, radio compass, Gee Mk II, the radar altimeter, Loran, M25, Rebecca Type IV, Eureka, BABS Type 31 used in conjunction with a normal Link trainer, simulated (SBA) let-downs and homings using cathode-ray D/F and Eureka beacons were all practised. The Controller also had to have a sound knowledge of airfield lighting equipment, meteorology, navigation and administration, watch-keeping duties and aircraft marshalling.

Airfield Controllers

Airfield Controllers were also trained at Shawbury, on a course which in 1951 lasted three weeks. This course was intensive and pupils learned about flare-paths, lighting systems, visual signals, pyrotechnics, visual and radio landing aids, aircraft recognition and identification, emergency and distress action and signalling as part of their training. They would visit the airfield caravan (a black and white chequered van at the commencement of the runway) for practical experience.

The Air Traffic Control Examination Board was formed in January 1955 to ensure that the standards of Air Traffic Controllers were maintained in all aspects of the job.

By 1958, due to the pressure of ATC courses utilising GCA and other radar navigational aids, it was decided to re-activate the airfields at Sleap and High Ercall. Cathode-ray direction finding (CRDF) equipment and a GCA caravan were installed for training. However, by 1960 High Ercall had closed, but Sleap continued as a satellite until 1964.

The school changed its name to the Central Air Traffic Control School on February 11th 1963 at the time when the Navigation Wing moved to Manby.

Boscombe Down and Regional Control 1938–1942

In September 1938, F/Lts. Bell and Bullmore were posted to Boscombe Down to set up a Regional Control Unit on the airfield. At this time the watch office [BN 307/A36 (419/29)] was a small detached bungalow sited half way along the line of original GS hangars. Here, with the aid of four civilian clerks, airmen and W/T equipment they set up their office.

The new watch office was only available as a service between the hours of 0900 and 1700 daily and only until mid-day on Wednesday, when the sports afternoon assumed a greater importance. One Controller did this shift with a civilian clerk and the other worked from 0900hrs on Thursday until noon on Saturday. They were responsible to the Air Ministry, which also employed the civilian clerks. Administration control was by Bomber Command, but they were on the strength of the Director of Navigation, attached to Boscombe Down. The war was soon to sort out all these anomalies as Regional Control became a normal function of a service aerodrome.

At the beginning of the war flying control became a 24 hour requirement which needed extra staff and several of the civilian clerks became Flying Control Officers in their own right after Sq/Ldr. Bullmore ran a couple of month-long courses.

One night in February 1941 when there was no flying due to freezing weather, Sq/Ldr. Bullmore heard an aeroplane to the south and mentioned this to his Control Clerk, Bert Rowden, who informed him that all Commands had cancelled night flying. At 2230 hours, the Southampton Police telephoned to say that an aircraft had been circling the town for over two hours. They thought that all was not well as it kept shutting off its engines as if to land, opening them up again when it entered the fog bank. Eventually, after much frantic telephoning, it was discovered that a Beaufort was long overdue at its base, St. Eval.

Shortly afterwards the Royal Observer Corps operations room at Winchester telephoned to say that an aeroplane, thought to be a Beaufort, had been on their plotting table for some time and seemed to be wandering aimlessly about the sky. Was there anything that Boscombe Down could do to help it? With the airfield fog-bound and all others similarly affected, not much could be done to land the aircraft safely.

By this time the Beaufort was circling the Needles off the Isle of Wight, but still not making use of the radio. Suddenly a thought occurred to Sq/Ldr. Bullmore: if an air-sea rescue launch could be despatched with a supply of signal rockets, perhaps the crew would realise that something was being done to help them. Hurried arrangements were made with RAF Calshot from which a launch was despatched to the Needles. Meanwhile the local ROC reported that they could see rockets being fired and that the Beaufort was circling the area. Finally, the ROC observers reported a crash out to sea and men shouting. An approximate position was given and was telephoned to Calshot, who directed the launch to the spot by radio to rescue the crew. A most satisfactory night's work that was to have a far reaching effect on the fortunes of RAF aircrew during the rest of the war.

As a result of this rescue, there was a sudden realisation that flying control could satisfy one aspect of flight safety which was peculiar to wartime conditions, that of helping lost or damaged aircraft to not only land safely, but also to find a satisfactory area in which to land.

Boscombe Down's Controller had already established an unofficial link with the ROC's operation room and as a result of the information gained during a visit with F/Lt. George Phillips on 27th January 1941 they built and operated a similar set-up in the new watch office. Here he plotted aircraft that seemed to be lost instead of being on a constant course for home.

A chance meeting during an evening's fishing at Stockbridge with the Chief Controller of the Fighter Command Sector Operations Room led to an invitation to visit Middle Wallop to see what went on. This was a real eye opener, as not only was the Winchester ROC area on display, but also the surrounding groups covering the whole of the south coast. Of course, this source of information was barred to him, as the operations room was for use in the offensive role and although the staff did what they could for lost aircraft it was not very effective through lack of specialised knowledge.

The real breakthrough came, however, during an opportunity to visit No. 10 Fighter Group Headquarters at Rudloe Manor. Since the Beaufort episode off the Isle of Wight, a lost Blenheim had been successfully landed on the race course at Cheltenham after the Home Guard commandeered cars and used their unmasked headlights to illuminate a suitable landing ground. The fact that these arrangements were directed by telephone from the watch office at Boscombe Down made the landing even more remarkable.

These rescue attempts had not gone unnoticed at Group HQ and when an opportunity presented itself, Bullmore grasped it with both hands. He explained that his unofficial link with the ROC at Winchester was enabling him to lay things on in a small way but only the sector operations room, with its operations board covering the whole of southern England up to a line across country through Rugby, could offer the scope required. When the AOC offered the use of his facilities at night, the offer was taken up at once. The Commandant of A & AEE, Air Commodore Sir Ralph Sorley, and Sir Quintin Brand, AOC 10 Group, agreed to let the Controllers give the experiment a try by taking turns to man the night watch at Rudloe.

Eventually, a Whitley which, when challenged, failed to give the colours of the day in reply, was shot down by a Beaufighter from Middle Wallop. The crew bailed out safely, but the aircraft was lost. This situation could have been saved had the Flying Control Officers been involved.

However, this finally persuaded the Air Ministry to try the experiment for three months despite an earlier refusal. The first watch on 22 April 1941 was uneventful, but George Phillips on the third watch received a call from the ROC at Winchester about an apparently lost Anson north of them. He alerted the Searchlight Liaison Officer and asked him to lay on a searchlight homing to Colerne aerodrome. This system consisted of a searchlight beam laid along the ground pointing in the direction of the airfield, where rockets were fired and the flare path lit. The pilot, having left his seat to bail out, was about to jump when he saw the beams and realised that someone was trying to help him. Crawling back to the cockpit, he was able to land the aircraft safely and as he finished his landing run both engines stopped - out of fuel.

In 1941 the standard procedure for an aircraft in distress to obtain searchlight homing was to circle for at least two minutes, fire the combination of coloured lights for the day and send a succession of dots on the navigation lights (later amended to the switching of navigation and downward recognition lights).

Any searchlight detachment seeing these signals, or on the order from Control, would expose the beam horizontally for 30 seconds in the direction of the selected airfield. In order to catch the pilot's attention the beam was elevated to 45 degrees and depressed again three times in succession. Finally the beam was left horizontal for a further 30 seconds.

The whole sequence was repeated until the aircraft flew in the correct direction, when the beam was kept on as a horizontal pointer for two minutes. Bullmore was instrumental in obtaining 1,200 surplus searchlights from Anti Aircraft Command which were supplied to RAF stations to form "canopies" of searchlights at airfields. Another 107 searchlights were installed at ROC posts at locations where there were large gaps between airfields. This scheme was allocated the code name "Sandra".

During these and other rescue operations, the direct telephone lines worked overtime, the ROC operations rooms and posts were used extensively, coastguard stations were alerted, and lighthouses were lit to enable bearings to be taken. The Home Guard, searchlight sites and every aerodrome in the south of England responded with enthusiasm and consequently the tally of aircraft and crews saved mounted nightly.

Although the centre of night flying liaison work in the South West had moved from Boscombe Down to Rudloe Manor, the Controllers carried out their normal work there during the day, travelling to Box each night to cover the vital period when aircraft were returning from operations. Squadron Leader Bullmore, Flight Lt. George Phillips and Pilot Officer Norman Thompson all did their turns.

Sq/Ldr Bullmore went on to establish the role of Flying Control Liaison Officer at 12 Group, Watnall, assisted by P/O Bert Bowden. Norman Thompson took over from Bullmore at Watnall after he went to the Air Ministry in February 1942 to be responsible for establishing FCLO sections in all remaining Groups of Fighter Command.

The original Regional Control cell at Boscombe Down can be said to have made a very important contribution to the development of Air Traffic Control in the early part of the war and was a valuable contribution to the war effort.

Information supplied by Norman Parker

If only I had known the significance of this building at Hawkinge when I photographed it in 1980. It was in fact the Watch office and has since been demolished.

Chapter 3

Air Traffic Procedure 1950

Local Control of Aircraft

Certain operating regulations were necessary to minimise accidents occurring on or in the vicinity of airfields. Examples were taxi-ing; obstructions such as vehicles; collisions between aircraft landing and taking off or in the approach; and breaches of discipline.

The Senior Flying Control Officer was directly responsible to the Station Commander for the local control of aircraft either permanently based on or temporarily using the station. Where permanent flying control staff were not available, Station Commanders simply delegated suitable staff to carry out local control of flying.

Flying Control Officer's (FCO) Duties

Normally in a typical 518/40 type control tower two Flying Control Officers sat at the control desk. One was responsible for aircraft on approach, the other for aircraft in the circuit. The Senior Flying Control Officer, later named Senior Air Traffic Control Officer, was responsible for marking out all bad ground, for controlling the activities of contractors from the point of view of obstructions and for the marking and daily checking of obstructions in cooperation with the works officer, who would obtain daily permission for the continuation of any work on the airfield. All relevant information was kept up to date on a plan of the airfield in the control tower and copies were located at all crew rooms, Airfield Controller's caravan and each dispersal point. Each runway was indicated by its QDM number and the runway in use was indicated by an arrow. Usually an NCO under the FCO's jurisdiction inspected the airfield at least twice daily, one before dusk prior to the commencement of night flying. For this purpose a car or jeep was made available to the flying control staff. The vehicle was also used to tow the runway caravan and fetch meals from the messes for the night duty staff.

The FCO was responsible for ensuring that all obstruction lights were in place and suitably hooded to prevent observation from above, and that aircraft were not parked in line, or within a distance of 200 yards either side of a recognised take-off and landing strip. He would delegate an airman to be stationed at the up-wind end of the runway in use throughout the daylight hours to control aircraft or vehicles moving across the end of the runway. At Thorney Island another airman was stationed inside a caravan positioned on the grass triangle between the intersecting runways, as there was a public road across the airfield to the church and officers' mess at West Thorney. He was equipped with a telephone to the tower, binoculars and a loud hailer to warn anyone near the runway to stay clear in the event of it being used.

The FCO was responsible for the Duty Flight, which looked after the reception and parking of visiting aircraft, the pilot of which had to report to the control tower immediately after taxi-ing the aircraft to the dispersal area. In addition, the FCO was responsible for the supervision of the Airfield Controller.

The FCO would detail the flarepath party to load up a truck with portable lighting equipment kept in the Night Flying Equipment Store (NFE) which included gooseneck flares, money flares, glim lamps and illuminated landing "T". Also on board would be a large "cotton reel" drum of telephone cable which gradually unwound as the lorry progressed along the landing strip and simultaneously distributed the portable lighting. The telephone cable was for communication between the Airfield Controller and the FCO. Where permanent runway and obstruction lighting was installed it could be controlled from the airfield lighting control panel in the control room.

Airfield Controller

The Airfield Controller, originally known as the Aerodrome Control Pilot, was positioned out on the airfield to the left of the downwind end of the runway in use, but not more than 50yds from the edge.

On grass airfields he usually sat inside a portable makeshift windbreak, normally a wooden box with handles and a rooftop astrodome, which could be removed and positioned elsewhere on the airfield depending upon which runway was in use. This was normally sited towards the downwind side of the airfield so that two or more aircraft could land simultaneously to the right of him and so that sufficient space was available on the left to enable an aircraft to take off.

On airfields with hard runways, a special caravan was placed on a concrete hard standing. Unusually, at Crail a small round concrete pill box was used, painted with a chequered pattern of yellow and black squares.

The Airfield Controller was responsible for placing the landing "T" to mark the runway in use. He had the power to refuse permission to land if an aircraft approached with undercarriage retracted, or if there was a danger of a collision. Also, he could refuse to allow an aircraft to leave the marshalling point or to take off if to do so would obstruct an aircraft approaching to land.

Any breaches of flying discipline were to be reported to the FCO including the use of non-standard signals or unusual aircraft movements. The Airfield Controller was also supposed to report any defects of night flying equipment or airfield lighting. He controlled the traffic on the perimeter track in the vicinity of the runway in use and the movement of vehicles requiring to cross the downwind end of the runway.

He was provided with the following:

1. Two signal lamps, one red and one green

2. Verey pistol with red cartridges only

3. Binoculars

4. The letters and colours of the day

5. Direct telephone and/or RT communication with the FCO in the tower

6. Plan of the airfield

7. Landing "T"

Procedure by Day

Taxi-ing and taking off

Pilots established R/T contact with the FCO before leaving dispersal and maintained a listening-out watch. Having left the dispersal they proceeded towards the marshalling point, where they awaited permission from the Airfield Controller to turn onto the runway. Permission was given by an intermittent green signal lamp, refusal by a steady red lamp signal. More care was needed on grass airfields and pilots were required to keep a particularly sharp look-out for aircraft landing. Final permission to take off was given by a steady green lamp signal. An intermittent red signal directed at an aircraft on the runway indicated that the aircraft was to be taxied clear immediately. Pilots could approach to land without permission. Refusal was given by a steady red lamp signal which denoted temporary refusal. An intermittent red lamp signal denoted total refusal. In cases of emergency a red Verey light was fired horizontally.

If a pilot on approach was refused permission to land, he was to open up again and rejoin the circuit unless he considered this procedure to be dangerous, in which case he simply completed his approach to land. Having landed, the pilot taxied at a safe speed to the perimeter track. On a grass airfield, the pilot brought the aircraft to rest and then turned 90 degrees to port. After carrying out cockpit drill the pilot made sure by visual observation that his aircraft would not cut across the path of another one that was landing or taking off. He then taxied to the airfield perimeter. On grass FTS airfields pilots taxied directly down wind after having received an intermittent green lamp signal from the Airfield Controller.

The rules for control by day did not apply to fighter aircraft under "scramble" conditions. Under these conditions the Flying Control Officer prohibited all movements of non-operational aircraft until the airfield was clear.

Procedure by Night

A blackboard in the control tower contained the following details of the airfield and was consulted by all pilots and marshalling personnel:

1. Layout of flarepath

2. Position of marshalling point

3. Position of obstructions and bad ground with details of lighting

4. Position of dispersed aircraft

5. Position and strength of wind

When R/T was not fitted aircraft left the dispersal according to a pre-arranged programme or on the receipt of instructions from the Flying Control Officer. Navigation lights were on while taxi-ing unless there was a possibility of intruder activity, when resin lights (where fitted) were used. Rear gunners carried a torch for use as an additional safeguard on the ground. On receiving instructions pilots taxied to the marshalling point, using the blue taxi-track if the airfield was equipped with airfield lighting Mk II, or on a similar track laid out with blue glim lamps. At the marshalling point the pilot carried out the necessary cockpit drill and then requested permission from the Airfield Controller by signalling his

distinguishing letter on the downward identification lights before he could go onto the flarepath. The Airfield Controller gave permission to proceed by repeating the distinguishing letter in green. Refusal was given by repeating the letter in red. Final permission to take off was given by a steady green lamp signal. An intermittent red signal directed at an aircraft on the runway or landing strip indicated to the pilot that he was to taxi clear of the runway immediately. An airman stationed at the marshalling point made sure that aircraft taxi-ing did not collide with other aircraft by using lamp signals.

On a hard runway airfield the FCO ordered the switching on of the outer funnel lights when an aircraft received permission to take off. If the visibility was less than 1,000 yards he also switched on the central and inner funnel lights.

Normal R/T procedure was used, and sometimes a combination of R/T and visual landing procedure. An aircraft requested permission to land by signalling his distinguishing letter on the upward and downward identification lights. The Airfield Controller gave permission as described above. On receipt of visual permission to land the pilot switched on the upward and downward identification lights. If for any reason a pilot was refused permission to land, he circled the airfield at 2,000 feet or as high as the cloud base permitted. If however there was more than one aircraft waiting to land the Controller gave pilots an order in which to land and heights at which to fly. The Controller switched on the funnel lights at the upwind end of the runway in case of an over-shoot.

If a pilot had to land immediately, he made a forced landing signal by either a series of short flashes on the identification or navigation lights, or on the signal lamp (followed by "F" if the floodlight was required) or by firing white or yellow cartridges. The Airfield Controller gave permission to land and reported the incident to the FCO. After making the forced landing signal the pilot switched on the navigation and downward identification lights and landed. Any pilot who had already been given permission to land before seeing the forced landing signal had to wait until the aircraft in distress had landed and was clear of the flarepath. He then repeated his request to land.

When for any reason an aircraft was refused permission to land by receiving an intermittent red lamp he was to proceed to a pre-arranged diversion airfield, or if no such instructions were laid down then he simply chose another airfield at his discretion.

Aircraft that landed at runway airfields were supposed to taxi to the end of the runway unless there was a runway intersection which should be used if this provided a shorter route to the dispersal or marshalling point. After landing at a grass airfield a pilot who wished to take off again turned to the left and kept well clear of the flarepath until he reached the take-off point. If he was returning to the dispersal he taxied to the end of the flarepath before turning off. Normally a look-out was positioned to have a good view of the upwind end of the runway in use and signalled to the Airfield Controller by an intermittent white lamp when the runway was clear.

Obstructed Runways

If a runway became obstructed during landing operations the FCO laid out and switched on five glim lamps with red domes between the totem poles, or across the downwind end of the runway. He then instructed the Airfield Controller to place the illuminated landing "T" on the grass to the right of the runway provided the grass surface was fit for landing. If the surface was unfit, or if the wind speed and direction precluded the use of an alternative runway, the aircraft was diverted to another airfield.

Methods of Warning Pilots that Intruders were in the Vicinity

Pilots on the ground were warned of intruder activity by an occulting hooded red light on the roof of the control tower and were instructed to taxi with resin lights when the red light was burning. No visual signal was to be made from the airfield itself to pilots waiting to land except in the case of EFTS airfields. At these locations the Airfield Controller was to flash a series of white dots by Aldis lamp to all visible aircraft. As a warning to airborne aircraft a triangle of three red lights located at each landmark beacon site was switched on. Aircraft were then to circle in the vicinity of the landmark beacon until the warning lights were switched off or on receiving further instructions.

Interior view of Uni-Seco control room at Tangmere, 1982.

Watch Office at Manby, 1980. (Similar to Thornaby)

Air Traffic Procedure at RAF Manby, late 1950s and early 1960s

RAF Manby up until the late 1960s was home to the School of Refresher Flying, operating Piston Provosts and later Jet Provosts and Varsity aircraft. They were flown by pilots who were returning to flying duties after ground tours.

The control tower was of pre-WW2 vintage, only had 250 degrees of visibility and was manned by three Controllers each operating on a different frequency. The Approach Controllers were responsible for maintaining separation between aircraft arriving, departing and transitting the airfield under their control by applying laid down separation standards. If the aircraft were flying in good weather conditions they could maintain their own separation from other aircraft by visual sighting.

In heavy cloud or poor visibility the Approach Controller ensured that aircraft were separated by 1000ft vertically (2000ft above 29000ft) or horizontally where possible by positioning over a radio beacon or other reporting points.

Aircraft requiring assistance to navigate to the airfield and descend through cloud to reach a position where they could continue visually to the runway and land were given a QGH approach, also known as a controlled descent through cloud.

The aircraft was homed to the airfield initially at a height predetermined by the Controller to ensure vertical separation from other aircraft with reference to the QGH procedure. The radar used, ACR7C, had a range of 20 miles and aircraft direction was controlled by means of a CRDF. When the aircraft transmitted on R/T a beam of light (or trace) was indicated on the display showing the heading to be flown to reach the overhead, where the signal was weakest, referred to as the cone of silence. This information was passed to the pilot by the Controller, who interrogated the pilot at intervals until the trace shortened or disappeared, showing that the overhead had been reached. The Controller then dispatched the aircraft on the outbound leg of the procedure, instructing the aircraft to call turning inbound towards the airfield at a height based on the commencing height.

The pilot was given instructions by the Controller on the heading to be flown both inbound and outbound based on the Controller's intepretation of the movement of the "trace" on the CRDF. On turning inbound the pilot continued his descent to a height known as the Break Off Height, which was based on obstacles such as high ground on the descent track. At this height the pilot hoped to see the airfield and therefore continue visually and land. If not he would not descend any further and would clear the area.

This method of recovery was useful, but relied on frequent checks on the trace, and if the frequency was busy with other aircraft calling for assistance the aircraft could wander off course. Therefore the area covered to decide the Break Off Point had to be large and could encompass many obstacles which a more precise approach would miss.

This was where the Radar Controller came into operation. He was able to see the precise position of the aircraft on the radar screen accurate to 0.25 mile and +-2 degrees to the approach to the runway marked on the screen. The pilot was informed of his position continously as well as the height he should be at for each range to maintain a 3 degree glide path, e.g. 4 miles 1250ft, 3 miles 950ft. This sort of accuracy demanded total commitment and only one aircraft could be controlled at a time. If the weather did not permit an aircraft to land from a QGH approach a landing was often possible from a radar approach and efficient co-ordination between the Approach and Radar Controllers enabled the aircraft to home to the overhead and hold to await its turn to commence a QGH/Radar approach.

The Aerodrome Controller was responsible for all aircraft, vehicles and personnel movements on the airfield, and all aircraft taking off, landing and flying in the visual circuit. This information was recorded on a large pin board with a diagram of runways, taxiways, etc. The actual positions of aircraft were shown by large map pins with the call signs of the aircraft, which were moved on receipt of R/T calls from the aircraft reporting their position, e.g. "Alpha 64 Downwind". Thus the Controller could confirm his visual sightings at any time.

Approach and Aerodrome Controllers were positioned side-by-side in the control room and the Radar Controller was in a cabin out on the airfield. They communicated with each other by intercom in order to co-ordinate the aircraft that each of them controlled. The facilities they had to assist them in their task included direct lines to other airfields, ATC Control Centres, and alternative R/T frequencies. The Aerodrome Controller had direct lines to the "Crash Crew". A back-up team of ATC Assistants manned ATC switchboards, monitored R/T frequencies, processed flight plans and generally eased the work load of the Controllers.

In the modern control tower at Manby Approach Radar Controllers were located on the first floor in the approach control room, where they manned radar surveillance consoles. The Approach Radar Controllers provided the separation for arriving traffic before handing over to a Radar Director who positioned the aircraft on final approach. At approximately 10 miles he handed over to the Talkdown Controller who used a precision approach radar (PAR) and guided the pilot to touchdown. The PAR had electronic lines drawn on the display, one representing the runway centre line and the other the 3 degree glide path. Continuous instructions were given to the pilot to ensure that the "blip" stayed on these lines, thus providing an accurate talkdown. The pilot turned left or right as instructed to stay on the runway centre line, and climbed or descended to remain on the glide path.

With radar direction of aircraft, the Controller could maintain separation more safely, and the number of aircraft recovered was higher than under the QGH radar method.

Ground to air signals were usually displayed in the signals area near the control tower on civil and service airfields to give warning to pilots of the prevailing conditions and precautions to be taken when landing and taking off. Other methods of signalling from ground to air (or vice versa) included W/T, R/T, the firing of pyrotechnics, morse code signals flashed on a lamp, the use of flags on the ground and sometimes the display of coloured lights. The majority of signals were, however, displayed horizontally on a black concrete signals square edged by a white border one foot wide with internal sides measuring 40ft for pilots in the air, or with the use of vertical symbols or flags on the signals mast for the pilots of aircraft within the manoeuvering area of the airfield.

A red square signal with sides 10ft long indicated that the special rules for air traffic in the vicinity of airfields open to the public were not in use. This signal was permanently displayed at RAF airfields.

Superimposing a diagonal strip on the red square signal indicated that temporary obstructions existed, such as the airfield being partly unserviceable and that special care was required in landing. Probably one of the most frequently used ground signals during the war and displayed when contractors were working on the repair of runways, cutting grass, etc.

Superimposing a yellow "X" on the red square signal indicated that there was a total prohibition of landing. Usually used when the runway in use was obstructed and for some reason the other runways could not be used.

Two yellow bars placed parallel to one another on the red square showed that only emergency landings were to be made and care should be taken as there were no emergency services available. Once a common sight on redundant airfields on Care and Maintenance.

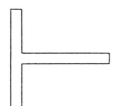

Landing "T"

First used during WWI, a white "T" of regulation size was installed by the Airfield Controller at the end and to the left of the runway in use. It was laid parallel to the runway and indicated the direction of landing. Another "T" was displayed in the signals square. When a change of runway was necessary the "Ts" were moved to the new position and a smoke-candle was lighted in the vicinity of the control tower. The under surfaces of both "Ts" were painted red for use in conditions of snow.

Sometimes due to a change of wind direction or because special exercises were taking place it was necessary to change from the normal left-hand circuit to a right-hand circuit. When this happened a red right-handed arrow was used in conjunction with the red square signal. A green flag was hoisted on the signal mast indicating to those on the ground that a right-hand circuit was in force. A red flag was hoisted when the left-hand circuit was restored. (Original red and yellow striped arrow shown)

Ground Signals at RAF Stations
Signals exhibited in the Signals Square

A white "dumb-bell" indicated that the airfield was unserviceable except for runways and taxiways. Landing and take-offs were to be made on runways only and aircraft were not to use the grass surface of the airfield for taxi-ing. Frequently used when grass airfields had concrete runways laid and there was a risk of aircraft becoming bogged down on grass (mud) areas.

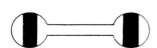

The superimposing of a detachable black cross bar, 5ft in length and 2ft wide on each side of the circular ends and at right angles to the length of the dumb-bell indicated that landing and take-offs were to be made on runways only. Aircraft could turn on to the grass with safety, the pilot being responsible for taking notice of any bad ground or obstruction markers that might be displayed. Bars were removed when the grass surface became unserviceable. Certain grass areas at some airfields were set aside for light aircraft. This became necessary to avoid the delay caused by slow taxi-ing light aircraft using a long concrete runway while heavier aircraft were waiting to land, disturbing the flow of heavy bomber traffic during the daytime.

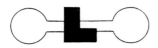

A separate landing area for light aircraft existed on this aerodrome, shown by white corner markings.

When bombing practice was being carried out a white hollow square was placed in the signals square, or placed inside the centre of the landing circle (as at Eastchurch). In the 1930s an arrow pointing to the bombing target was situated near the watch office. Pilots who wished to land at an airfield with this signal displayed kept a sharp look-out for aircraft bombing or diving and avoided the target area. The target to be bombed consisted of a solid white square 15ft x 15ft situated at the most suitable spot on the airfield. In addition to the solid white square at some stations was a chalk silhouette of an aircraft used for diving practice.

A red "G" on a triangular white background indicated that the airfield had been subjected to a gas attack. Aircraft could land but must taxi up the upwind edge of the airfield and remain there until further orders.

A red "G" with a red strip underneath on a triangular white background indicated that the airfield had been subjected to a gas attack and that aircraft were not allowed to land.

Ground Signals at RAF Stations
Signals exhibited in the Signals Square

A red diamond on a white horizontal square replacing the red square in a corner of the signals square, or a red diamond on a white flag indicates that permission must be obtained before joining the circuit or before starting to taxi or take off. Now the only ground signal displayed at RNAS airfields.

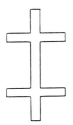 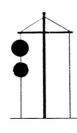

A double white cross indicated that glider flying was in progress. Used in conjunction with two red balls hoisted on the signals mast.

A single yellow cross was used to indicate the cable dropping area.

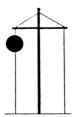 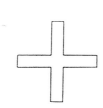

A single black ball hoisted on the signal mast and a white cross on the ground indicated that parachute dropping was in progress. When these signals were displayed pilots were not to taxi their aircraft, take off, or land. Pilots already in the air were to fly to a distance not less than two miles from the centre of the airfield and to a height of not less than 1,500 ft.

A large yellow pyramid with sides six feet long hanging from the signals mast indicated that a standard beam approach landing was in progress. There was never an appropriate horizontal signal for the signals square.

A white flag on the signals mast indicated full dual and solo flying. Flying Training Schools.

A black flag on the signals mast indicated "no flying today". Flying Training Schools.

A black and white horizontally striped flag on the signals mast indicated dual flying only. Flying Training Schools.

Signals associated with the Signals Mast

Marshalling Point

At junctions of runway and taxiway the marshalling point was indicated by a solid white line, one foot wide, painted across the taxiway at right angles to the centre line and 225ft from the nearest runway end. A two foot square yellow board with the runway number in black numerals was displayed 225ft either side of the runway and 75ft from the outside edge of the taxiway.

Their purpose was to indicate the point on the taxi-track, prior to turning on to the runway in use, where pilots must halt their aircraft, make any last minute checks and await the "GO" signal from the caravan Controller's green Aldis light.

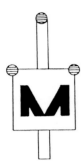

A similar board bearing the letter "M" in black was displayed at the marshalling point of grass airfields. Both these types of boards could be illuminated by three 15-watt blue pygmy lamps which were connected to the flarepath circuit. They also acted as a guide at night for taxi-ing to the correct end of the runway.

When the airfield was finally abandoned the signals square and windsocks were removed. A white "X" with arms 60ft long, 5ft wide was also painted on the ends of all the runways indicating that the airfield had been abandoned and that no landing should take place except in an emergency. Runways at some disused airfields had a white bar painted beneath the cross at the end of the runway indicating that the runway had been inspected every six months and found to be serviceable for emergency use at any time.

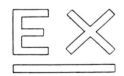

After the war at a few abandoned airfields, explosives were stored on the disused runways. Here a white letter "E" was painted by the white cross at the end of the runway. No landing should have been attempted at these airfields. An example was Attlebridge.

50ft

A white five-pointed star on grass airfields indicated that the airfield was divided in half by an imaginary line and aircraft must take off on the left and land on the right.

Windsocks

The site of the main windsock on the airfield was marked by a white 20ft diameter ring one foot wide.

Air Traffic Signals not associated with the Signals Area or Mast

Signals square showing runway arrangement. Fairwood Common, 1982.

single row of thirty 40-watt blue lamps mounted on a timber framework. The overall size of the letters was 11ft 6ins high by 5ft 6ins wide. The bulbs were shielded so that they could not be seen from the side or overhead. This sign was fed via a switch from the control tower, independent of any other lighting circuit.

Illuminated Identification Panel

Where a number of airfields were located so close together that their circuits overlapped, there were often occasions when pilots were confused as to which airfield they were approaching. Consequently a design of night identification panel was devised, consisting of an illuminated sign, showing the two identification letters of the airfield, the overall length of each letter being 20 feet. The light fittings were 15-watt pygmy lamps spaced one foot apart and supported on a timber or steel framework mounted on the ground at an angle of 60 degrees. At those airfields equipped with an illuminated outer circle the panels were connected to the outer circle circuit and, being close to the end of the line and requiring an extra load of 600 watts, resulted in dim lights. At those stations where there was no outer circle, a single panel similar to that described but mounted horizontally on the ground was provided for installation in the ground signals square in front of the control tower.

Other signals

The firing of a red signal or the display of a red flare on the ground by day or night indicated to aircraft in flight that they were not to land for the time being. An intermittent red beam directed at an aircraft in the circuit meant that landing was prohibited and that it was to divert to another airfield.

In order to warn an aircraft that it was in the vicinity of a prohibited area by day, a series of black or white rockets was fired at intervals of ten seconds. By night the warning consisted of a series of ten second rockets bursting white lights or stars, or the direction of a white beam at the aircraft. Bursting green lights or stars by day or night was a request for an aircraft to land.

During the day when the runway was being changed, a smoke candle was lit in the signals area. Aircraft were not permitted to land until the candle was doused and the new direction of landing was indicated by the landing "T" in the signals square and at the end of the new runway. The smoke candle was left burning until the Controller's van had reached its new position. The smoke stream across the airfield was a good indication of the new landing direction.

Dispersals

Each dispersal was identified by illuminated indicators consisting of a tin plate box 9.5 inches square by 13.5 inches high with holes drilled in it in the pattern of a digit designating the dispersal number. In practice however the fitting was usually made locally from discarded four-gallon petrol cans and 15-watt pygmy lamps. The indicators were connected to the taxi-track lighting circuit, one on either side of the dispersal at the junction with the taxi-track.

Illuminated Control Tower Sign

At certain airfields, to enable the control tower to be located at night, an illuminated "C" panel was devised. This was installed vertically, the "C" being outlined by a

Air Traffic Signals not Associated with the Signals Area or Mast

Runway Markings

Since the mid 1950s runway ends have been marked by two white painted numbers indicating the magnetic bearing of approach to the nearest ten degrees, e.g. QDM 142 degrees = runway 14, or QDM 315 degrees = runway 32. They are painted 75 feet up from the runway threshold. Each figure is 30 feet long, 15 feet wide and equidistant from the runway centre line and is underlined by a white bar. The magnetic bearing of the runway in use was also displayed on top of the control tower on yellow boards eight feet square in such a way as to be visible from all parts of the perimeter or taxiway.

The centre lines of the main and secondary runways are indicated by a broken white line 15 feet long and one foot wide at intervals of 40 feet. Where a taxiway crosses the end of a runway, the runway centre line ends 15 feet before the taxiway. At intersection centre lines of subsidiary runways the line ends 15 feet from the centre lines of main runways.

Taxiways

Taxiways have their centre lines marked by a broken yellow line ten feet long and four inches wide at intervals of 25 feet (on bends the length of intervals is sometimes reduced, depending on local requirements) and are carried past the ends of runways without alteration of spacing. The broken centre lines of taxiways which intersect runways or other taxiways stop before reaching the edge of the intersecting runway or taxiway.

Light Aircraft Landing Area

Light aircraft landing lanes were marked by white strips 20 feet long and three feet wide to indicate the landing area.

Bad Ground, Obstructions, etc.

Unserviceable areas on an airfield due to bad ground or to the presence of working parties, immobile aircraft or obstructions were marked by either white or yellow two-foot squares. These were laid vertically and horizontally on the boundary between good and unserviceable ground so as to be visible to pilots in the air and those taxi-ing aircraft on the ground. White or yellow crosses were also placed on the ground itself or, in some cases, a single white cross in the centre of the bad area with white strips three feet wide marking the boundary of the bad ground thus giving an indication of the shape of the area.

Obstructions such as vehicles could be marked by a yellow double disc marker or a yellow three-sided marker buoy set on a pole attached to a rounded base.

Airfield Closure

When the control tower was not manned the ground signals should have still indicated the correct state of the aerodrome. Therefore the landing "T" was covered or removed from the runway and signals square and the "land emergency only" signal displayed instead. The runway control caravan was removed from the runway and the QDM boards from the control tower.

Airfield Identification Codes

A system of two-letter codes was adopted as a means of visual confirmation of an airfield's identity. Characters taken from the airfield name were displayed horizontally, normally in or close to the signals square. Each letter was 10ft long.

As more airfields were constructed during the war it became difficult not to duplicate codes already selected and letters which had no obvious connection with the airfield name were used, such as I, J, U, V, X or Z. Furthermore, some airfields shared a common code.

In the early 1950s with many airfield closures, it became possible to reallocate surviving airfields with a more rational system of codes linked to their actual names. For example, Aldergrove in 1944 was JV but became AG in 1952.

Some airfields however, which had a code made up of letters within the airfield name, were given codes with inappropriate letters, such as Turnhouse, which in 1944 was TS and in 1956 was WF.

Airfield Identification Codes

Airfield	ID Code 1944	ID Code 1956
Desford	A	A
Abingdon	AB	AB
Aldergrove	JV	AG
Anthorn	–	AH
Acklington	AI	AL
Ansty	AT	AT
Bishops Court	IC	BA
Binbrook	BK	BK
Benson	EO	BO
Bramcote	BR	BR
Bassingbourn	BS	BS
Brough	BU	BU
Rochester	C	C
Castle Bromwich	CB	CB
Church Fenton	CF	CF
Castle Archdale	QA	CM
Chivenor	IV	CN
Cranwell South	CP	CP
Coltishall	CS	CS
Cottesmore	CT	CT
Culdrose	–	CW
Coningsby	CY	CY
Calshot	KT	CZ
Dishforth	DH	D
Debden	DB	DB
Kete	–	DL
Doncaster	DK	DK
Driffield	DR	DR
Duxford	DX	DX
Derby/Burnaston	DY	DY
Inverness/Dalcross	DZ	DZ
Croydon	–	ED
Elstree	–	EL
Renfrew	ER	ER
Birmingham/Elmdon	EX	EX
Ford	FD	FD
Feltwell	FL	FL
Fairoaks	FQ	FQ
Full Sutton	FS	FS
Finningley	FV	FV
Eglinton	GN	QM
Hornchurch	HC	HO
Horsham St. Faith	HF	HF
Halfpenny Green	HG	HG
Hamble	HJ	HJ
Hawarden	HK	HK
Hemswell	HL	HL
Hullavington	HV	HV
Honiley	HY	HY
Stretton	JA	JA
Bristol/Whitchurch	JB	JB
Exeter	EX	JC
Southampton/Eastleigh	JD	JD
Isle of Man/Ronaldsway	JE	JE
Sumburgh	JF	JF
Gatwick	JL	GK
Enstone	EN	JN
Wolverhampton	JP	JP

Airfield	ID Code 1944	ID Code 1956	Airfield	ID Code 1944	ID Code 1956
Liverpool/Speke	JQ	JQ	Stradishall	NX	SS
Prestwick	JR	JR	Sywell	SX	SX
Aberdeen/Dyce	DY	JV	Shawbury	ZY	SU
Jurby	JY	JY	St. Eval	ZE	SZ
Worksop	KP	KP	Thornaby	TB	TB
Kinloss	KW	KW	Tangmere	RN	TG
Lyneham	YM	L	Ternhill	TR	TH
Lindholme	LB	LB	Thorney Island	TC	TI
Leconfield	LC	LC	Topcliffe	TP	TP
Lichfield	LF	LF	Upwood	UD	UD
Leeming	LG	LI	Usworth	UW	UW
Langham	LJ	LJ	Valley	VY	V
Linton-on-Ouse	LO	LO	London Airport/Heathrow	–	VA
Lee-on-Solent	LP	LP	Jersey	–	VC
Little Rissington	LR	LR	Guernsey	–	VE
Llanbedr	LW	LW	Stansted	KT	VF
Leuchars	LY	LY	Hurn	KU	VH
Cambridge	M	M	Holme-on-Spalding Moor	HM	VT
Machrihanish	MA	MA	Ballykelly	IY	VK
St. Merryn	MF	MF	Cranfield	CX	VP
Middleton St. George	MG	MG	Squires Gate	ZG	VQ
Martlesham Heath	MH	MH	Blackbushe	VY	VY
Merryfield	IA	MJ	Waddington	WA	WA
Moreton-in-Marsh	MO	MO	Nutts Corner	XU	WC
Manston	MQ	MQ	Wymeswold	WD	WD
Marham	MR	MR	Turnhouse	TS	WF
Milltown	IT	MV	Waterbeach	WJ	WJ
Middle Wallop	MW	MW	Wellesbourne Mountford	WM	WM
Manby	MY	MY	Watton	WN	WN
Newcastle/Woolsington	NE	NE	Northolt	NH	WD
North Luffenham	NL	NL	Woodvale	OD	WQ
North Weald	NQ	NW	West Raynham	WR	WR
Oakington	OA	OA	Wattisham	WT	WT
Odiham	OI	OI	Cardiff/Rhoose	–	WV
Panshanger	PG	PG	Tiree	TI	ZT
Pembroke Dock	PM	PM	Bovingdon	BV, BZ	ZZ
Pershore	PR	PR			
Wick	QZ	QZ			
Redhill	RI	RH			
Stornoway	XZ	RI			
Weston-super-Mare	RM	RM			
Rufforth	RU	RU			
Scampton	SA	SA			
Strubby	NY	SB			
South Cerney	SC	SC			
Southend/Rochford	RO	SD			
Shepherds Grove	HP	SG			
Syerston	YM	SJ			
Swanton Morley	SM	SM			
St. Mawgan	ZM	SN			
Sculthorpe	SP	SP			
Swinderby	NR	SQ			

Darky

From 1941 the RAF began to install TR9D HF short range radio sets at airfields to help with aircraft in distress. This was a simple transmitter/receiver working on 6,440 Khz and had a useful range of 10 miles and the scheme was given the code "Darky". At Boscombe Down there was a hostel for the use of pilots who found it necessary to use Darky in order to find the airfield. In the autumn of 1942 it was decided by the Director General of Airfield Safety to extend Darky to include 45 ROC posts (extended to 50 in 1944) in areas where RAF coverage was poor. Each ROC Darky was allocated to a parent RAF station and maintained a listening watch from sunset to sunrise.

My work used to take me down to the A361 road and as I drove between Burford and Lechlade in Oxfordshire, I used to look over to my left to catch a glimpse of Broadwell tower. Sometimes, when I had time to spare, I turned off down a side road which had been built across the airfield and stopped where this road passes close to the tower. Looking at the rendered brick shell, I remembered how different it was in 1946.

On completing an R/T Operator's course at No. 1 Electrical and Wireless School, Cranwell, in July 1946, I was posted to Broadwell, where I was sent to work in Flying Control. I found that although the tower was of the standard wartime type, it was operated by a group of men who gave it a special personality of its own. In charge was the Senior Flying Control Officer (SFCO) who had a small office at the top of the stairs behind the watch office. Each watch was run by one of the Flying Control Officers, who were all commissioned pilots. To assist the Duty Flying Control Officer (DFCO), there was an ex-aircrew NCO in the tower and another in the caravan at the end of the runway in use. The third member of the watch office team was the R/T Operator who logged all the R/T messages and made most of the routine transmissions himself. The VHF receivers were located in the W/T office, which was behind the watch office and was manned by the W/T Operator. Downstairs, there was a crewroom, kitchen, toilet and storerooms. These facilities were used by the duty crew who provided the men to man the crash tender, marshal visiting aircraft, change the runway boards on the side of the tower, alter the signals square, and let off pyrotechnics as required by the DFCO. But above all, they brewed char at frequent intervals and cooked supper when night flying was over.

The Controller's desk was in the centre of the watch office and was fitted with panels displaying routine navigational and operational information. I still have a penknife with both blades broken by a clumsy DFCO who borrowed it to remove a stubborn drawing pin from one of the charts. The desk was fitted with R/T handset, GPO telephones and a telephone connected to the caravan by landlines. The latter were always being cut by the grass-cutting machines out on the airfield and we were forced to communicate with the Airfield Controller by R/T. The rear wall of the watch office, to the left of the door was covered by a large map of the British Isles showing all the airfields in use. The R/T Operator's desk was to the right of the door and, further to the right, there was a hatch through the wall into the W/T office. On the left-hand wall, as you looked out over the airfield, there was a large blackboard on which the details of all aircraft flying from or to Broadwell were chalked up. In the opposite corner, between the front and side windows, there was a console which controlled the runway lighting with an illuminated diagram above it which showed the lights in use on a plan of the airfield.

The first thing I was taught was always salute when entering the watch office to take over a duty shift, although no one ever paid any attention to you. I suppose that it may have been inherited from the naval tradition of saluting the quarter deck on boarding a ship. The R/T Operator's next duty was to go into the W/T office and check the tuning of the VHF receivers (R1132). He then

sat down at his desk and signed on duty in the R/T logbook. As he sat at the desk he had two candle-stick type microphones in front of him with their corresponding loudspeakers in cabinets behind them; these were for the Transport Command Approach VHF Channel A (120.96 Mc/s) and the RAF Universal Airfield Control VHF Channel B (117.9 Mc/s). To his right, on the wall, there was another loudspeaker with the corresponding microphone on a shelf below; this was for Local Airfield Control HF Channel (5063 kc/s). He also had a pair of earphones round his neck with the corresponding microphone on the shelf; this was for the Darky Emergency HF Channel (6440 kc/s). No one ever used the HF channels while I was on duty, except a Polish pilot who always used the Local Airfield Control HF Channel for all his R/T messages. This made communication with him rather difficult as there was always static on the HF channels and his English was atrocious.

When an R/T Operator came on in the morning, he spent the first hour or so answering calls from the aircraft as the wireless mechanics went round doing their DIs (daily inspections). Later, the aircraft called up for taxi clearance and then took off for operational or training flights. All the routine messages were handled by the R/T Operator, the DFCO dealt with any which required his special attention, and all messages in and out were logged by the R/T Operator. During the evening, the operational aircraft returned from their scheduled services and afterwards night flying training kept the tower busy until about midnight. When all the aircraft landed, the W/T Operator would tune in to AFN (American Forces Network) and at 2345 hours we liked to listen to the smooth strains of "The Vocal Touch", followed at 2400 hours by the more strident tunes of the famous "Midnight In Munich". By this time, we would be tucking into a plateful of bacon, eggs, beans and chips, with sometimes a sausage as a special treat. Afterwards, camp beds were put up in the appropriate rooms; the DFCO in the SFCO's office, the W/T Operator in the W/T office, the R/T Operator in the watch office, and the rest of the crew downstairs in the crewroom. I always tried to get my bed as near to the centre of the room as possible as earwigs climbed the walls during the night and fell off the ceiling before they reached the middle. I can still hear the soft hiss of the VHF loudspeakers and the plop as another earwig hit the lino.

Broadwell, at that time, was in No. 46 Group, Transport Command, and was the base for No. 271 Squadron flying Dakotas (coded YS/-, call sign OFB/-) on various transport duties in Europe. Broadwell was the squadron's base for servicing and training, but all scheduled services were flown from Croydon or Blackbushe. No. 271 Squadron had an excellent war record flying from Doncaster initially and then from Down Ampney. Flt. Lt. Jimmy Edwards won his DFC and Flt. Lt. Lord, a posthumous VC with the squadron. Earlier, Broadwell had opened in No. 70 Group, but transferred to No. 46 Group in January 1944. Nos. 512 and 575 Squadrons arrived in February with Dakotas and remained until August 1945. Nos. 10 and 76 Squadrons were at Broadwell during August 1945 but were replaced by No. 77 Squadron at the end of the month, and then No. 271 Squadron replaced No. 77 in September 1945.

In October 1946, rumours began to circulate that the station was to close and everyone was going to Bicester. A scouting party actually flew across there in a Dakota and returned with gloomy tales of a grass airfield, old barrack blocks and bags of bull. However, at the end of the month, I was posted to Watton and did not see the final days of Broadwell. No. 271 Squadron was renumbered as No. 77 Squadron in December 1946, and moved to Manston at the end of the month. Broadwell finally closed down completely in March 1947.

Now, as I stand looking at the blank windows of the tower, sometimes filled with hay, I hear the crackle of the R/T "Oboe Fox Baker Tare – This is Broadwell Tower – You are clear to join circuit – QFE 29.45 – Over". As night falls, I hear the old tunes from AFN and smell the bacon frying. After that there is only the plop of an earwig, and then – "Broadwell Tower Out".

Brian Martin 1992.

This article originally appeared in an ARG Newsletter in 1978.

At 1 FTS, Moreton-in-Marsh, the control tower, type 518/40, was never greatly modified from its original condition. This is an attempt to record the life and times of working in the tower during 1953/54.

The "nerve-centre" was the upper-floor control room, where two Control Officers sat at a console, which was probably of post-war construction. One Controller was responsible for aircraft approach, the other for aircraft in the circuit or on the ground. Behind the control room, on the left of the central passageway, was the radio "shack", where all VHF radio calls were monitored (of which more later). On the right was the crew-room, where people lounged and brewed tea when not on duty. Behind this was the office of the SATCO (Senior Air Traffic Control Officer).

On the ground floor, at the front, the large full-width room had been subdivided to form, on the left, an office for the officer comanding HQ Flight, and on the right an office containing very little but the switchboard. Behind, on the left of the corridor, was the Met. Office, manned by two or three civilians, and on the left, near the rear door, was the office used by the NCOs, usually a Flight Sergeant and a Corporal, one of whose jobs it was to prepare duty rosters and ensure that they were adhered to.

The minimum number of staff required for duty at any one time, apart from the two Controllers, was eight, but this was reduced to four or five during the lunch-time period when there was less flying activity, or at night.

This number was made up as follows:

(a) Two airmen acting as radio operators in the "shack". Their job was to monitor all four VHF frequencies: 117.9 Mhz (RAF common frequency used by non-Flying Training Command visiting aircraft); 115.56 Mhz, FTC common frequency; 122.4 Mhz and one other – these two were the local and approach frequencies, but I can't remember the full details. The Controllers listened out on these two channels only. When a visiting aircraft using one of the other frequencies called up it was the job of the radio operator to acknowledge the call, giving the runway in use, barometric pressure, runway length and airfield elevation and then notify, via an intercom system, the Controller who would then plug into that channel and take over. The airmen also gave taxi-ing instructions to all based aircraft.

(b) One airman who sat at a desk alongside the control console and kept a record of which pilots were airborne in which aircraft, for the benefit of the Controllers. This was a very sleep-inducing job in warm weather.

(c) One airman who operated the switchboard downstairs and who dealt with requests from other airfields to send aircraft to Moreton. These were referred to the Duty Controllers, who seldom refused permission. The airman also dealt with our own aircraft visiting other airfields in the same way, and maintained the visiting aircraft log book. The switchboard was connected to the RAF/ATC system, with a direct line to the control centre at Uxbridge and connection with the station's main switchboard.

(d) One airman and one NCO who manned the runway control caravan alongside the runway in use. This was equipped with the local VHF frequency, and a land-line to the tower. The airman kept a check on take-off and landing times, while the NCO's brief was to ensure that no aircraft landed minus undercarriage or with any other problem. He was equipped with red and green Verey pistols to fire in an emergency.

(e) One airman to do general clerical work such as amending radio facility charts. This job was the first to be dispensed with in any staff shortage.

(f) One airman to act as driver of the Land Rover which was permanently allocated to Air Traffic Control, much to the disgust of all other sections of the station, who had to rely on the MT section for transportation. The Land Rover took the Duty Controller on his daily inspection of the airfield, towed the runway caravan, fetched meals from the messes when night flying took place, and generally made itself useful. It was equipped with a Pye VHF set for contact with the tower. The driver might also be called upon to marshal visiting aircraft, although this was normally the job of the HQ Flight Duty Crew.

When I arrived at Moreton on 17 April 1953 there were 16 airmen on the ATC staff, which meant that about half of us had no full-time work to do, but by the summer of 1954 there was a definite shortage. As the station was due to close in the spring of 1955, however, no action was taken to put the situation right.

Three airmen were seconded to ATC from other sections. One was a direction finder (Homer) operator, who sat in solitary splendour in a van on the other side of the airfield and provided, by operating an ancient bit of equipment manually, compass bearings on airborne aircraft to the Approach Controller as required. Another chap was an electrician whose job was to charge and replace the batteries in the portable runway lights (glims) which were used to supplement the built-in taxiway lights. The third chap was a teleprinter operator who sent and received the few flight plans we ever bothered to compile.

During the period in 1953/54 when RAF Edgehill was in use as a satellite, two or three extra airmen and a SNCO were needed for daily detachment to that airfield.

No CRDF or radar was ever installed at Moreton, but the Approach Controllers were highly experienced in handling QGHs. This involved using the SBA equipment, a relic of the war with which Moreton was equipped.

John Hamlin 1991.

When I entered the world of ATC in the early 1950s things were very much the same as they had been during the latter half of the war years and I think that the best way to start this article is to describe the layout of a typical control tower and what took place therein.

Ground Floor

Across the width, at the front of the building, was the Met. Office with a total staff of around 8 civilians, divided into shifts. Their job was to provide hourly Met. reports to ATC and to brief the aircrews. They also fed the local weather statistics into the National Network.

To the left, and to the rear of the Met. Office was the radio equipment room within which were the line amplifiers, relay racks, standby radio emergency sets and the accumulators for same. The VHF transmitters and receivers were located at remote sites that could be anywhere up to three miles from the airfield and the line amplifiers mentioned acted as an interface. Not a single tape recorder in sight! There were usually two signals technicians in attendance.

Behind the radio room was the airfield lighting relay room with its racks of heavy duty relays and stepping motors. Two civilian AMWD electricians operated from here.

To the right, and behind the Met. Office was the GPO equipment room where all the telephone lines terminated, together with relay racks for the ATC telephone switch boards.

To the rear of the above was the airmen's and officers' toilets, plus a store cupboard.

First Floor

Across the full width at the front was the main control room with a large control desk in the centre. This desk was occupied by two ATC Controllers, usually of commissioned rank. One was known as the Approach Controller, the other as the Local Controller.

Two loudspeakers were mounted in this desk for the monitoring of the VHF radio channels but no headphones were then in use and the microphones were of the "candlestick" variety as used in the old 1930s telephones. Also on the face of the desk were the Wind Direction and Speed Indicators. Each Controller had in front of him an aide-memoire board which he stuck magnets to or mapping pins into, each representing an aircraft in its relative position. Incidentally the squadrons used silly names as callsigns, such as "Plantout", "Sunray" or "Wells".

There was a centre console that carried the FGRI 5417 R/T control panel that provided only four VHF radio channels. Also on this console was the Hadley Intercom, with extensions to such places as the runway caravan, fire section, Wing Co Flying, station CO, ops room, Met. office etc. There was also the station tannoy microphone and the emergency radio selectors. There were two discrete intercom boxes to the GCA truck and the manual D/F, plus telephones to Watnall (Nottingham) Control Centre, the SSQ and the ATC switchboard. It was at this console that the supervisor sat, (usually a Flt. Lt.) known as the DATCO.

In the rear corner of the room was the rather antiquated airfield lighting panel and on the rear wall was a blackboard for displaying the details of aircraft that were due to arrive or depart that day. Next to this was a huge map of the UK with its compass rose and a distance measuring tape. All military airfields were marked on this map and it was constantly being referred to.

Near the door leading to the verandah were the green and red Aldis signalling lamps and the Verey pistol with a selection of coloured cartridges.

To the rear, and to the left of the control room, was the monitor and movements room where there were two consoles. The one facing the control room (above which was a window and a sliding panel) had two loudspeakers for the monitoring of the "RAF Common" frequency of 117.9 Mhz and the "Command Common" of 107.28 Mhz. An airman or airwoman operated these channels and passed elementary information to the aircraft. The other console faced the door and here were two clerks who worked the ATC telephone switchboard and dealt with visiting pilots, but most important of all, they made the tea!

To the right, and to the rear of the main control room, was the Squadron Leader SATCO's office (usually an ex-pilot) who dealt mainly with policy and officers' rostering.

To the rear of the SATCO's office was an Admin. Office with a sergeant in attendance who dealt with all admin. matters and the rostering of NCO and other ranks. This was a full time job as there were around 40 on the staff as shift work was involved.

Up on the Roof

At the rear was a small room with double doors that was used by the Met. people for the filling of Met. balloons from the hydrogen cylinders. Also on the roof was the scaffolding frame for holding the runway-in-use boards. These were large yellow boards with black figures which had to be changed when a different runway was brought into use, no mean feat on a windy day. The standby aerials were mounted up here also.

Outside the front of the tower was the signals square and the Met. Office instrument enclosure, whilst to the left was a small pyrotechnic store.

Airfield Sited Equipment

Out in the centre of the airfield was the VHF manual D/F homer mounted on a vehicle chassis known as RVT105. This was operated by signals personnel who rotated its aerial to obtain an aircraft's bearing relative to the airfield. This information was then passed to the Approach Controller via land lines. One can imagine how slow such a procedure was and it was painfully inadequate for jet aircraft working.

Part way down each runway, and slightly to the left, was a hardstanding where the GCA trailers were accurately placed. This was American equipment known as MPN 11 and on loan to the RAF at a limited number of airfields. It contained three radar systems, one that surveyed 360 degrees out to a distance of twenty miles, one that scanned a narrow horizontal arc along the line of the runway, and one that scanned a narrow vertical arc along the line of the runway. This system enabled an aircraft to be talked down onto the runway, but the three Controllers had to work in very hot and cramped conditions inside the trailer.

On the perimeter of the airfield was the DME (distance measuring equipment) which was a modernised high powered version of the wartime Eureka beacon. This enabled an aircraft to obtain its range from the airfield up to 150 miles distance. It was also possible to "home" onto this beacon, all without any assistance from ground personnel.

To help in the recovery of fighters a device known as the voice rotating beacon was in use and this was housed in trailers parked on an old dispersal point. This too was a pilot interpreted system which used a VHF radio channel to radiate a steady tone signal for 350 degrees of its aerial rotation. In the gap of the other 10 degrees was a lady's voice, taken off a disc, that spoke the compass bearing of the direction that the aerial was pointing at that time. Unfortunately the rotation speed was only one revolution per minute which could be an awful long time for a pilot to wait to know his relative bearing to the station when travelling at 500 miles per hour in a Meteor. Needless to say this system only lasted a few years.

At some airfields, especially within Transport Command, a low power H/F short wave transmitter radiated a coded signal which enabled aircraft crews to use their radio compass to obtain a bearing from it. Sabre jets incidentally were also fitted with a radio compass.

Better Facilities

The first improvement in Nav. Aids at RAF airfields was the introduction of the CRDF. This automatic DF system enabled the Approach Controller in the control tower to see the bearings of an aircraft displayed on a cathode ray tube in front of him, even though the processing equipment was housed in a brick building in the centre of the airfield.

It may be relevant, at this point, to explain the duties of the Approach Controller. He was responsible for aircraft flying outside the three mile radius of the airfield and his main task was informing pilots which way to steer their aircraft to reach the overhead by passing to them over the R/T the bearings presented to him on the CRDF indicator. Once overhead the pilot was given a predetermined course to steer. This heading was known as the "safety lane" and was in a direction free from hills and other airfield lanes. Once established on this heading a pilot was told to commence descent to around half his starting height. When he reached this low level, he was instructed to turn onto a reciprocal heading and then descend to 2000ft. This procedure brought the aircraft safely down through cloud and in visual contact with the airfield.

All this time the Controller would be checking the bearings of each radio transmission made by the pilot, offering him corrections as necessary. This could really

be a hot seat if the weather began to deteriorate when every aircraft was shouting for recovery and a Controller could soon become saturated if more than four aircraft requested this QGH service at the same time.

If the pilot requested a "talk down" then the GCA Director in the trailer would "pick off" the aircraft from the safety lane when he identified it on his radar display. Once he had aligned the aircraft up at six miles from touch-down he would hand it over to the Talk-Down Controller who would then use his radio to give guidance to the pilot right down to the end of the runway.

The duties of the Local Controller, who also operated in the main control room, were dealing with the aircraft within three miles radius of the airfield. His main task was giving aircraft permission to take off or land and passing such details as the barometric pressure, runway in use and conditions. He was also responsible for knowing what was taking place on the landing ground, including vehicle movements and contractors at work.

The fire section in the 1950s was still part of the guard room and this is where the fire crew and fire engines remained until being called forward to the control tower via the use of intercom or tannoy. During high intensity flying periods the foam producing vehicle and the rescue jeep would stand alongside the runway caravan at the end of the runway.

At airfields that did not possess the luxury of a GCA, the wartime BABS system was still in use but help was on the way. The British had developed the wartime SBA by increasing its radio frequency into the VHF band. This enabled a vertical beam as well as a horizontal beam to be employed. This system was known as ILS (Instrument Landing System) and the pilot could be guided by instruments in his cockpit down to within half a mile of the runway end. The large semi-circular aerial system which generated the horizontal beam was located at the downwind end of the runway, whereas the single pole aerial for the vertical beam was located at the upwind end of the runway. Unfortunately this system could only be used on one runway in one direction.

The Parting of the Ways

Cossor Radar Ltd. had developed a precision approach radar plus a 360 degrees surveillance radar as two separate systems. This act brought about a complete rethink to the way Air Traffic Control operated, as these new radars of the 1960s now brought the radar screens into the control tower for the first time. This meant that the main control room had to be blacked out and a separate visual control room (VCR) provided for the Local Controller. As an interim measure a crude greenhouse structure was erected on the control tower roof. Much later on, a new air conditioned room with sloping glass windows took its place, if the engineers thought that the existing building would carry the weight. At Linton-on-Ouse a steel support frame had to be provided alongside the original building, on top of which was bolted the new VCR.

Another major change to take place around 1960 was when NATO decided that all military aircraft radios would move up to the UHF frequency band, but as no British equipment was yet available American gear had to be borrowed. A new direction finder working on this band was eventually produced, known as CADF (commutated aerial D/F). A brick building with a 20ft diameter metal mesh disc on its roof appeared on all airfields.

At fighter stations large concrete hardstandings were provided at each end of the runway. This enabled fighter aircraft to scramble much more quickly when they were parked here and connected via umbilical cable to the ops centre, enabling pilots to be briefed while sitting in the cockpits. The ATC also monitored what was going on as he had the final word on giving permission to take off, on yet another intercom box.

The poor relation in receiving navigational aids was always Flying Training Command and they had to make do with only a low powered surveillance radar known as ACR7. There were two versions of this equipment; one was transportable and therefore had its display inside the trailer where the Controller had to operate under very cramped conditions. The other version had its radar head equipment out on the airfield in a small cabinet but its display was back in the control tower approach room.

Moving into Top Gear

By the late 1960s most airfields had been provided with a high powered surveillance radar known as AR1. It was located in a brick building with the revolving aerial on top of its 40ft lattice tower, which was a common sight at most airfields. This radar had a range of 70 miles and could have as many display units as one liked to install in the approach room. Because of its excellent range and "off set" facility, this radar would often be shared by more than one station. The Approach Controller was provided with a display and was now able to see his aircraft in their controlled descents and this almost rendered the radio D/F obsolete.

The precision radar "talk down" aspect was being provided by the Cossor 3B or 3C as the American MPN 11 had long since been returned to the States. These Cossor radars had their relevant vertical and horizontal displays in the comfortable approach room but the main equipment was mounted on a turntable close to the intersection of the runways. One version could be rotated remotely but the older model had to be turned by hand, not an enviable task on a frosty morning.

Things had also been improving for the Local Controller as he now had an assistant for the control of aircraft movements on the ground and a separate radio channel was utilised for this. A new purpose built fire section building had been erected adjacent to the control tower or in some cases, like Leeming, at the far side of the airfield. The rescue service vehicles now had mobile radio telephones fitted and a special bird scaring team was formed with a vehicle fitted with a loudspeaker, over which was played tape recordings of birds in distress. The runway caravan was now purpose designed and fitted on a Commer vehicle chassis and not the hotch potch lashup that had been used previously.

On airfields that had poor visual contact with certain runway approaches a closed circuit TV and camera was fitted and at others, such as Dishforth and Finningley, complete new visual control towers were built at the other side of the airfield.

The old Eureka/DME was replaced by TACAN, which enabled a pilot to find both his bearing and range from the beacon. At some major stations, secondary radar was fitted which triggered a transponder in the aircraft. This, in turn, sent back a digitally coded signal which, when decoded, applied the details of the aircraft and its height onto the radar tube alongside its blip. Even the basic Jet Provost was fitted with this equipment so almost all military aircraft could now be identified instantaneously.

The remote radio and transmitting sites had been moved back within the airfield boundary and aircraft now carried a radio that could be used on 1,700 channels. Multi channel tape recorders now record every word that is spoken within Air Traffic Control either on telephone, intercom or radio. Aircraft movements and timings are stored in computers and more and more VDUs are appearing in control rooms.

Final Thoughts

Air Traffic Control is a far cry from how it had been in the late 1940s, when it had taken many minutes to identify an aircraft's position and there was no chance of a landing back at base if the visibility had fallen below half a mile or so.

Gone were the days when the "Met. Man" had to launch a balloon to find the cloud base; all he has to do now is look at his cloud base recorder which uses infra red light to constantly measure both the base and thickness of cloud. He does not need to trudge outside to read his thermometers as these are now displayed electronically. Instead of having to draw weather maps from figures received by a teleprinter, the maps now come to him ready made via a Fax machine.

The airfield lighting is no longer a matter of turning big wheels, throwing heavy switches and kicking the cabinet. Now it is all done by remote control with the touch of a button, where high intensity lighting can be turned up or down as easy as winking.

Gone too are the old wartime ex-aircrew lags who used to form the backbone of the control staff. Now they have bright new Controllers who entered the ATC trade from the outset and a high percentage are females. Even the Squadron Leader SATCOs are bare chested with no war medals or aircrew wings and, to me, they are looking younger every year, or is it that I am growing old?

Guy Jefferson BEM

Guy was a civilian radio/radar engineer at Linton-on-Ouse for 35 years.

The Watch Office before the Expansion Period

The origin of the watch office and control tower on military airfields can be traced back to 1918, when the first of the "control tops" was built above one of the brick door gantries of a General Service shed, possibly at Beaulieu. Bircham Newton also had a control top, although it may have been built in the early 1920s. It was in fact larger than the one at Beaulieu and took up the whole of the area above the door gantry. It may have been used in conjunction with the Duty Pilot's Office to drawing number 2072/26, built when the station was first remodelled in 1929. The station was rebuilt during the early part of the expansion period and the aeroplane sheds and the Duty Pilot's office were demolished. This was in preparation for the construction of the latest "C" type hangars and a new watch office with tower (Fort) to drawing number 1959/34.

One early example of an attempt to standardize buildings was drawing number 1072/26, which has the title "Pilots' Room at Fighter Stations and Accommodation for Officer of Watch at Bomber Stations". The bomber station building was a single storey detached building, brick built with a pitched roof and comprising two rooms: the watch office, with an unsupported bay window, and rest room at 19ft 6ins by 16ft. This was in fact very similar to drawing number 2072/26. The fighter station pilots' room, however, was completely different as it was 61ft long by 20ft wide, built of brick cavity walls with a steel framed pitched roof clad with diamond shape asbestos tiles. The main entrance at the front led into an "L" shape corridor and the rooms consisted of watch office with bay window, rest room, toilets, pilots' room with dormer window and a locker room. The door nearest the bay window gave access to a heating chamber, the floor level being some three feet below ground level. Strangely, it is not known which airfields had this type of watch office accommodation.

Drawing number 2072/26 (Type Design), Office for Duty Pilot, is similar to the Bomber Accommodation for Officer of Watch (drawing 1072/26) except that its bay window used a different type of casement and was supported by a brick wall. Everything else was the same and in detail consisted of the following: normally built of unrendered cavity brick walls 19ft 6ins by 16 ft; roof of timber purlins and rafters clad with rough timber boarding covered with diamond shape asbestos tiles; ceiling of flat asbestos sheeting. The entrance, from a side elevation, led into a small lobby, and on the left was a toilet. The main room consisted of the Duty Pilot's office and at the rear was a rest room. Heating was by a pair of corner fireplaces. They were built at Bircham Newton, Hendon, Hornchurch, Martlesham Heath, Mildenhall (built 1931 and replaced 1940/41 by 5845/39), Netheravon, Upavon, Upper Heyford and Wittering. It is quite likely, although not confirmed, that none of the above survive.

There was very little in the way of alterations and additions to this building, as they were simply replaced by the watch office with tower. However, at Martlesham

Heath and Upper Heyford, a flare path trolley and shelter were built as an extension to one side wall in 1927/28.

Drawing number 1597/27 was exclusively for Tangmere and had the title "Pilots' and Locker Rooms, Flight Offices and Watch Office". New accommodation for pilots of two squadrons was provided within a pair of rooms built of stud partitions and matchboard inside the General Service aeroplane repair shed (ARS), one either end of the shed against the south facing wall. This meant that one of the shed doors at either end was permanently closed. The new accommodation contained pilots' room and locker room, took up five bays of the shed and was 20ft wide. The existing south annexe of aeroplane sheds Nos. 1 and 2 contained offices for the three Flights of each squadron. The detached watch office was the result of a conversion of the old Flight office and was located in front of the eastern-most shed (No.3). This consisted of a brick built structure with cavity walls and a close coupled roof. The entrance was roughly in the centre of the front elevation and led into a lobby area. The rooms consisted of the watch office with bay window and a rest room. Heating was by a pair of fireplaces positioned back-to-back. Another entrance on the front elevation only gave access to a fuel store. It is believed that this building, along with the aeroplane sheds, was destroyed as a result of enemy action during the Battle of Britain.

Expansion Period Buildings Watch Office with Tower (Fort type)

Construction of expansion period airfields first commenced in 1935, most of the preliminary site investigations and design having been carried out in 1934. New Type Design permanent stations were commenced at Marham, Feltwell, Cranfield, Harwell, Stradishall, Waddington, Church Fenton, Thorney Island and Odiham. Alterations and additions to existing stations to replace unsatisfactory accommodation commenced at Catterick, Hornchurch and Turnhouse.

In 1936 reconstruction work was undertaken at Castle Bromwich and in 1937 additional accommodation was built to replace unsatisfactory buildings at Bicester, Cranwell, Bircham Newton and Felixstowe. Also in this year a new combined aircraft storage unit and flying training school was started at Cosford. All these stations had in common a watch office with tower (1959/34) in permanent brick construction.

1936 also saw airfield planning and site investigations for new Type Design stations commence at Debden, Dishforth, Driffield, Finningley, Hemswell, Leconfield, Scampton, Upwood and Wyton. Additional accommodation was provided at the existing stations of Digby and Wittering. In 1937 plans of new stations to be built using similar standard designs were prepared and contracts placed for Bassingbourn, Benson, Brize Norton, Cottesmore, Honington, Wattisham, Watton and West Raynham. All these stations had in common a watch office with tower (207/36) in concrete construction.

This watch office Type Design, now commonly known as the "Fort" type, was the first serious attempt at having a standard design of airfield watch office for military airfields at home and abroad (e.g. Seletar, Malaya). This building was a considerable advance on previous designs and therefore replaced the earlier 1920s multi-functional (pilots' room/watch office) 1072/26 and Duty Pilot's office 2072/26 designs.

Its shape resembles a child's toy fort, consisting of a large (approximately square shape in plan) ground floor building 28ft by 22ft supporting a central observation tower. The original 1934 revised design to drawing numbers 1959/34 and 1960/34 was an unrendered brick built structure. The type of brick chosen was of a class in keeping with other station buildings and conformed to architectural requirements approved by the Royal Fine Arts Commission and the Society for the Preservation of Rural England. Walls of the main building were 15ins thick with a two inch cavity, while the cavity walls of the tower were 11ins wide. A combination of the load bearing walls of the main building, reinforced concrete roof and four cased steel beams in a square pattern supported the weight of the tower. Alternatively it could be built without a tower to drawing number 2062/34, and was structurally designed to carry the weight of a tower should one be built at a later date and therefore both these designs were the first to anticipate some measure of a future development in airfield control. The only airfield known to have this watch office type was Hornchurch, but it is not known whether the tower was added at a later date.

An alternative development of this building type to drawing number 207/36 was constructed entirely of concrete in lieu of brick (examples include Digby and Watton). 207/36 buildings are associated with technical accommodation built of concrete in lieu of brick and this included the "C" type hangars, which were steel framed clothed with reinforced concrete. The pre-cast concrete walls of both the main building and the tower were ten inches thick and were internally lined with pioneer blocks. The tower comprised eight reinforced concrete columns with pre-cast walls which were supported by four reinforced concrete upstand beams; all floors were also pre-cast. The internal arrangement of the rooms of both designs was the same.

The entrance to both types was located on the right hand elevation whereas, curiously, another door at the rear only gave access to the airmen's toilets. On the left hand side of an entrance lobby were the officers' toilets and further along a door gave access to a spiral staircase that connected the ground floor with the first and second floors of the tower. The front part of the ground floor was the watch office for the Duty Pilot, with large steel sliding and folding casement windows running the whole width of the building. A pyro cupboard was built into the wall to contain signal cartridges (red, green and white) and other signalling projectiles. The Duty Pilot's rest room was located at the rear of the watch office on the left hand side.

The spiral staircase gave access to the first floor of the observation tower which was only used for storage as its ceiling height was only 6ft. At this level was a door which gave access to the roof of the main building. Further up the staircase was the observation room, which had windows on all four sides but only allowed a good view immediately in front of the tower, its rear and side views being obscured by other buildings. A cat-ladder connected the observation room with the roof of the tower which, like the main building roof, had a parapet wall on all four sides.

The watch office at Thorney Island was destroyed (or partially destroyed) along with a "C" type hangar during the Battle of Britain. When concrete runways were laid in 1941 a new watch office was built on the opposite side of the airfield at West Thorney. At Upwood the fort was demolished in 1942 and the new tower (343/43) opened in January 1944.

Structural Alterations

It become apparent when permanent runways were built at many stations that the existing observation tower was too small to be fitted out with the necessary control equipment for runway lighting. Furthermore, the building was usually sited close to the centre pair of "C" type hangars and viewing was limited to the area immediately in front, side viewing being restricted by the outer-most hangars and the area behind the "Fort" by the technical buildings. Therefore, at some stations the "Fort" was abandoned and a new watch office built in a better position, examples being Burtonwood, St. Athan, Upwood and Watton. At some airfields where it was decided to retain the original building an option was to structurally alter it by building a larger control room. One method was to completely remove the tower and replace it with a larger brick built control room to drawing number 4698/43, examples of which were Cranfield, Driffield, Hemswell, Leconfield and Stradishall. This new control room took up two thirds of the roof space and the remaining area became a balcony using the existing parapet wall and railings. Access to this new addition was via either the spiral staircase which had been removed from inside the building and repositioned against a side wall, or by a new purpose built brick staircase as used at Stradishall and Leconfield. At Cranfield a Seco additional control room was anchored to the roof of the new extension before this too was replaced by a modern VCR, and at Hemswell QDM boards were fitted above a small signalling penthouse on the roof of the original control room. At Harwell the tower was removed and a new control room built above the walls of the ground floor structure. This was larger than the control room 4698/43.

Another alternative was to retain the tower and simply build the new control room around it. This strange idea happened at Bassingbourn, where the new control room was built above the existing parapet wall of the main building up to the level of the tower's observation windows. A balcony was added to the front elevation, supported by steel scaffolding, access being via a steel ladder connecting with the ground. Evidence of the original tower can still be seen inside the control room. At a later date a new observation room penthouse was added on top of the old tower. This building was replaced by a new structure in 1956.

Where it was decided to retain the original "Fort" building without any major structural alterations the QDM boards were simply bolted to the wall of the tower as drawing number 1358/44. Post war, at Hemswell and Leconfield an extension consisting of a new control room was built against a side elevation. Later still Leconfield went one stage further by having a modern VCR anchored to the roof of the extension similar to that built at Kinloss and Coningsby when these buildings were modernized. At Cranfield the Seco control room was removed and a modern VCR was fitted instead with access from a spiral staircase inside an extension at the rear of the building. Three buildings are still used for air traffic control: Cosford, Cranfield and Leconfield. A number of "Forts" are still extant (1991) at Bassingbourn, Bicester, Bircham Newton, Catterick, Felixstowe, Harwell, Hemswell, Odiham, Watton, Wattisham and West Raynham, although Cranfield and Harwell are under threat of demolition.

Watch Office with Tower (Fort Type) Known Drawing Numbers

Airfield	Drawing No.	Replacement Building
Bassingbourn	207/36	2548c/55
Benson	Unconfirmed	2548c/55
Bicester	1959/34	None
Bircham Newton	1959/34	None
Brize Norton	Unconfirmed	5223A/51
Burtonwood	207/36	15371/41
Castle Bromwich	1959/34	12779/41
Catterick	1959/34	None
Church Fenton	1959/34	
Cosford	1959/34	None
Cottesmore	207/36	?
Cranfield	1959/34, FCW 5066, 4698/43, 1125/44	None
Cranwell	Unconfirmed	2548c/55
Debden	207/36	None
Digby	207/36	None
Dishforth	Unconfirmed	2548c/55
Driffield	207/36, 4698/43	None
Felixstowe	1959-60/34	None
Feltwell	1959-60/34	None
Finningly	207/36	2548c/55
Harwell	1959/34, 4698/43	None
Hemswell	207/36, 4698/43	None
Honington	207/36	Unknown
Hornchurch	2062/34	
Leconfield	207/36, 4698/43, 5871c/55	None
Lee-on-Solent	1959/34	
Marham	1959-60/34	294/45
Martlesham Heath	207/36	12779/41
Mildenhall	1959/34	5845/39
Odiham	1959/34	FCW 4514
St. Athan	1959-60/34	12096/41
Scampton	207/36, 4698/43	2548c/55
Stradishall	207/36, 4698/43	None
Thorney Island	Unconfirmed (Blitzed)	No. unknown
Upwood	207/36	12779/41, 343/43
Waddington	1959/34	5845/39
Watton	207/36	12779/41
Wattisham	207/36	No. unknown
West Raynham	207/36, 4698/43	294/45
Wittering	207/36 other numbers unknown	
Wyton	Unconfirmed	2328/39

Drawing No.	Comments
1959/34	General arrangement, revised design 1934
1960/34	Details
2062/34	Watch Office without Tower
ME450/35	Internal wiring
207/36	Concrete design
4698/43	Tower removed, new control room
ME 6732	Internal wiring for new control room
1125/44	Details unknown
1358/44	Addition of QDM boards
FCW 5066	Details unknown

Credit is due to Ron Blake for the description "Fort Type" (Disused Airfields as a Planning Resource – 1978)

Watch Office with Tower; tower removed and new control room built. West Raynham 1993

Bircham Newton 1929
Plan showing remodelled Station buildings including the control top (26)
and position of watch office (25)

Bircham Newton was remodelled in 1929/30. However, the construction of the watch office 2072/26 was soon to become obsolete, as by 1937 work had commenced on reconstructing the Station which included the demolition of this and the General Service sheds when these buildings were deemed unsatisfactory.

1. Former aircraft repair shed in use as MT shed
2-4. General service sheds (double bay)
5. MT shed and yard
6. Main stores
7. Engine test bed
8. Barrack blocks (new)
9. Barrack blocks (old)

10. Ablutions
11. Maintenance contractors yard
12. Latrines
13. Boiler room
14. Workshops
15. Parachute store
16. Inflammable store
18. Lubricant store
19. Photographic block

20. W/T lecture block
21. Station offices
22. Squadron offices
24. Lecture room/library
24. Gymnasium/cinema located in ARS annexe
25. Watch office 2072/26
26. Control top (above)

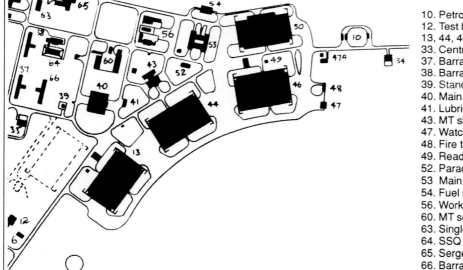

10. Petrol bulk installation
12. Test butt 3958/37
13, 44, 46, 50. "C" type shed 3270/35
33. Central heating station 2918/36
37. Barrack block type "Q" 444/36
38. Barrack block type "R" 2357/36
39. Standby set house 607/36
40. Main stores 4287/35
41. Lubricant store 307/36
43. MT shed
47. Watch office (with tower) 207/36
48. Fire tender shelter & NFE store 4264/35
49. Ready use (RU) pyro store 4264/35
52. Parachute store 175/36
53 Main workshops 4923/35
54. Fuel store
56. Works services building
60. MT section (11 bay) 6234/36 and 5907/36
63. Single sergeants' quarters 4042/36
64. SSQ and decontamination centre 7503-4/37
65. Sergeants' quarters 3484/36
66. Barrack block 444/36

Plan showing Upwood Technical Site 1939 (part)

The watch office with tower was quite often built central to the "C" type hangars. Alternatively it was built on one side of the crescent formed by the hangars and apron area.

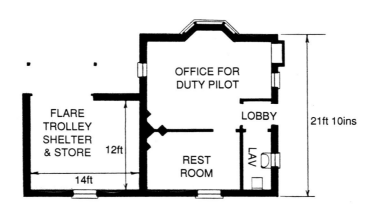

FLARE TROLLEY SHELTER & STORE

OFFICE FOR DUTY PILOT

LOBBY

LAV

REST ROOM

12ft

14ft

21ft 10ins

Office for Duty Pilot
with addition of flare trolley shelter and store, UHD/348/29 (2072/26), Upper Heyford.
Ground floor plan. Brick cavity walls.

WATCH OFFICE

LOBBY

REST ROOM

LAV

OFFICERS LAV.

**1959/34
or
207/36**

Ground floor plan. Brick cavity walls
or concrete construction

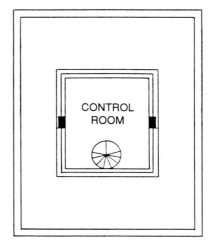

CONTROL ROOM

Second floor plan

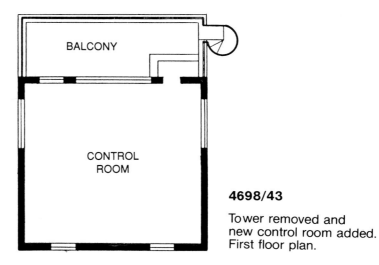

BALCONY

CONTROL ROOM

4698/43

Tower removed and
new control room added.
First floor plan.

Watch Office with Tower

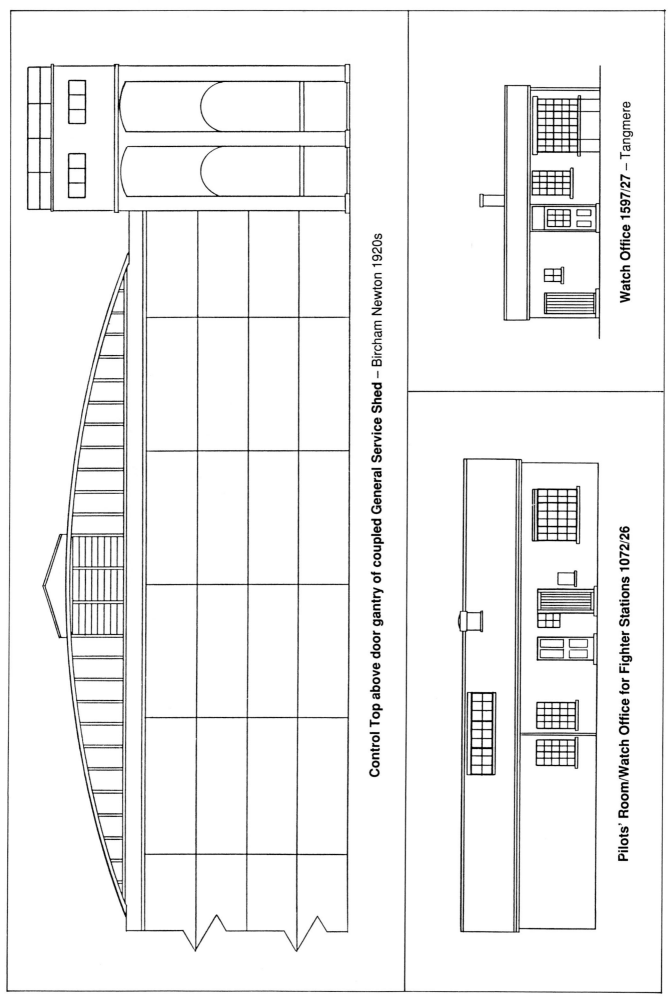

Control Top above door gantry of coupled General Service Shed – Bircham Newton 1920s

Watch Office 1597/27 – Tangmere

Pilots' Room/Watch Office for Fighter Stations 1072/26

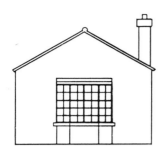

Watch Office for Duty Pilot 2072/26

Watch Office, North Coates
Type A timber hutting

Timber framed panel walls covered externally with rebated weather boarding. Timber trussed and panel roof boarded and felted.

Watch Office for Duty Pilot 2072/26, Hendon. Photographed shortly before demolition in 1989.

Watch Office, North Coates, 1980. (Type "A" hutting)

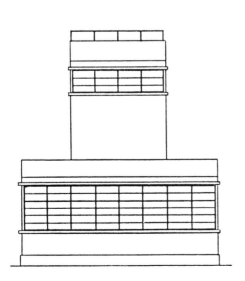

Watch Office with Tower 1959-60/34
Brick design

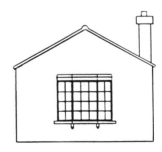

Accommodation for Officer of Watch at Bomber Stations 1072/26

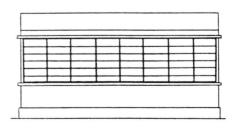

Watch Office without Tower 2062/34
Hornchurch

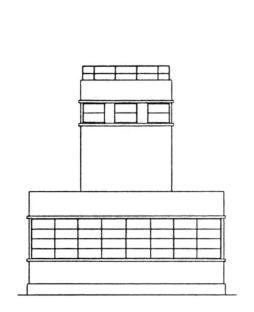

Watch Office with Tower 207/36 – Watton
Concrete design

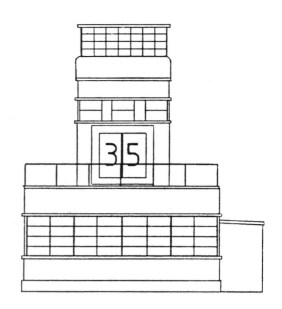

Watch Office with Tower 207/36 and 1358/44
Concrete design. With new control room and QDM
boards – Debden.

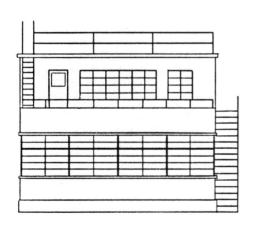

Watch Office with Tower 207/36 and 4698/43
Tower removed and new control room added,
Stradishall

Watch Office with Tower 1959/34, Bicester 1980. Brick construction.

Watch Office with Tower 207/36, Watton 1980. Concrete construction.

Watch Office with Tower 207/36. Tower removed and new control room constructed (4698/43), with later two storey side extension. Hemswell 1980.

Watch Office with Tower 1959/34. Tower removed and new control room built (4698/43) with later two storey side extension and new VCR. Cranfield 1991.

Chief Flying Instructor's Block at Flying Training Schools

The construction of new Flying Training Schools was one of the earliest requirements of the expansion programme. Although many of the basic Type Design buildings both domestic and technical found on operational airfields were suitable for stations of this function, a number of new standard designs particularly suited for them was required. These comprised the aircraft repair shed (ARS), engine test house, ground instruction block and the FTS type watch office which also contained the Chief Flying Instructor's office.

Construction started in late 1935 on a new FTS airfield at Ternhill and at Hullavington and Shawbury in 1936. In this year the planning and construction of aircraft storage units was commenced at those airfields where the ASU and FTS shared the same airfield. The combined FTS/ASU station at Little Rissington and the FTS station at South Cerney were both started in 1937.

Drawing 5740/36 shows the original design with a single storey wing on either side of a central tower and looking rather similar (although somewhat larger) to the watch office with tower 1959/34. It is not known (because the airfield site plans only refer to 5740/36 and clearly there should be other drawings) whether the few examples of buildings constructed on permanent Flying Training School Stations were originally built as shown or not. Alternatively the extra rooms at first floor level could have been built at a later date, as the front elevation at first floor level is different at Little Rissington from that at Hullavington. Furthermore, the first floor extension at Little Rissington is built in rendered brick similar to Ternhill and the remaining external wall area is unrendered brick. I would expect the whole fabric to be consistent if built as a two storey building with a tower. This is also true at Hullavington, except that it was built with Bath Stone in keeping with the traditions of the Cotswold countryside, while at first floor level the later part of the building is rendered.

At Shawbury one side at first floor level was used as the "live" control room while the room at the top of the tower was used as a synthetic control room for training Flying Control Officers. Hullavington was supplemented by a new control room mounted on top of a steel tower adjacent to the original building, similar to the one at Warton.

The building measured 53ft 4ins x 39ft and 31ft to the top of the tower. The cavity walls of the original building were 15ins wide. Floors were reinforced concrete screeded to receive lino and were supported by internal walls and brick piers. Stairs were precast concrete. Heating was by radiators fed by the central heating station.

The internal arrangement of the original building was as follows: the main entrance was at the rear with a lobby leading into a passageway; immediately on the right were toilets and on either side was a clerk's office, the one on the left being smaller to accommodate a pyro cupboard with access from the passageway. In the centre of the passageway was the staircase. Central to each wing was an office for civilian assistants, while at the front on the right was the Chief Flying Instructor's office and on the left was the Commanding Officer's office. In the centre of the tower was the watch office, the first floor of which was taken up by the staircase and a rest room. The second floor was the observation room (17ft 6ins x 14ft 6ins), from which a ladder gave access to the roof.

In recent times Little Rissington has had a two storey building attached to a side elevation. South Cerney and Hullavington are largely unaltered, while Ternhill (the first to be built) has been modified in such a way that it is difficult to recognise it as belonging to this type. Some time ago the windows of the Chief Flying Instructor's and Commanding Officer's offices were removed and two brick piers inserted with new window frames fitted between them. In the centre of the front elevation a new entrance and lobby was built. The right-hand first floor room on the front elevation is now windowless, probably for the use of radar monitoring equipment. Finally a modern timber and glass VCR has been built on top of the tower.

RAF Hullavington control tower with aircraft repair shed behind, 1991. Photo: J. Temple

Chief Flying Instructor's Block 5740/36
Permanent brick. Original design.

Chief Flying Instructor's Block 5740/36,
Little Rissington, with first floor extension.

Chief Flying Instructor's Block 5740/36,
Hullavington, with first floor extension.

Watch Office with Meteorological Section – all designs

Introduction

This group of buildings is an example of how late expansion period permanent designs were adapted from peacetime to wartime conditions. With anticipation of war the design branches of the Air Ministry had to utilize forms of temporary buildings as a means of speeding up construction and for the economical use of building materials.

Kirton-in-Lindsey was the first Type Design station with the later "C" type hangars (protected type, some-times unofficially known as "C1" type). Work started in 1938 and preliminary site investigations and planning were also undertaken at Coltishall, Horsham St. Faith and Colerne. Construction commenced in 1939 at Binbrook, Bramcote, Lindholme, Middle Wallop, Newton, Topcliffe and Leeming. Additional buildings were also built at the existing stations at Leuchars, Linton-on-Ouse, Waddington and Wyton. All these Stations had in common an all concrete watch office with meteorological section (2328/39). Wick and St. Eval had the new "C1" type hangars (although not protected) with timber accommodation and timber watch office (2423/39).

Immediately upon the outbreak of war, at those stations then uncompleted it became necessary to introduce austerity measures and the construction of Coningsby, North Luffenham, Swinderby, Waterbeach, Oakington, Middleton St. George, Swanton Morley, West Malling and Ouston began, not with "C" type hangars but with another product of the expansion period, "J" type hangars, and supplemented with temporary hangars (T2). Middleton St. George is interesting as the station had a mixture of "C1", "J" and T2 hangars, caught in the transition from peacetime to wartime with the corresponding change in hangar types. Furthermore, a change in construction from concrete to permanent brick was adopted for the watch office (5845/39). New accommodation was added to existing stations at Abingdon and Mildenhall, again in brick construction.

By 1940 further austerity measures became necessary and a temporary brick watch office (518/40) was designed on similar lines to the all-timber building (2423/39). The aircraft storage units at Llandow, Lichfield, Hawarden and High Ercall were the first with this new building. They were built with both permanent and temporary hangars and accommodation. The operational airfields at Chelveston, Chipping Warden and Honeybourne (to name a few) had a single "J" type hangar supplemented by T2 hangars and temporary accommodation. Finally, stations such as Ayr, Bovingdon, Tealing and Tain are a few examples of airfields with temporary hangars and temporary accommodation, but still having a watch office with meteorological section.

All Timber Construction 2423/39

Despite post war modifications, at first glance the building at Wick looks like a typical 518/40 brick built building, and it is not until one approaches it that it becomes obvious that it is in fact built entirely of timber.

This building (37ft x 44ft) was built on only two locations in the UK (as far as is known). These were St. Eval and Wick, both of which had permanent "C1" type hangars but with the remaining technical and living accommodation in timber hutting. The only surviving example is at Wick, which was re-clad in 1968 and the original steel windows replaced. Not much is known about its construction except that, as with all the technical accommodation, it was built of timber framed panel walls covered externally with rebated weather boarding and in this case lined internally with plasterboard. Floors were of timber framed and boarded units supported by RSJs. The timber used may not have been the high class Canadian cedar used previously on "A" and "B" type hutting, as by 1939 there was the beginning of an acute timber shortage resulting in the use of cheaper and inferior quality timber.

Concrete Construction 2328/39 and Brick Construction 5845/39 ("Villa" type)

Brick and concrete designs within this family were similar in appearance and were designed as permanent buildings. Built on attractive lines, with a large proportion of the front elevation covered with metal folding windows, the control room had typical 1930s streamlined wrap-around curved windows at the corners. This was both attractive and functional as it allowed more room on the balcony for personnel to turn the corner and gain access to the door to the control room. The watch office on the ground floor extended forward and supported the balcony above. This had a large number of closely spaced balustrades and rails, again typical of contemporary architecture of the period. In contrast, the roof of 2328/39 had a concrete parapet wall all the way round, while 5845/39 had a brick parapet wall on the front elevation and steel railings around the remaining roof area. Quite a number of buildings have been painted and therefore an easy way of distinguishing between the two types is to see if the parapet wall extends all the way round the roof (concrete) or if it is only on the front elevation (brick).

2328/39 was built entirely of reinforced concrete (except for brick internal walls). All external walls were 14ins wide, thickly reinforced with steel bars, especially around window openings and beams, which were all cast in situ using plywood shuttering. 5845/39 had cavity brick walls, 15ins wide, while floors and staircase were reinforced concrete slab work similar to 2328/39. On the roof of both types was a huge reinforced concrete upstand beam running the width of the building. Many buildings were not completed until the close of 1940; in fact Oakington was not finished until January 1941 despite the station opening in July 1940.

West Malling and Leuchars had an additional night figher control room built against the balloon filling room on the roof to drawing 10342/42. Horsham St. Faith had a Seco control room built on top of the roof of the staircase tower. As far as known all buildings survive except Mildenhall, and many are still used for air traffic control, mainly those which have had a modern VCR installed on the roof or, in the case of Linton-on-Ouse, built on a steel girder frame next to the original building. Some have been replaced by modern control towers, such as Abingdon, Leeming, Leuchars and Waddington. Those under threat are Lindholme, Binbrook and West Malling.

Temporary Brick Construction 518/40 & 8936/40

Drawing No. 518/40 shows a temporary brick and timber building, based on the previous all-timber design 2423/39. This new building type was built after 1941 on many OTU airfields to drawing numbers 518/40 and the superseding drawing 8936/40. 518/40 called for 9ins solid brick and rendered walls with timber joists and floor-boards for first floor, balcony and roof and included a timber staircase. Drawing 8936/40 called for only the floor above the watch office room and balcony in timber, the remaining floor area, roof and staircase to be in pre-cast concrete slab work. This was achieved by replacing the internal 4.5ins walls with load-bearing 9ins walls to support the heavier floor. At Ibsley, timber was replaced altogether at first floor level by concrete and this was one of the few with a concrete balcony. It is not known exactly how many (if any) buildings were built just to 518/40 alone. (Unfortunately the airfield site plans quite often only quote 518/40 and not the deviation and superseding drawings and therefore are not quite correct.)

Despite the fact that it was only designed as a temporary structure the basic design was well ahead of its time. In fact, so much so, that this building type did not require structural modifications or extensions (until after the war). The only wartime modification was the addition of a further control room to drawing 10342/42 for night operations, and this could be built straight on to the concrete roof. Perhaps one reason for its success is that it was based around previous permanent expansion period designs, one characteristic of which was the staircase and main entrance lobby being partially located inside an extending annexe in the centre of the rear elevation. This enabled more floor area inside the building for rooms and associated stores for the Met. Section office and a large control room, big enough for the installation of modern air traffic control equipment.

The following description of the room arrangement is typical of the previous designs within this group. The main entrance was located on the right-hand side of the extending annexe, the left-hand door only giving access to the cylinder store. A central corridor led to the front of the building with rooms either side. On the right was the Duty Pilot's rest room, then airmen's toilets and side entrance passage. Then came a switch room and officers' toilets. On the left after the staircase was a Met. store and a further store cupboard and then a large "L" shaped forecast room. In here would be a mercury column barometer, charting bench and cupboard. Access to the teleprinter was through this room. The front elevation contained the watch office, 12ft x 36ft, with pyro store in one corner. On the rear wall was the "aerodrome instructions board".

Up the stairs to the first floor and on the right was the Met. Officer's bedroom. Then came the Control Officer's rest room, while on the left was a narrow store room and then a large signal office. At the front of the building was the control room, 20ft x 36ft. In here would be the "aerodrome state board", Control Officer's desk, plotting table, recorder table, Lorenz control panel and airfield mimic panel. On the front elevation were large sliding and folding windows. Double doors on both side walls gave access to the balcony.

The staircase continued up to the roof where there was a balloon filling room. A copper pipe opening could supply hydrogen for balloon filling from the cylinder store on the ground floor.

An additional control room for night operations could easily be added to the concrete roof to drawing number 10413/42, as seen at Barrow. Bovingdon had an extended watch office on the front elevation and a small brick additional control room on the roof, but this was rare. The only known building at an RAF station to have a modern VCR was Pershore and this had to be additionally supported by four cased steel columns to carry the weight.

Today, 1992, many buildings survive, most without the timber balcony, the joists having rotted away and failed where they extended out from the building. The following are still extant:

Andreas	Limavady
Ballyhalbert	Llandow
Barrow	Marston Moor
Bottesford	Pershore
Bovingdon	Rednal
Carlisle	Shipdham
Fairwood Common	Shobdon
Goxhill	Silloth
Hawarden	Tain
Honeybourne	Tealing
Hurn	Westcott
Ibsley	Wymeswold

Watch Office with Meteorological Section
Brick, Timber or Concrete Construction
Known Drawing Numbers

Airfield	Drawing Numbers	Airfield	Drawing Numbers
Abingdon	5845/39	Newton	2328/39
Binbrook	2328/39 & 5871c/55	North Luffenham	5845/39, 5871c/55
Bramcote	2328–2330/39	Oakington	5845/39, 5871c/55
Colerne	2328/39	Ouston	5845–5847/39
Coltishall	2328/39, 8786/39	St. Eval	2423/39
Coningsby	5845/39, 5871c/55	Swanton Morley	5845/39
Horsham St. Faith	2328–2330/39	Swinderby	5845/39
Kirton-in-Lindsey	2328/39	Syerston	5845/39
Leuchars	2328/39	Topcliffe	2328/39
Leeming	2328/39, 5871c/55	Waddington	2328/39 replaced 1959/34
Lindholme	2328/39, 5871c/55	Waterbeach	5845/39
Linton-on-Ouse	2328/39, 5871c/55	West Malling	5845/39
Middleton St. George	5845/39, 5871c/55	Wick	2423/39
Middle Wallop	2328/39, 5871c/55	Wyton	2328/39, 5871c/55
Mildenhall	5845/39		

Drawing No.	Date	Comments
2328/39		General arrangement. Concrete design
2423/39		General arrangement. Timber design
3876–3878/39		Foundations, stairs and walls, etc. Concrete design
5845/39		General arrangement. Brick design
12995/39	9.39	Detail of WT insulators
5871c/55		VCR. General arrangement

Watch Office with Meteorological Section 2423/39. Timber construction, Wick 1991

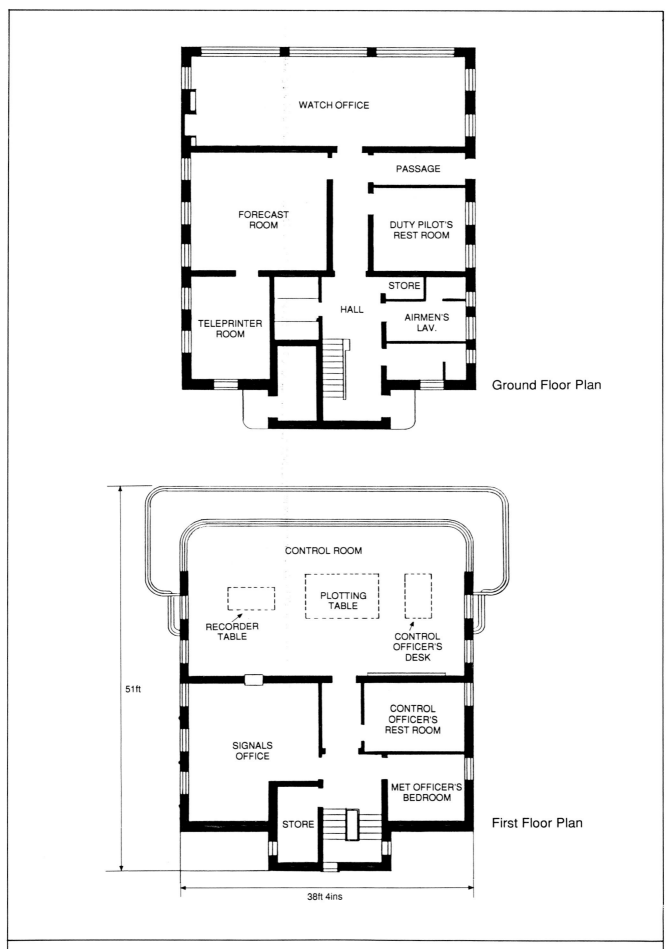

WATCH OFFICE

PASSAGE

FORECAST ROOM

DUTY PILOT'S REST ROOM

STORE

HALL

TELEPRINTER ROOM

AIRMEN'S LAV.

Ground Floor Plan

CONTROL ROOM

RECORDER TABLE

PLOTTING TABLE

CONTROL OFFICER'S DESK

51ft

CONTROL OFFICER'S REST ROOM

SIGNALS OFFICE

MET OFFICER'S BEDROOM

STORE

First Floor Plan

38ft 4ins

Watch Office with Meteorological Section. Concrete Design 2328/39 (Brick Design similar)

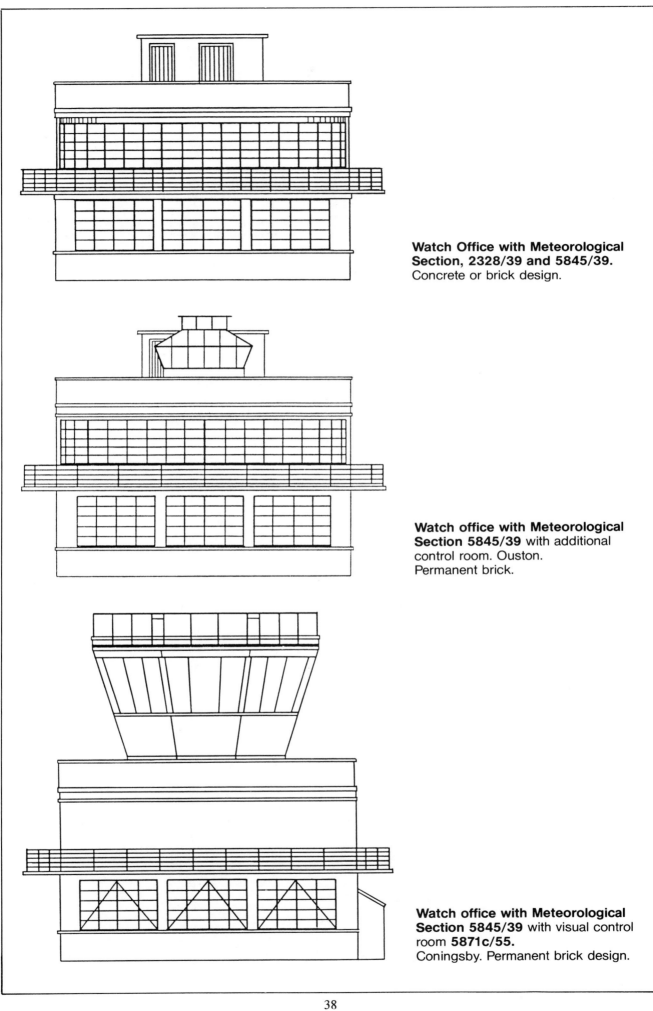

Watch Office with Meteorological Section, 2328/39 and 5845/39. Concrete or brick design.

Watch office with Meteorological Section 5845/39 with additional control room. Ouston. Permanent brick.

Watch office with Meteorological Section 5845/39 with visual control room **5871c/55.** Coningsby. Permanent brick design.

Watch Office with Meteorological Section 5845/39, Colerne. Photo: Julian Temple

Watch Office with Meteorological Section 5845/39, with small VCR, Ouston. Photo: Julian Temple

Watch Office with Meteorological Section 2328/39, Topcliffe, 1981. Concrete construction.

Watch Office with Meteorological Section
Temporary Brick Construction
Known Drawing Numbers

Airfield	Drawing Numbers	Airfield	Drawing Numbers
Andreas	518/40, 10413/42	Lichfield	518/40
Atcham	518/40	Limavady	518/40
Ayr	518/40, 16406/40	Llandow	518/40
Ballyhalbert	518/40, 8936/40	Long Kesh	518/40, 16406/40, WA6/1090
Barrow	518/40, WH 53/42	Marston Moor	518/40
Benbecula	?	Milfield	518/40, 8936/40
Bottesford	518/40	Molesworth	518/40
Bovingdon	518/40, 8936/40	Moreton-in-Marsh	518/40, 8936/40
Carlisle	518/40	Pershore	518/40, 8936/40, 5871c/55
Charterhall	518/40	Peterhead	518/40, WA15/782/41
Chelveston	518/40	Polebrook	518/40, 3446/42
Chipping Warden	518/40	Portreath	518/40
Eglinton	518/40, 8936/40	Rednal	518/40, 8936/40
Elsham Wolds	518/40	Riccal	518/40
Enniskillen	518/40	Shipdham	518/40, 8936/40
Fairwood Common	518/40, FCW 4952	Shobdon	518/40
Foulsham	518/40, 5217/41	Silloth	518/40
Goxhill	518/40, 8936/40	Skaebrae	518/40
Hardwick	518/49, 5966/43	Snaith	518/40, 8936/40
Harrowbeer	518/40	Tain	518/40, 8936/40
Hawarden	518/40, 8936/40 + modern VCR	Tealing	518/40, 8936/40
High Ercall	518/40, 8936/40	Tempsford	518/40, 3446/42
Holme-on-Spalding Moor	518/40	Thurleigh	518/40
Honeybourne	518/40, 16382/40, 8936/40	Upper Heyford	518/40
		Wellesbourne Mountford	518/40
Honiley	518/40, 8936/40	Westcott	518/40
Hurn	518/40	Wing	518/40
Ibsley	518/40, 8936/40	Wymeswold	518/40

Note: The above is a guide based on site plans held at RAF Museum, Hendon and fieldwork.

Drawing No.	Date	Comments
518/40		General arrangement
8936/40	6.40	Deviation, precast concrete floor, etc. supersedes 518/40
ME 11237/40		Internal wiring
16406/40		Details unknown
ME 14317/41	24.11.41	Internal wiring, superseding ME 11237/40
WA6/1090		Details unknown
WA15/782/41		Details unknown
WA53/42		Details unknown
3446/42		Details unknown
10413/42		Additional control room
ME 2316/43	3. 6.43	New control room wiring
1358/44		Addition of QDM boards
5871c/55		VCR general arrangement

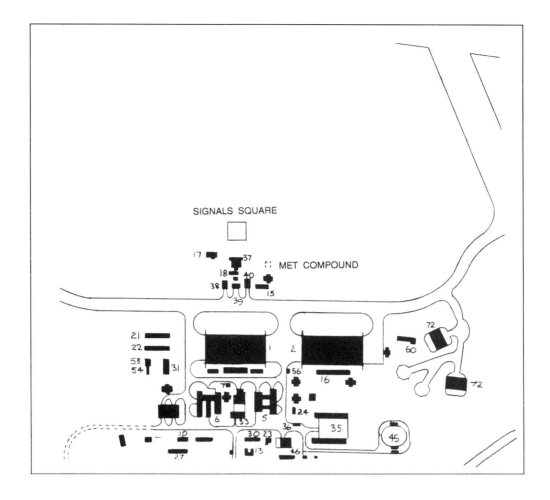

SIGNALS SQUARE

MET COMPOUND

1-2. T2 aircraft hangar
5. Main workshop 9380/40
6. Main stores 9379/40
7. Bulk oil installation 1127/40
10. Gas defence centre 48/40
13. Sub station 16457/40
15. Squadron offices 9376/40
16. Flight offices and workshops 12982/40
17. Battle HQ (used as speech broadcasting) 2239/41
18. Night duty hut
21-22. Flight offices 12982/40
23-24. Technical latrine
27. Lecture block 12979/40 and 4930/41
30. Cine camera gun workshop 12983/40
33. Link trainer (3) 7790/40
35. MT shed 12980/40
36. MT petrol installation
37. Control tower and met section 518/40 and 8936/40
39. NFE store 9386/40
40. Floodlight trailer and tractor shed 9386/40
45. Petrol installation 3386/41
53. Signal section
54. Signal section stores.

Plan showing High Ercall Technical Site (part) 1944
and position of Watch Office with Meteorological Section

High Ercall was a typical example of a very late expansion period airfield built with a mixture of permanent and temporary hangars and technical accommodation.

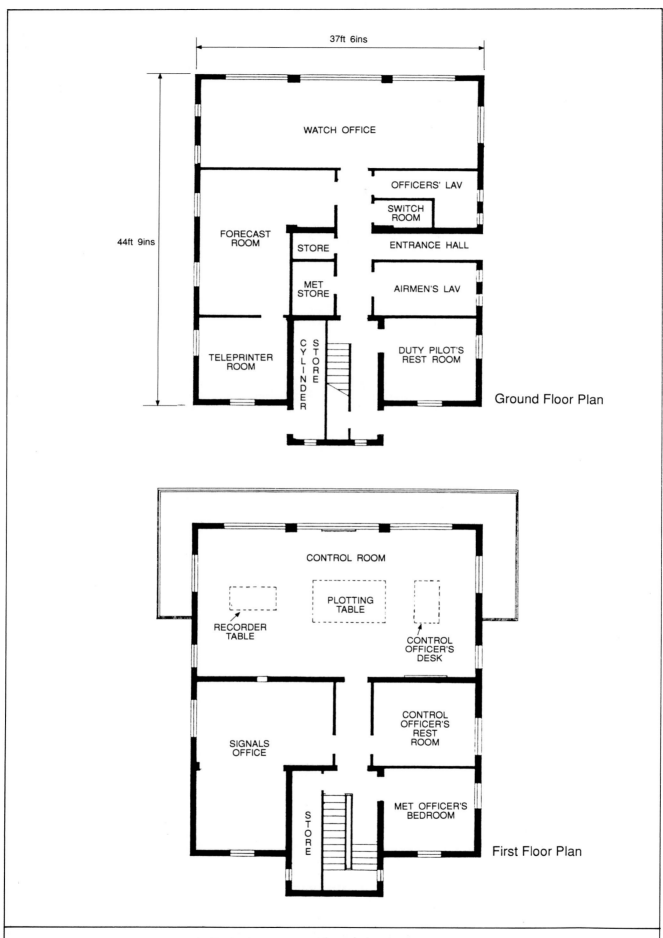

37ft 6ins

44ft 9ins

WATCH OFFICE

OFFICERS' LAV

SWITCH ROOM

FORECAST ROOM

STORE

MET STORE

ENTRANCE HALL

AIRMEN'S LAV

TELEPRINTER ROOM

CYLINDER STORE

DUTY PILOT'S REST ROOM

Ground Floor Plan

CONTROL ROOM

RECORDER TABLE

PLOTTING TABLE

CONTROL OFFICER'S DESK

SIGNALS OFFICE

CONTROL OFFICER'S REST ROOM

STORE

MET OFFICER'S BEDROOM

First Floor Plan

**Watch Office with Meteorological Section
Temporary brick construction 518/40**

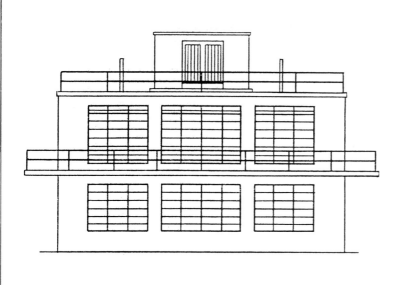

Watch Office with Meteorological Section 518/40. Temporary brick and wood construction.

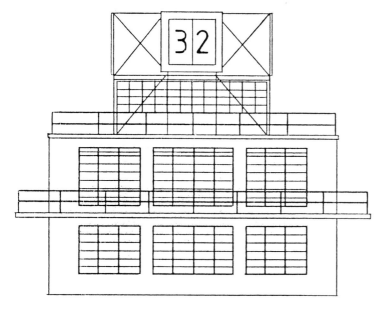

Watch Office with Meteorological Section 518/40, 8936/40, 10413/42 and 1358/44 with additional control room and QDM boards.
Temporary brick and wood construction.

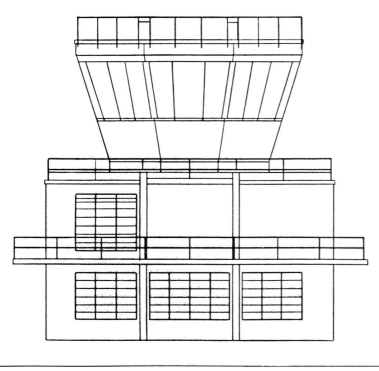

Watch Office with Meteorological Section 518/40, 8936/40 and 5871c/55. Temporary brick construction with concrete floors and additional supports for new visual control room. Pershore.

Watch Office with Meteorological Section 518/40 and 8936/40 with concrete floors and balcony. Ibsley 1990.

Watch Office with Meteorological Section 518/40 and 8936/40 with part timber and concrete first floor. Tealing, 1984.

Watch office with Meteorological Section 518/40 and 8936/40, Holme-on-Spalding-Moor, showing extent of timber floor in control room. Note the folding windows.

Watch Office for Fighter Satellite Stations

This small design of watch office to drawing numbers 14383/40, 17658/40, 18441/40 and 3156/41 was constructed on early WW2 fighter satellite grass airfields and, strangely enough, the sector fighter airfields at Biggin Hill and North Weald. They were single storey and built of 9ins cement rendered brick with a number of gas control vents, the bricks laid fair face inside ready for painting. The flat roof was constructed of reinforced concrete protected from the weather by a layer of asphalt. The entrance, complete with gas proof door, was located at the rear of the building and was protected by a brick traverse blast wall housing a chemical closet at the rear. The front elevation had three window openings and both side elevations merely had a single window located at the front, while the rear of this small building was blind. Inside, on the left-hand corner of this single 15 ft square room was a pyro cupboard with a steel gas proof door. The only furniture was a table, chairs and small control desk positioned against a side wall where earthenware pipes entered the room for perimeter control and communication cables. Heating was achieved by 9ft and 12ft long tubular electric heaters. The only known difference between drawings 14383/40, 17658/40, 18441/40 and 3156/41 is that the window height of 3156/41 is four feet while the other drawings show three feet. This is clearly an anomaly as it seems they were all built four feet high.

Extensions to Existing Structure

Mainly as a result of permanent runways and the installation of airfield lighting, the first stage of extending this building type was the addition in 1942 of a switch room (6ft 2ins by 7ft) to drawings numbers 1536/42 and ME 3651/42. This new extension was built against a side elevation in 4.5ins brick and on some buildings the blast wall of the original building was extended to protect the entrance to the switch room. Inside the switch room was a trench containing the incoming mains electric cables which were connected to the necessary switch-gear, fuse box, main distribution board for airfield lighting, watch office lighting and heating switches.

At Stapleford Tawney the grass airfield was retained and so this watch office did not need any further extensions. Around 1942 at those airfields which were upgraded and had runways built it became apparent that this building type either with the switch room extension (Kinnal), or not (Calveley), was inadequate as an office or flying control. Several options were possible: the construction of a new building to the latest design (e.g. Condover), or alternatively, the provision of an observation room extension to the existing structure.

The former was probably the most popular of the two and a replacement building was constructed to one of the following drawings numbers: 12096/41 (Cark), 12779/41-343/43 (Calveley), 13726/41 (Longtown), or Navy type (Fearn) depending on how it was decided that the airfield was to be developed. The original building was relegated to other uses, e.g. fire section office at Lulsgate, battery charging at Culmhead or balloon filling hut at Calveley. Alternatively where the existing building was to be extended, one method was to build the new observation room on top of the concrete roof of the original building as at Matlask and Dale. At Matlask the new extension was simply built above the walls of the original building and was therefore the same size. The corners of the side and front elevations contained large windows giving a reasonable view of the landing ground while, curiously, at Dale the observation room was much smaller than the original building. Both Matlask and Dale were, however, soon replaced by new structures.

Alternatively, from October 1942 at day fighter OTU satellites and fighter satellite airfields that were to be converted to forward fighter satellites drawing number 7332/42 was used. This was for the alterations and additions to provide a two-storey extension and was used in conjunction with drawing number 2658/42. It comprised a new structure built against the opposite side wall to the switch room in 9ins cement rendered brick, and consisted of two 15ft square rooms one above the other. The original watch office was converted to a signals office, the pyro cupboard having been removed and rebuilt on the first floor of the new extension as this room now became the new watch office/observation room. The gap where the pyro cupboard had been in the original watch office was made larger and a door was inserted which led to a new NFE store room. In some cases the observation room had large windows on all four walls offering a good all round view of the landing ground. However, at Balado Bridge the rear was blind.

At the rear of the building a steel ladder connected the ground with the roof above the chemical closet, giving access to the observation room via a side door. Another ladder gave access to the roof of the observation room. Standard tubular steel railings were fitted along the edge of the roof of the original building only. Most buildings enlarged in this way were not altered any further.

Yet another alternative similar to drawing number 5966/43, as used for example at Lympne and North Weald, was the installation of a Seco control room which was simply anchored to the concrete roof of the existing structure. This was similar to that erected on top of other type design buildings.

Post War

Probably the last building of this type to be used for the purpose of flying control was at Lympne, which was replaced by a new building in 1967. The last on a military airfield was at North Weald, which became redundant in 1952 when replaced by a modern control tower. A few buildings survive today (1991) including those at Balado Bridge, Cark, Condover, Culmhead, Fearn, Great Orton, Kinnal, Ludham, Montford Bridge, Perranporth, Stapleford and Winfield. All these are derelict, being too small for any modern day practical use.

Watch Office for Fighter Satellite Stations
Known Drawing Numbers

Airfield	Drawing Numbers	Replacement Building	Airfield	Drawing Numbers	Replacement Building
Angle	14383/40	Unknown	Great Sampford	17658/40	None
Balado Bridge	4520/41, 8142/41, 7332/42	None	Ibsley	17658/40	518/40
Biggin Hill	7335/42	5223A/51	Kinnal	4520/41, 1536/42 7332/42	None
Calveley	17658/40	12779/41	Lasham	Unknown	13726/41
Cark	14404/40	12096/41	Llandwrog	18441/40	12779/41
Charlton Hawthorne	17658/40	Unknown	Longtown	17658/40	13726/41
Chedworth	2658/42, CH205	Unknown	Ludham	3156/41, 1536/42	343/43
Condover	17658/40	13726/41	Lulsgate	3156/41	12779/41
Culmhead	14483/40	12779/41	Lympne	2658/42	None
Dale	2658/42	Navy Type	Matlask	18441/40, 7332/42?	343/43
Dunino	4520/41	Navy Type	Merston	18441/40	None
Dyce	2706/41	Unknown	Montford Bridge	17658/40, 7332/42	None
Fairlop	14483/40	Unknown	North Weald	17658/40, 2658/42?	5223A/51
Fearn	17658/40, 4520/41	Navy Type	Perranporth	14435/40, 7335/42	None
Fordoun	3156/41	Unknown	Stapleford Tawney	17658/40, 1536/42	None
Fowlmere	17658/40	12779/41	Stretton	3156/41	12779/41
Fraserburgh	17658/40, 2706/41, 7332/42	Unknown	Wellingore	2658/42	Unknown
			Westhampnett	17658/40	13726/41
Great Orton	3156/41	None	Winfield	Unknown	Unknown

Drawing No.	Date	Comments
14383/40	1940	General arrangement
ME 17252/40		Internal wiring
17658/40	12.40	General arrangement
18083/40	12.40	Reinforced concrete details
18441/40	12.40	Supersedes 14383/40 (GA)
2706/41		Details unknown
3156/41	2.40	Supersedes 17658/40 (GA)
4520/41		Details unknown
8142/41		Details unknown
1536/42	2.42	Addition of switch room. Deviation to 3156/41
2658/42		Deviation. Addition of observation room
ME 3651/42	7.5.42	Internal wiring (additional switch room)
7332/42	10.42	Addition of observation room
7335/42		Details unknown

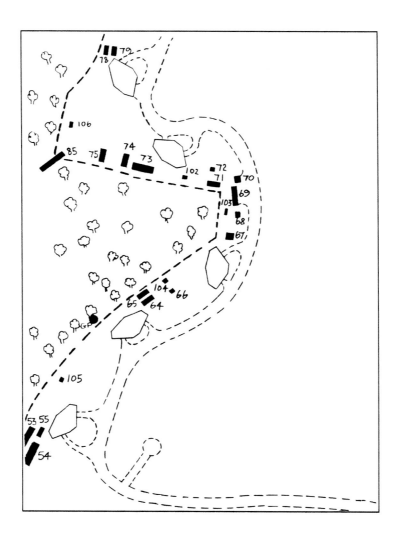

53. Store 11049/41
54. Flight offices 6370/40
55. Latrines and drying room 1556/41
64. Gas clothing store, Nissen
65. Lubricant and inflammable store, Nissen
66. Fire hose store
67. Reserve water tank
68. Speech broadcasting building 5648/41
69. NFE store and workshop 196/41
70. Watch office 17658/40
71. Store
72. Fire hose store
73. Flight office 6370/40
74. Latrines and drying room 1556/41
75. Sleeping shelter 11049/41
78-79. Decontamination centre, Nissen
85. Barrack hut
102-105. Latrines

Stapleford Tawney Satellite Fighter Station
showing position of watch office 17658/40, associated buildings and dispersed aircraft pens

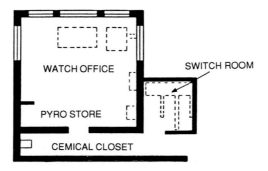

Watch Office for Fighter Satellite Stations 17658/40 with addition of switch room 1536/42.
Temporary brick construction.

Ground Floor Plan

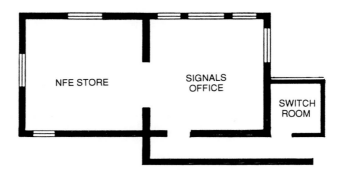

Watch Office for Forward Fighter Stations with addition of observation room 3156/41, 1536/42 and 7332/41.

Ground Floor Plan

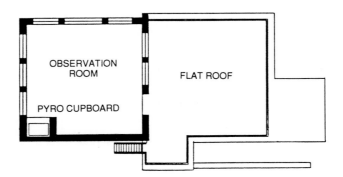

Watch Office for Forward Fighter Stations with addition of observation room 3156/41, 1536/42 and 7332/42.

First Floor Plan

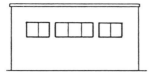

Watch Office for Fighter Satellite Stations 17658/40 or 18441/40 or 3156/41.

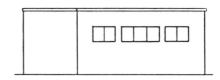

Watch Office for Fighter Satellite Stations 1536/42. Addition of switch room.

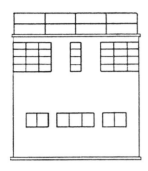

Watch Office for Fighter Satellite Stations 18441/40 and ?, with addition of observation room, Matlask.

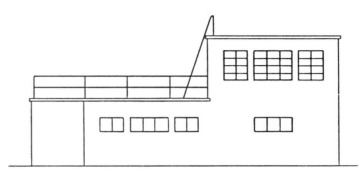

Watch Office for Forward Fighter Satellite Stations 3156/41, 1536/42 and 7332/42. Addition of observation room.

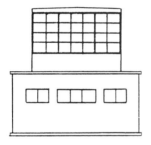

Watch Office for Fighter Satellite Stations 2658/41 with addition of Seco control room, Lympne.

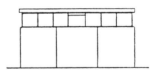

Watch Office at Macmerry. Drawing No. unknown.

Unconfirmed Watch Office for Satellite Landing Grounds. Drawing number unknown. Kirkton.

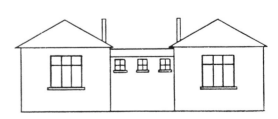

Ministry of Aircraft Production Office for Satellite Landing Grounds. Drawing number unknown. Bodorgan.

Watch Office for Fighter Satellite Stations 14483/40. Culmhead, 1984.

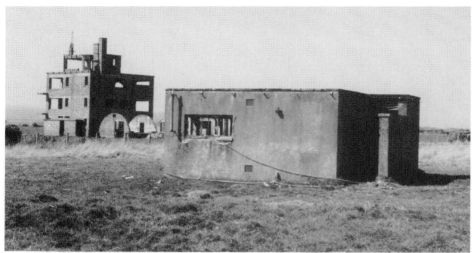

Watch Office for Fighter Satellite Stations 17658/40 and replacement Navy tower. Fearn, 1991

Watch office for Fighter Satellite Stations 4520/41, 1536/42, converted to Forward Fighter Satellite Station watch office 7332/42, showing addition of switch room, NFE store and observation room extension. Kinnal, 1984.

Watch Office, Macmerry, 1982.

Watch Office with Operations Room etc. for Bomber Satellite Stations.

This group of buildings was the result of alterations and additions to the structure of a 4.5ins brick hut watch office which was originally constructed from 1940 on early bomber satellite airfields to drawing numbers 15898/40, 15956/40 and 17821/40. They were of similar appearance to any other early cement-rendered temporary brick buildings of 18ft span and a pitched roof. This version became the Type A and was 60ft long, and from June 1941 was structurally altered to a much improved design. New Type B buildings constructed after this date were built to a similar design but were 78ft long. Both these types were divided into watch office, operations room and crew briefing room.

Many surviving examples structurally altered later in the war still retain evidence of their original features. At Long Marston for example, the words "Watch Office" are still visible painted in white letters beside the watch office windows.

In the original form the watch office of both types soon became inadequate to cope with the increased aircraft movements, offering very little visual coverage of the airfield. Also with the construction of concrete runways and the installation of permanent runway lighting, the existing building became obsolete as an office for flying control. Thus, to combat the continuing development of the war-time airfield, at some locations the original Type A buildings were altered by as many as three distinct phases of reconstruction and the Type B by two phases of reconstruction.

Reconstruction Phase 1 Type A and Construction of Type B.

The first option for Type A buildings to drawing number 7344/41 was to rebuild the ground floor operations room to include a PBX, speech broadcasting installation and teleprinter room. A switch room containing the main fuses was located against the PBX outside wall with a traverse blast wall extended from it. The watch office and crew briefing room retained their 4.5ins brick walls while those of the operations room and PBX etc. were increased to 13.5ins brick. A flat concrete slab roof was added on top of the thicker load-bearing walls and then, curiously, in some cases a pitched roof using brick spandrels in lieu of steel or timber trusses was added on top of this and blended in with the existing pitched roof above the crew room and watch office.

As with all operation rooms, this part of the building was perfectly sealed against a possible gas attack and was built with gas tight doors and air locks. The incoming electrical mains and standby supplies entered the building underground to the fuse box located in the switch room and then on to the lighting, heating, airfield lighting and main distribution boards located in the watch office in Type A buildings, or PBX room in Type B buildings. Type A buildings had an operations/PBX room constructed in the centre of the original structure between the watch office and crew room, with the PBX half perpendicular to it, therefore being "T" shape in plan. The Type B building was simply built from scratch to the latest Type A standard to drawing number 7345/41 with both operations room and PBX in the same plane of the original building. The operations room part of the building could be identified by its tapering narrow slit windows and examples can still be seen at Seighford and Ingham.

Reconstruction Phase 2 Type A, and Reconstruction Phase 1 Type B.

The next rebuilding phase, around 1942, was the addition of an observation room extension to both types to drawing number 13079/41. This was constructed above either the PBX or operations room and involved removing the existing pitched roof above that part of the building to which the new extension was to be added. The new observation room was built in 9ins brick onto the exposed concrete roof and supported by the load-bearing walls of the room below. All four walls had a minimum of two large windows, allowing a much improved view of the landing ground. The observation room contained a control desk, table and Airfield Lighting Mark 2 control board. Heating was by several electric tubular and panel type heaters.

Outside, a red obstruction light was mounted on top of the roof on the airfield elevation. Entrance to the observation room was via either a steel ladder (Blyton) or brick staircase (Kirmington) to a small concrete balcony which was supported by a brick traverse blast wall and protected the entrance to the teleprinter and PBX rooms on the ground floor. The brick staircase was built with a parapet wall offering some protection against enemy aircraft to personnel climbing the stairs or on the balcony. Where steel ladders were used, in some cases the blast wall was extended in height to give protection. Further local variations included either a pitched roof above the watch office and crew briefing room (old) as seen at Ingham or, as at Tibenham, the wall thickness was increased to support a flat concrete roof in lieu of a pitched roof. A combination of both can be seen at Edge Hill.

The early watch office at Docking which can be classified as belonging to this group is probably the only example where the original building (Type A) was extended by having a two storey extension built against the watch office elevation. It is not clear why this building should be any different to other buildings in this group and it was obviously of limited success as the building was eventually replaced by a new one to drawing number 343/43 and became the BAT Flight Office.

Also during this stage the crew briefing room became a kitchen in one half, complete with a large kitchen range, and toilets in the other. A corridor connected to a new crew briefing room was either a temporary brick hut (Long Marston) or a 24ft span Nissen hut (Grafton Underwood) located either beside or behind the former crew briefing room. This new room had a raised dais at one end with a blackboard against the rear wall which the crew would face during a briefing. Very few buildings seen today still have the attached crew briefing room left standing, although examples survive at Seighford (Nissen) and Long Marston (brick). A detached Met. office and signals block to drawing numbers 2338/42 and ME 15670/41 in either 24ft span Nissen hut or temporary brick construction was sometimes built nearby and contained Met. room, two rest rooms and signals room.

Reconstruction Phase 3 Type A, and Phase 2 Type B

Many bomber satellite airfields had the type of watch office/operations room described above and generally the structure proved adequate for the local airfield control and operations, requiring no further enlargement (e.g. Seighford). However, at certain airfields that were upgraded from bomber satellite to Class A bomber airfields, a new operations block to the latest 1943 Type Design (288/43) was constructed on a new dispersed administration site. Futhermore, some airfields had extended runways which made the existing watch office/observation room inadequate. There were then two alternatives – either to abandon the existing building or to enlarge the first floor observation room once more. If the watch office was to be abandoned, as happened for example at Kimbolton and Saltby, it was often relegated to the single function of speech broadcasting. The replacement would be built to the latest standard Type Design which was either 15371/41 (12779/41 with narrow window openings in the watch office and control room) or, alternatively, if it was constructed after 1943, drawing number 343/43 was used. It is interesting to note that the operations room and its ancilliary rooms, including the crew briefing room Nissen hut, were very similar in design to the operations room complex to drawing number 13023/41 and 13742/41 which were built on a few bomber OTU satellite airfields that had other designs of watch office, e.g. Burn and Turweston.

Choosing the other option to drawing number 4170/43 involved doubling the size of the existing observation room, by building onto the remaining pitched roof above either the operations room or PBX. The new extension therefore adjoined the existing observation room, and the dividing wall was removed to create a large room now called the "control room". Some buildings had a standard brick and steel signalling penthouse which was also common to other types of watch office. This was a 4.5ins brick structure with 9ins brick corner piers supporting a steel framed glasshouse with a flat roof. This was built on top of the roof above the control room and tubular steel railings were fitted around the roof edge. QDM (runway heading) boards were fitted probably to drawing number 1358/44 in a prominent position near the penthouse. About this time at some airfields the watch office became the meteorological office and airfield flying control was transferred to the new control room upstairs. A few buildings where the observation room was not extended into a large control room had instead a Seco control room to drawing number 5966/43 built above the observation room. Examples of this were at Attlebridge and Bungay.

At Rufforth (7345/41 and 13079/41) the temporary brick watch office room was demolished and a new two storey structure built in its place, the upper level being the control room. This was taller than the existing observation room and therefore the railing around the roof edge finished at the rear wall of the new control room. On the front elevation a reinforced concrete balcony was included at first floor level similar to other building types, complete with an access door from the side walls of the control room. A similar scheme may have happened at Wigsley except that the new addition was far larger than that at Rufforth. In the late 1960s a timber and glass VCR was added on top of the control room at Rufforth, access being from a door at the rear with steps down to the roof of the former observation room below, where a vertical ladder gave access to a side balcony, and then timber steps led down to ground level. Today the VCR and former crew briefing room have been removed but the main structure survives.

The watch offices at Warton and Skellingthorpe were unusual because the four corners of the control room had windows covering both walls of the corner, achieved by having large concrete lintels supported by the load bearing walls, thus requiring no structural corners. When Warton became an air depot a fifty feet high steel cross braced girder tower was erected against the rear elevation with an additional control room perched on the top although this could not be used in adverse weather conditions. Access was from a side door at first floor level and three flights of ladders. Unfortunately at Warton the watch office, which had been used for fire crew accommodation, was demolished in 1988. At Waltham, a timber balcony at first floor level was added to the front elevation, with access from either a steel ladder from the ground or by two doors, one at either end of the control room. Another steel stair gave access from the balcony to the roof. This balcony idea seems to have been repeated elsewhere such as East Moor and Skellingthorpe but with concrete balconies.

At those stations where the operations room was still used, the crew briefing room Nissen hut was in some cases doubled in length. Furthermore, at some airfields, such as Rufforth, new Seco huts were erected nearby as RAF and WAAF rest rooms (8ft 3ins walls) and new signal rooms containing DTN/PBX and traffic and teleprinter rooms (11ft-7ins walls) to drawing numbers 4702/43 and ME 6026/43 were also erected.

Because the central structure was built with reasonably thick walls (ops room/observation room etc.) and the side rooms had thin walls, on those buildings that were allowed to decay it is quite often the case that surviving buildings only consist of the stronger portion until this too is eventually demolished. It has certainly been true of a number of buildings, for example Great Massingham, Kirmington, Saltby, Tholthorpe and Warboys. The remaining structure, not looking anything like it should, has confused many a researcher in the past. Furthermore, because there were so many different local variations it is easy to misinterpret any one of the buildings within this group as being in a group of its own. One other source of confusion can be contemporary photographs. For example, a photo taken of the watch office at Edge Hill in 1942 will look completely different from one taken in 1990, simply because in 1942 the building only had an observation room and in 1990 we see the building with a control room, a room twice that size. At airfields such as Tholthorpe it is still possible with a little bit of effort to establish the correct identification during fieldwork by looking for evidence of the former watch office, crew rooms etc., in the form of brick foundations or roof outlines on the surviving structure. It is then that questions such as the type of building and how much alteration the building suffered can finally be answered.

It is not known which watch office of this type was last used on an active basis for military flying control, but one of the last was Graveley. A few buildings survive today and include Alconbury, Attlebridge, Docking, East Moor, Edge Hill, Graveley, Ingham, Langar, Long Marston, Rufforth, Seighford, Stratford on Avon, Tholthorpe and Waltham.

Watch Office with Operations Room, etc. for Bomber Satellite Stations Known Drawing Numbers

Airfield	Drawing Numbers	Replacement Watch Office	Airfield	Drawing Numbers	Replacement Watch Office
Alconbury	7345/41, 13079/41	343/43	Ingham	7345/41, 13079/41, TD346, TD 361	None
Atherstone	Unknown	None	Kimbolton	7345/41, 13079/41	12779/41, 15371/41
Attlebridge	17821/40, 7344/41, 13079/41, 5966/43	None	Kirmington	Unknown, 13079/41	None
Balderton	15898/40, 7344/41, Unknown	Unknown	Langar	15898/40, 7344/41, 13709/41, 4702/43	None
Bardney	7345/41 (proposed but not built)	13726/41	Long Marston	7345/41, 13079/41, 4170/43	None
Blyton	7345/41, 13079/41, TD346, TD361	None	Maghaberry	Unknown, 13079/41	12779/41
Bodney	15898/40	343/43	Marsworth	Unknown, 13079/41, Unknown	None
Bourn	Unknown, 13079/41, 4170/43	None	Mount Farm	M/4109/41	None
Bungay	Unknown, 13079/41, 5966/43	None	Oakley	Unknown, 13079/41, Unknown	Unknown
Docking	Unknown, 15898/40	343/43	Oulton	15898/40, Unknown	12779/41
Downham Market	7345/41, 13079/41	None	Rufforth	7345/41, 13079/41, Unknown	None
East Moor	Unknown, 13079/41, 4170/43	None	Saltby	15975/40, 13079/41	12779/41, 15371/41
East Wretham	15898/40, 7344/41, Unknown	Unknown	Seighford	7345/41, 13079/41	None
Edge Hill	7345/41, 13079/41, 4170/43	None	Skellingthorpe	Unknown, 13079/41?, 4170/43?	None
Elgin	13079/41, 4170/43, WA15/14/44	None	Stanton Harcourt	15898/40, 7344/41, 13079/41	343/43
Forres	7345/41, WA15/14/44	Unknown	Templeton	7345/41, 13079/41, 2338/42	None
Grafton Underwood	15898/40, 7344/41, 13079/41, 4170/43	None	Tholthorpe	Unknown, 13079/41	343/43
Graveley	7345/41, 13079/41, 4170/43	None	Tibenham	7345/41, 13079/41	None
Gt. Massingham	15898/40, 7345/41, 13079/41, 4170/43?	None	Waltham	7345/41, Unknown	None
Hampstead Norris	M/4109/41, HN7307/42	Unknown	Warboys	15898/40, 7344/41, 13079/41, 4170/43	None
Harlaxton	15898/40, 7344/41, Unknown	None	Warton	7345/41, Unknown	**
Hinton-in-the-Hedges	15896/40, M/4109/41, Unknown	Unknown	Woodhall Spa	15956/40, 7344/41 Unknown	Unknown

**Used in conjunction with steel frame tower until replaced by modern building.

Drawing No.	Date	Comments
15898/40		Type A General arrangement/Plan
15975/40		Details unknown
15956/40	11.40	Type A Plan
17821/40		Type A Plan
M4109/41		Details unknown
7344/41	6.41	Type A, load bearing walls to operations room
7345/41	6.41	Type B, watch office and operations room
ME 7769/41	10.41	Internal wiring
13079/41	10.41	Addition of observation room (Types A and B)
ME 15670/41	30.7.42	Internal wiring superseding ME 7769/41
2338/42		Details unknown
HN7307/42		Details unknown
4170/43	7.43	Addition of control room
5966/43	24.1.44	Additional Seco control room to 13079/41
ME 6026/43	6.10.43	Internal wiring to control room, etc.
ME 6334/43	7.10.43	Internal wiring to control room and signalling penthouse
ME 8265/43	24. 1.44	Internal wiring to Seco control room
TD 346		New control room
TD 361		Details unknown

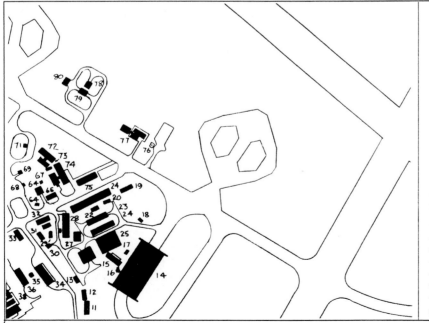

11. Barrack hut, Laing 13903/40
12, 17, 20, 29, 64, 73 Latrine 17822/40
13, 34. M/E plinth
14. T2 hangar 3653/42
15, 16. Link trainer 4189/42
18. RU pyro store 548/42
19. Office
23, 24. Armoury 9882/42 and 3939/43
27. Maintenance staff block 1277/41
28. Maintenance office
30. Store
31. Fire party hut 2995/42
32. Guard house 17825/40
22. Picket post
36. Gas respirator store 13730/41
38. Main stores 2981/43
66. Fire tender house
67. Speech broadcasting building 8492/43
68, 69, 71 Petrol installation
72. Photographic block 4781/42
74. Crew locker/drying room
75. Armoury 17824/40
76. Sleeve streamer mast
77. Control tower 17821/40 and 1700/43
78. Fire tender shelter 12410/41
79. Floodlight trailer and tractor shed 12411/41
80. NFE store 12411/41

Plan of Attlebridge
showing position of watch office and technical buildings

When originally built as a satellite airfield the technical accommodation facilities would have been limited but, as the airfield was developed, buildings such as fire tender shelter, floodlight trailer/tractor shed and NFE store were added.

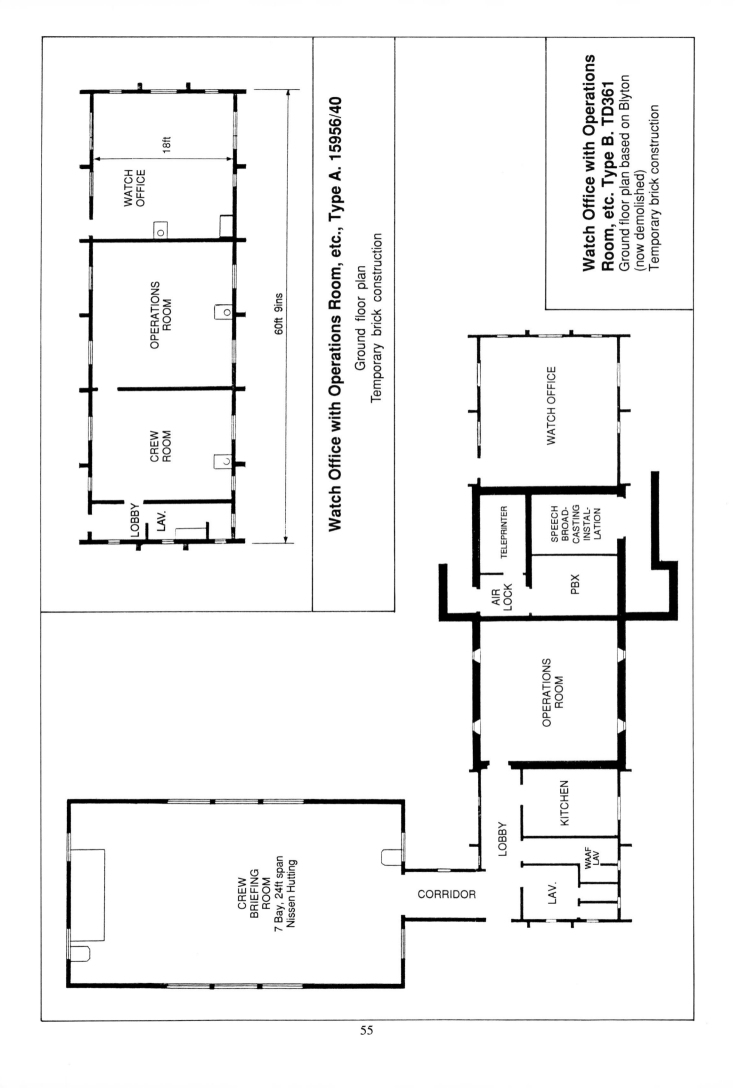

Watch Office with Operations Room, etc., Type A. 15956/40
Ground floor plan
Temporary brick construction

WATCH OFFICE

18ft

OPERATIONS ROOM

60ft 9ins

CREW ROOM

LOBBY

LAV.

Watch Office with Operations Room, etc. Type B. TD361
Ground floor plan based on Blyton (now demolished)
Temporary brick construction

WATCH OFFICE

TELEPRINTER

SPEECH BROAD-CASTING INSTAL-LATION

AIR LOCK

PBX

OPERATIONS ROOM

KITCHEN

LOBBY

WAAF LAV

LAV.

CORRIDOR

CREW BRIEFING ROOM
7 Bay, 24ft span
Nissen Hutting

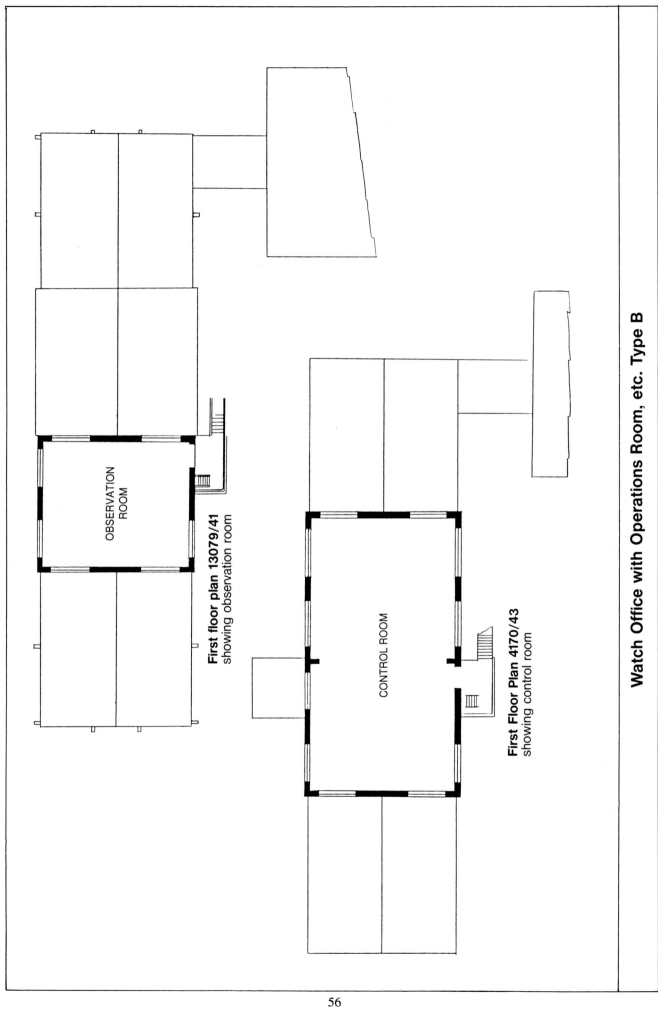

First floor plan 13079/41
showing observation room

First Floor Plan 4170/43
showing control room

Watch Office with Operations Room, etc. Type B

OBSERVATION ROOM

CONTROL ROOM

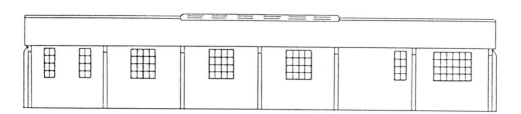

Watch Office for Bomber Satellite Stations, Type A. 15898/40
Temporary brick construction. Docking.

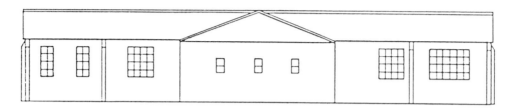

Watch Office with Operations Room, etc. Type A. 15898/40 and 7344/41, Harlaxton

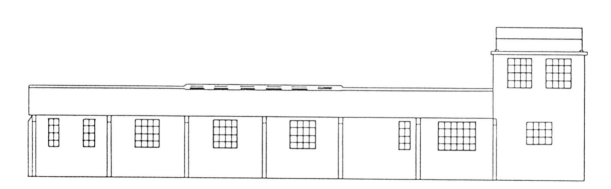

Watch Office for Bomber Satellite Stations, Type A. 15898/40
With observation room. Docking.

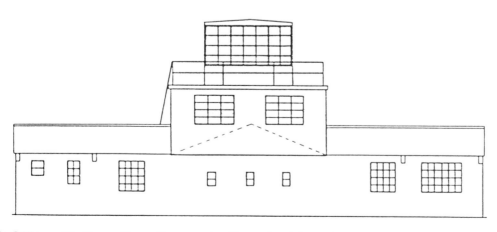

Watch Office with Operations Room, etc. Type A. 17821/40, 7344/41, 13079/41 and 5966/43
With observation room and additional control room. Attlebridge.

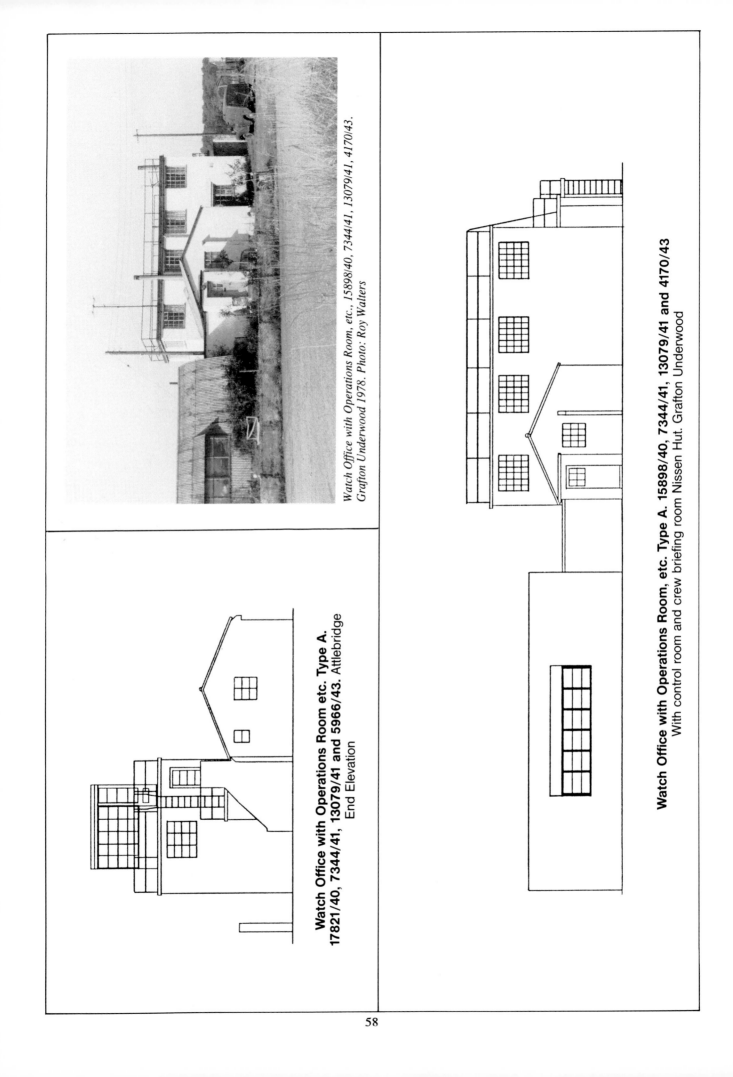

Watch Office with Operations Room, etc., 15898/40, 7344/41, 13079/41, 4170/43. Grafton Underwood 1978. Photo: Roy Walters

Watch Office with Operations Room etc. Type A.
17821/40, 7344/41, 13079/41 and 5966/43. Attlebridge
End Elevation

Watch Office with Operations Room, etc. Type A. 15898/40, 7344/41, 13079/41 and 4170/43
With control room and crew briefing room Nissen Hut. Grafton Underwood

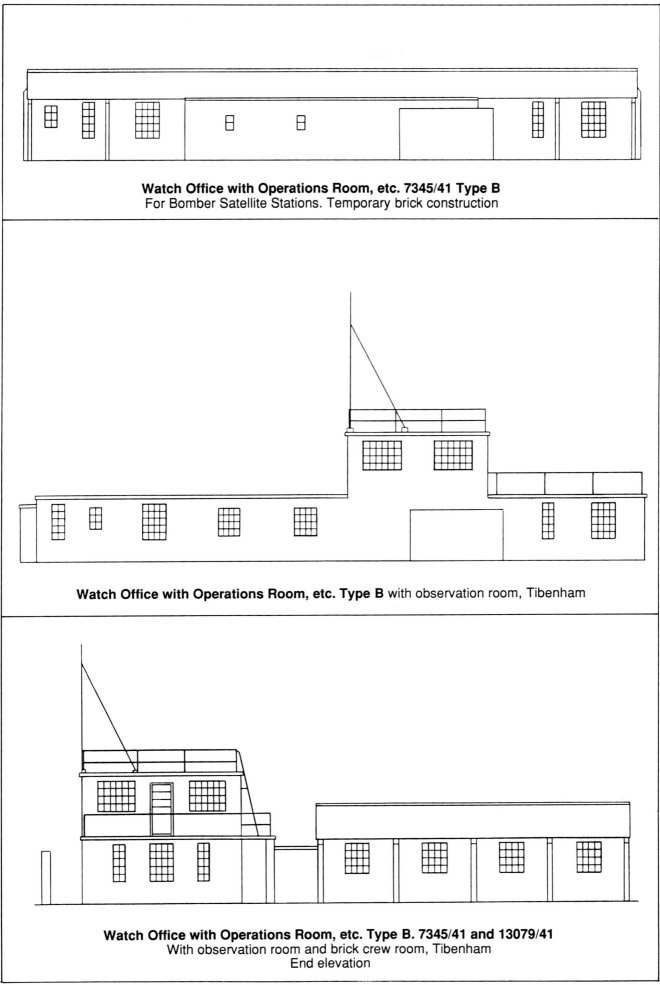

Watch Office with Operations Room, etc. 7345/41 Type B
For Bomber Satellite Stations. Temporary brick construction

Watch Office with Operations Room, etc. Type B with observation room, Tibenham

Watch Office with Operations Room, etc. Type B. 7345/41 and 13079/41
With observation room and brick crew room, Tibenham
End elevation

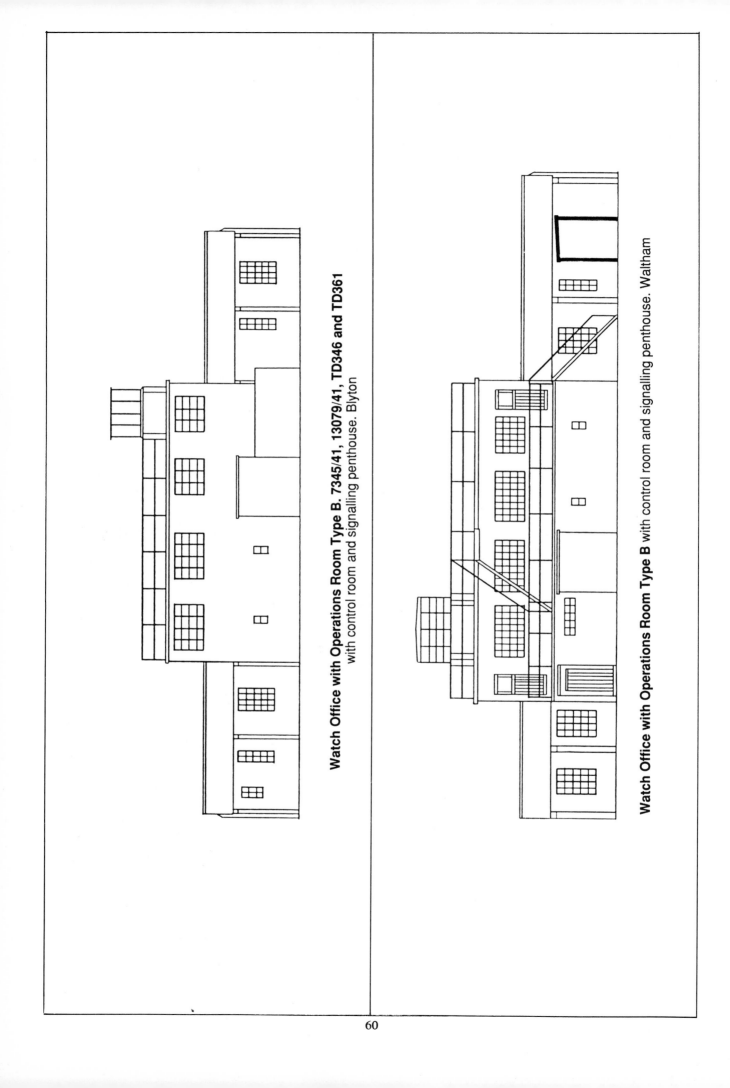

Watch Office with Operations Room Type B. 7345/41, 13079/41, TD346 and TD361
with control room and signalling penthouse. Blyton

Watch Office with Operations Room Type B with control room and signalling penthouse. Waltham

Watch Office with Operations Room, etc. 7345/41 and 13079/41 showing addition of observation room. Seighford, 1984.

Watch Office with Operations Room, etc., showing two storey extension and modern timber and glass VCR. Also note Seco huts for new signals, teleprinter and rest rooms to 4702/43. Rufforth, 1980.

Watch Office with Operations Room, etc., Warton, 1949 with control room on top of steel girder tower. Photo: British Aerospace, Warton.

Elementary Flying Training Schools 1934-1950

Elementary and Reserve Flying Training Schools were formed from 1934 to undertake the training of pilots and RAF Volunteer Reserve. They were designed to relieve service flying training schools of the preliminary part of the pilots' training. The number of schools was increased through the expansion period until by 1939 there were 31 in operation for the RAF, operated by civilian companies under contract to the Air Ministry. New facilities were provided and the design of buildings was subject to scrutiny and approval by the Directorate of Works.

Pre-war RAF E & R FTS stations like Grimsby (1938) tended to have "A" type hutting. At the outbreak of war many disbanded and a few survived as Elementary Flying Training Schools. New accommodation was mainly designed and constructed by the Directorate General of Works. One watch office, 641/41, as seen at Shellingford, took the form of a standard rendered brick hut (40ft long and 18ft wide) with piers supporting steel roof trusses, covered with corrugated asbestos sheeting. The front elevation had two main rooms, each with a bay window, (15ft x 12ft) and located in each bay was a table shaped to fit. The left-hand room had a large pyro cupboard so presumably this room was the watch office while the other was the Chief Flying Instructor's office. There was one other room of function unknown. Entrance was at the rear which led into a corridor leading to all rooms. After 1943 a change of construction from temporary brick to 24ft span Nissen hutting took place at new airfields. No. 3 EFTS at Shellingford closed in March 1948 and by February 1950 all had closed.

Watch Office and Chief Instructor's Office, Halfpenny Green 1984.

Watch Office and Chief Instructor's Office (641/41), Shellingford 1991, consisting of a standard rendered temporary brick hut 40ft long, 20ft wide with two main rooms, both with bay windows (one having pyro cupboard) and one further room. Similar to Wolverhampton and Halfpenny Green.

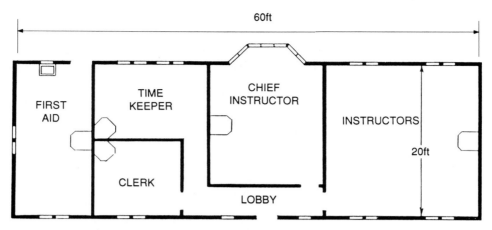

Chief Flying Instructor's office, Grimsby. Ground floor plan

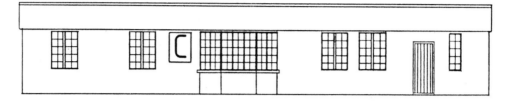

Chief Instructor's Office, Grimsby. Type A timber hutting

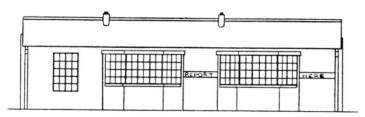

Watch Office 641/41, Shellingford.
Temporary brick construction.

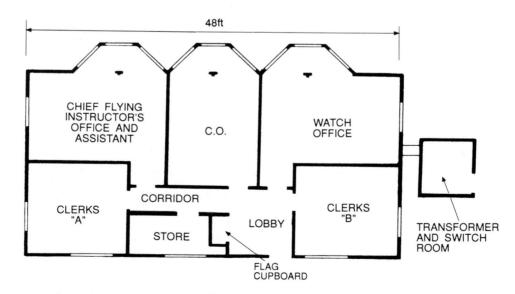

Watch Office for Central Flying School, Air Gunnery School, Bombing & Gunnery School and Air Observer School Stations. 24ft span Nissen Hutting 2847/42, 1534/42, 13739/41, ME 16017/41 3.4.42

Similar to 2846/42 and 14525/41 which was 36ft long and had two bay windows only (CO's office omitted) for EFTS, CGS AND AONS Stations

Watch Office for Night Fighter Stations

Original Design

This group of buildings is based on construction characteristics similar to drawing number 12096/41 for night fighter stations and therefore includes the drawing FCW 4514. Although not all airfields within this group were used as fighter airfields, all the buildings were constructed of permanent brick, with all four walls 13.5ins thick, supporting reinforced concrete floor, balcony and roof. The roof and balcony were reinforced with concrete downstand beams and, strangely, in most cases the roof was further reinforced with a single concrete upstand beam spanning the width of the building above the control room. It was probably built in this way so that there would not be any restriction in height inside the control room. Furthermore, some buildings had very thick concrete floors and balcony, being some nine inches thick, as seen at Elvington. At Kings Cliffe a huge reinforced concrete lintel spanning the width of the building was built above the control room windows to drawing number FCW 4524.

The rear of the building was practically blind, except in some cases for a small window on the ground floor opposite the staircase. A steel ladder bolted to the rear wall was originally the only access to the roof as there was no ladder from the balcony. However, some buildings were later modified by having a steel ladder either on one side of the balcony similar to later designs such as 12779/41, but fitted on the opposite side as seen at Coleby Grange. Alternatively, at Fiskerton a vertical steel ladder was simply bolted to the front elevation. The window openings of both watch office and control room were exactly the same size except the side wall containing the pyro store. A rare modification to the deviation drawing number 16560/41 at a few airfields such as Scorton was the reduction of the openings to receive narrow window frames to the watch office and control room, similar to deviation drawing 15371/41 that affected the 12779/41 watch office and also included the provision of individual RT chambers in the wireless operators' room.

In this building the main entrance, at the rear, led into a lobby area and corridor. Immediately on the left was the concrete staircase connecting with the first floor. Having the staircase on the left is a characteristic of this type, as all other designs had a right-hand staircase. There was no separate switch room and so the electric mains and standby power entered the building to a switching area under the stairs. Opposite the staircase were the toilets for both airmen and officers and opposite here was a store room. The next room on the right was a rest room and opposite this was the meteorological office. At the front was the watch office room complete with pyro cupboard in one corner, and between the watch office and restroom on the right was a side entrance. The staircase led to an "L" shape landing and corridor, the Controller's rest room was first on the right and next to it was a store room. Opposite was the wireless operators' room containing three cubicles. The front half of the building was the control room, the wireless room wall having three hatches, one from each cubicle. Curtain rails were located in the ceiling, allowing the entire room to be blacked out.

Steel doors, one either side, gave access to the balcony. Both balcony and roof had steel railing around the edge. The Yorkshire Air Museum at Elvington have refurnished the control tower with fixtures and fittings from the war period including teleprinters, aerodrome mimic board (replica) and radio equipment.

Some airfields such as Coleby Grange had a steel framed concrete panel additional control room to drawing number 10413/42 which was fitted to other building types on airfields used for night fighter operations. An alternative additional control room similar in size but of Seco construction was available, as built at Tangmere, although this may have been built post-war.

The building at Ford was extended in 1953, when a brick kerb was built above the existing roof up to the level of the upstand beam, and a floor was laid above it with a balcony and new second floor control room. An additional control room was then added on top of the new extension. On the left hand side elevation between the first and second floors an annexe was constructed, supported by a retaining wall. The rear of the building was also extended, creating a huge control tower more in line with a true Navy building.

A light timber and glass VCR was constructed above the rear half of the watch office, behind the concrete upstand beam, at Church Fenton. Although the drawing number is unknown, it was similar to that built above other watch office types at Topcliffe, Rufforth and Strubby.

Clearly this building type was inferior to the standard watch office designs, as many of its features are not found on later drawings; the upstand concrete beam on the roof, the absence of the ladder on the balcony connecting with the roof, and the staircase being on the left are a few examples. Furthermore, this building was soon to become obsolete and was replaced by a new design similar to other standard watch offices being constructed around 1942.

Today several buildings of this group survive, and a few are still used for air traffic control including Church Fenton, St. Athan, Wickenby and Woodvale. Bradwell Bay, Cark, Hibaldstowe and Rattlesden are all dwellings. Elvington is a museum, and Grove and Odiham are offices. Charmy Down, Kings Cliffe, Melbourne, Skipton-on-Swale, Tangmere, Twinwood Farm and Woolfox Lodge are all derelict.

Superseding Design

From March 1942 the Type Design 12096/41 was superseded by a new standard design to drawing number 15684/41 (TD446). This building was similar in size, appearance and internal arrangement to the standard bomber satellite watch office 15683/41.

Despite the obvious similarities, not so obvious was its construction, which was quite different. Nine reinforced concrete columns and beams and all four brick walls 13.5ins thick provided the loadbearing structure that supported the reinforced concrete balcony, floor and roof. Usually the walls were left unrendered as this was unnecessary when the walls were so thick. Just why night fighter stations had to have a watch office built of this type of permanent construction is unclear. Long narrow windows were provided for the control room, the watch office room having shorter windows of the same width.

For a description of the internal arrangement see New Bomber Satellite Watch Office.

An obstruction warning light was fitted at roof level on the front elevation and operated by a switch in the control room. Where an additional control room was required drawing number 10413/42 was used similar to other night fighter stations, although there is no evidence that they were ever built above this type of building. Indeed, the only confirmed airfield to have this building type was at Winfield, where it replaced a fighter satellite watch office. However, according to the airfield site plans held at the RAF Museum, both Winkleigh and Zeals were supposed to have had this type, but this may not be the case as the window arrangement is somewhat different and they are both cement rendered.

Watch Office for Night Fighter Stations
Known Drawing Numbers

Airfield	Drawing Numbers	Airfield	Drawing Numbers
Bradwell Bay	12096/41	Melbourne	FCW 4514
Burn	12096/41	Odiham	FCW 4514?
Cark	12096/41, W/451/41	Pembrey	12096/41
Castle Donington	12096/41, 10413/42	Ramsbury	12096/41
Charmy Down	FCW 4514, 10413/42	Rattlesden	4533/42
Church Fenton	Number unknown	Scorton	12096/41, 16560/41
Coleby Grange	12096/41, 10413/42, TG46	Skipton-on-Swale	12096/41
Darley Moor	FCW 4514	St. Athan	FCW 4514?
Dunholme Lodge	12096/41	Tangmere	12096/41
Elvington	4532/3/43	Twinwood Farm	12096/41
Fiskerton	12096/41	Winfield	15684/41
Ford	12096/41 + extra storey	Winkleigh	15684/41
Greenham Common	12096/41	Winthorpe	12096/41
Grove		Woodvale	12096/41
Hibaldstow	FCW 4514, FCW 4914, TD 246	Woolfox Lodge	4532/3/43
Hunsdon	12096/41, 10413/42	Wrexham	12096/41
Kings Cliffe	FCW 4514	Zeals	15684/41
Little Horwood	12096/41		

Drawing No.	Date	Comments
2723/41		Reinforced concrete details
12096/41	8.41	General arrangement
15684/41	3.42	Superseding 12096/41
16560/41	1.42	Deviation, reduced windows to 12096/41
ME 1710/42	11.3.42	Internal wiring
ME 3989/42	1.6.42	Internal wiring to 15684/41
10413/42		Additional control room
ME 2316/43	3.6.43	Wiring of additional control room
FCW 4514		Details unknown
FCW 4914		Details unknown
TD 246		Details unknown

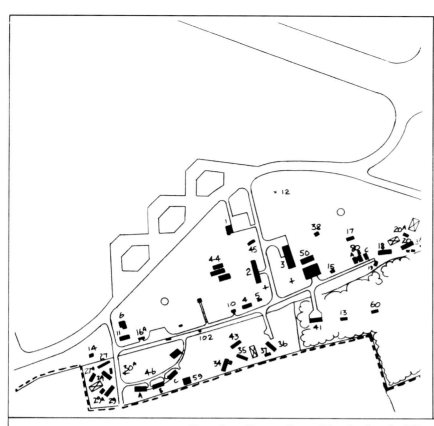

1. Control tower (watch office) 12096/41
2. SHQ 14376/40 + 158358/40
3. Armoury/NFE 15838/40
4. Lubricant store 15839/40
5. Technical latrine
6. Sub station
7. Fuel compound
9. Petrol (MT) compound
10. Bulk oil
11. Guard house
12. Sleeve streamer mast
14–15. M/E plinth
16A. MT p[etrol installation
17. Parachute store 11137/41
18. Defence unit officers' quarters 13903/40
19. Defence unit latrines
20. Defence unit sergeants' quarters
20A. Dinghy store
24, 27, 29, 29A. Defence unit quarters, etc.
30A. Latrines
34, 35, 36. Defence unit quarters, etc.
37. Latrines
38. Single Link trainer 10040/41
41. Gas defence centre 48/40
43. Defence unit
44. Intelligence office & crew briefing
46. AOC equipment stores 1502/41
50. ME plinth
60. Battle HQ 110081/41
80. Searchlight site HQ hut
A, B, C. Accommodation
102. MT Petrol Installation

Bradwell-on-Sea Technical Site (part)

This plan shows part of a night fighter airfield with a 12096/41 watch office, built with its own vehicle park hard standing. Hangars were mainly EO blisters dispersed around the airfield with a single Bellman.

Note the large amount of Defence Unit accommodation, most of which was Laing hutting. This was because of its location in the Blackwater estuary and the possibility of attack from enemy craft coming up the river.

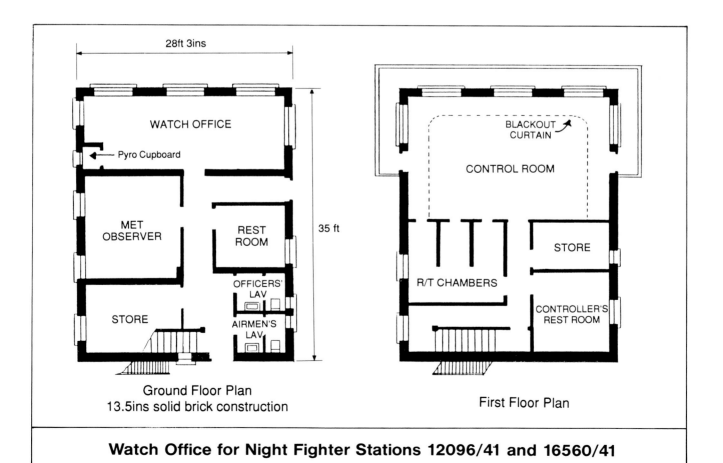

Ground Floor Plan
13.5ins solid brick construction

First Floor Plan

Watch Office for Night Fighter Stations 12096/41 and 16560/41

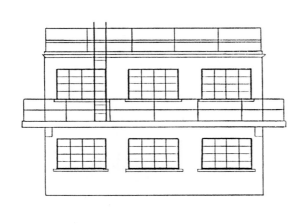

**Watch Office for Night Fighter Stations
12096/41**
Permanent brick
Fiskerton

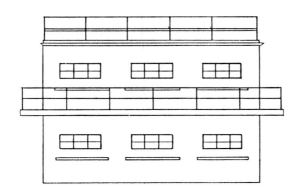

**Watch Office for Night Fighter Stations
12096/41 and 16560/41**
Original window frames removed and replaced
with smaller frames.
Scorton

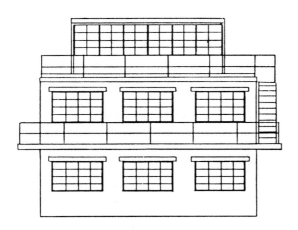

**Watch Office for Night Fighter Stations
12096/41, 10413/42 and TG46**
with addition of new control room and steel
balcony stair.
Coleby Grange

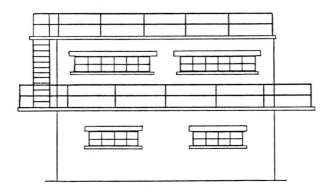

**Watch Office for Night Fighter Stations
15684/41.** Replacement design.
Permanent brick and reinforced concrete.
Winfield.

Watch Office for Night Fighter Stations 12096/41, Burn 1977.

Watch Office for Night Fighter Stations 15684/41, Winfield 1980.

Watch Office for Night Fighter Stations FCW 4514, Kings Cliffe 1980. Note the reinforced concrete beam above the control room windows and the reinforced concrete upstand beam on the roof.

Watch Office for Night Fighter Stations 12096/41, Woodvale 1977, showing early VCR. Photo: Aldon Ferguson.

Watch Office for all Commands

This Type Design building was originally an attempt to standardise flying control buildings on OTU and other training airfields in late 1941, and construction commenced in early 1942 to drawing number 12779/41. With the exception of satellite airfields, it was probably adopted in late 1943 as the standard flying control building for all Commands to drawing number 343/43.

The two storey square-shaped building (35ft x 33ft 6ins) was built in 9ins brickwork except for the front elevation which was built of 13.5ins brick. As with most temporary brick buildings, all external walls were cement rendered, although Debach and Matching Green were exceptions. The flat roof, balcony and first floor were built of reinforced concrete and the control room floor originally comprised timber floor boards battened to the concrete floor beneath.

Between 1942 and March 1943, this building was constructed at many airfields to the earlier drawing of 12779/41, which had large window frames for the watch office and control room. At some airfields, however, such as Kimbolton and Rougham, the window size was reduced to drawing number 15371/41. There the original window frames were removed and the openings bricked up with straight-joint brickwork except for a narrow opening which was the same width and height at all openings. The reason for this practice is unclear although it could be that the operations from the airfield were mainly conducted at night. After 1943 most of the buildings constructed to the earlier drawing of 12779/41 with large window frames were refitted with smaller frames to the watch office and control room to drawing number 343/43 and all new buildings constructed from March 1943 were built to this drawing, which superseded 12779/41. Today it is possible to see evidence of this practice. For example at East Kirkby the replacement brickwork between the original and new window openings consisted of 9ins brick instead of 13.5ins, thereby leaving a brick width's scar on the front elevation. However, it is more common to see this evidence inside the building than on the outside wall. At some airfields such as Bodney the external evidence is the original window sills still in-situ a few brick courses below the replacement sills. Another sign to look out for is where the cement render has fallen in the area where the original window frames would have been, exposing the straight-joint brickwork and giving an outline of the former opening. Furthermore, if the building was built to 12779/41 the staircase window will be eight feet long and if built to 343/43 it will be only four feet long. Finally, the centre window on the front elevation of the watch office on the ground floor sometimes had five panes instead of the usual four if built after 1943. Not all buildings were amended to 343/43 however, those at Catfoss and Membury retained the larger window frames.

Internal arrangement

The main entrance at the rear of the building led into a central corridor with rooms leading off either side. To the right of the entrance was a pre-cast concrete staircase connecting the ground floor with the first floor. Further along the corridor were toilets and opposite these and the staircase was the Met. Office. In here in one corner was a partititon behind which was the teleprinter, connected to the Defence Teleprinter Network (DTN). Beyond the toilets and on the same side was the switch room to which the only access was from outside the building. Opposite this room was the Duty Pilot's rest room, after which was the watch office room, generally used by the Duty Pilot on training airfields. In one corner stood the pyrotechnics cupboard. Most rocket projectiles, however, were kept inside two specially constructed detached pyro stores, each located a short distance either side of the watch office.

The staircase led to a first floor landing and corridor. Opposite the landing was the signals office which faced the Controller's rest room. At the end of the corridor was the control room with a PBX located in one corner, partitioned off in fibre board. Two exits, one on each side wall, led directly on to a concrete balcony. A steel ladder connected the right hand side of the balcony with the roof and the usual tubular steel railings were fixed to the balcony and roof edge.

A few buildings had a small Seco control room or signalling penthouse installed on the roof, but this seems to be rare; an example was at Framlingham, where a replica has been built. Similar brick built additional control rooms were used as an alternative to the Seco type; at Stretton, for example, one was built on the left-hand corner of the building with QDM boards anchored to the railings. At Alconbury one was built similar to that shown on drawing number 4170/43 (ops room type watch office) located on the right-hand corner. Alternatively, if the airfield was to be used at night an additional control room to drawing number 10413/42 was constructed in the centre of the roof above the existing control room and consisted of a steel frame clad with cement rendered 4.5ins brick. In conjunction with this new room was drawing number 1358/44 which was for the erection of QDM boards. These consisted of a braced tubular steel frame erected on three sides of the new control room supporting hinged timber number boards located above the roof of the new control room. The number plates were hinged in two leaves and were operated by a rope from roof level.

One design which appears to have similar characteristics to this building type as seen at Findo Gask and Dumfries was built with three storeys instead of the usual two. The ground floor consisted of a main entrance through double doors at the rear, with an "L" shape corridor leading to a side exit. There were two rooms on the ground floor with access from here, one of which contained toilets. A further room, the switch room, only had access from outside the building similar to two storey buildings. A concrete staircase led up to the first floor. The front room was the watch office with pyro store in one corner, and here the walls were rendered up to dado height and painted green while the fair face bricks above were painted cream. There were two further rooms of exact function unknown (probably Duty Pilot's rest room and Met. Office) and toilets above those on the floor below. A cupboard was located opposite the rear room. Behind the toilets at the rear was a staircase leading to the second floor signals office, control room and balcony. It is interesting to note that both the watch office and control room had larger window frames at one time, as evidence can be seen of the original outline of the windows. The usual steel stair allows access to the roof, where a 9ft square steel QDM frame is still in situ. It is not clear why Findo Gask should have had such a large control tower. The owner is currently seeking planning permission to convert the building into a house.

Post War Alterations

At some post war airfields it became necessary, in order to bring the building up to modern air traffic control standards, to build a visual control room (VCR) on top of the existing building. One method, as built at Kinloss to drawing number 3957/58, was as follows:

Holes were cut through the concrete slab of the first floor and roof and then through the concrete floor in the former watch office down to the original foundations. Four new RSJ stanchions were then erected and RSJ beams were bolted on to the stanchions to provide a load bearing structure to which the VCR could be anchored. This allowed the VCR to be positioned at the front end of the building so that the timber floor could be extended out from the front elevation to provide a balcony complete with a steel handrail to match the existing. The drawing used for the VCR was 5871c/55 in common with many other buildings modified to include a VCR, e.g. Watton, or the latest design of control tower then being built and commissioned, such as Dishforth. This room, octagonal in plan, was steel framed and clad with anti-glare glass. The entrance was at the rear of the room, where new timber stairs connected with the first floor signals office. This enclosed staircase was erected inside a 4.5ins brick stairwell. A steel heating and ventilation duct was fitted on the left-hand side and connected with the AC plant equipment on the ground floor.

On the first floor, the former control room became the approach control room and was fitted out with the necessary radar equipment. The teleprinter was moved from the ground floor and repositioned behind a breeze block partition in the former signals office next to the new staircase. The Controller's rest room became the Senior Air Traffic Controller's office (SATCO). On the ground floor the watch office room became the technical apparatus room, the Duty Pilot's rest room became the GPO equipment room. The Met. Office became the new AC plant room, containing air supply fan, compressor, condenser and coolers. Outside, a single storey building was erected against the entrance to the mechanical and electrical (ME) switchgear room. This was the "A" centre and its equipment translated the requirements which the Controller had selected from the control desk into coded signals which were sent out via underground cables to the selected "B" centre (electrical power substations) located near the ends of the runway. This allowed the economical distribution of electrical current and was, and still is, called the Unit Control System.

At Watton a more substantial loadbearing modification was required, consisting of four external cased steel concrete columns and four internal columns supporting a new brick built octagonal room above which was mounted the VCR. The floor was extended around all eight sides thus forming a complete balcony. Alternatively, a light timber VCR was built at Strubby and West Freugh, consisting of a timber framed structure clad with timber boarding and glazed with 0.375ins thick green tinted glass. At Strubby, the VCR measuring 22ft by 17ft was built at the rear left hand corner, mounted directly on to the roof. It is believed that the building did not require any structural modification other than the removal of a section of the existing concrete roof for access from the floor below. This was similar to that built above other watch office buildings modified in the late 1950s, and included Church Fenton and Rufforth, although these seem to be smaller.

Buildings Today

Being the most common type of watch office built, quite a number survive (1991) and a few are still used for air traffic control, including:

Barkston Heath	Merryfield
Bentwaters	Mona
Dunsfold (until recently)	St. Angelo
Duxford	Stansted
Halfpenny Green	Sumburgh?
Kinloss	West Freugh
Leicester East	Woodbridge
Llandwrog	

Other buildings still extant include the following:

Acaster Malbis	Jurby
Alconbury	Keevil
Aldermaston	Kingston Bagpuize
Ashbourne	Llanbedr
Aston Down	Langham
Banff	Lavenham
Beccles	Little Snoring
Bodney	Little Walden
Boreham	Ludham
Broadwell	Maghaberry
Bruntingthorpe	Martlesham Heath
Calveley	Matching Green
Catfoss	Membury
Chedburgh	Mullaghmore
Church Lawford	North Creake
Culmhead	Oulton
Dallachy	Rackheath
Davidstow Moor	Rougham
Debach	Sandtoft
Deenethorpe	Shepherds Grove
Docking	Silverstone
Dounreay	Snitterfield
Dumfries	Stretton
Dunkeswell	Strubby
Earls Colne	Tholthorpe
East Kirkby	Tilstock
Errol	Toome
Findo Gask	Turnberry
Framlingham	Upottery
Full Sutton	Warmwell
Gosfield	Watton
Haverfordwest	Wheaton Aston
Hixon	Wigtown
Husbands Bosworth	Wombleton.
Hutton Cranswick	

Approximately half the above are derelict, such as Findo Gask and Ludham; most of the others are used as offices for light industry, examples being Ashbourne, Membury and Little Walden. Mullaghmore, Toome, Turnberry and Sandtoft are dwellings and East Kirkby and Framlingham are both museums.

Watch Office for all Commands
Known Drawing Numbers

Airfield	Drawing Numbers	Airfield	Drawing Numbers
Acaster Malbis	343/43	Framlingham	12779/41, 15371/41, 5966/43
Alconbury	343/43	Full Sutton	343/43
Aldermaston	12779/41, 343/43	Glatton	12779/41, 343/43
Andrewsfield	12779/41, 343/43	Gosfield	343/43
Angle	12779/41, 14741/41	Great Dunmow	12779/41, 343/43
Ashbourne	12779/41, 343/43	Greencastle	12779/41, 343/43
Aston Down	12779/41, 343/43	Halesworth	12779/41, 343/43
Banff	12779/41, 343/43	Halfpenny Green	12779/41
Babdown Farm	12779/41, 343/43	Harrington	12779/41, 343/43
Barkston Heath	12779/41, 343/43, 5871c/55	Haverfordwest	12779/41, 15371/41
Beaulieu	12779/41, 343/43	High Roding	12779/41, proposed but not built
Beccles	12779/41, 343/43	Hixon	12779/41, 343/43
Bentwaters	12779/41, 343/43	Holmsley South	12779/41, 343/43
Birch	12779/41, 343/43	Horham	12779/41, 343/43
Blakehill Farm	343/43	Hornchurch	12779/41, 343/43
Bodney	343/43	Husbands Bosworth	12779/41, 343/43
Boreham	12779/41, 15371/41	Hutton Cranswick	12779/41, 343/43
Bottisham	15371/41	Jurby	12779/41, W451/42
Boxted	12779/41, 343/43	Keevil	12779/41, 343/43
Brackla	12779/41, 343/43	Kingston Bagpuize	343/43
Broadwell	343/43	Kinloss	12779/41, 3957/58
Bruntingthorpe	12779/41, 15371/41	Kimbolton	12779/41, 15371/41
Burtonwood	12779/41, 15371/41	Langham	12779/41, 4702/43
Calveley	12779/41, 343/43	Lavenham	12779/41, 10302/42
Carnaby	343/43	Leicester East	12779/41, 343/43
Catfoss	12779/41	Leiston	12779/41, 343/43
Chedburgh	343/43	Little Snoring	12779/41, 343/43
Chalgrove	343/43	Little Walden	12779/41, 343/43
Chilbolton	12779/41, 343/43	Llanbedr	12779/41
Chipping Ongar	12779/41, 343/43	Llandwrog	12779/41, 343/43
Church Lawford	343/43	Lulsgate Bottom	12779/41, 343/43
Croughton	12779/41	Ludford Magna	12779/41, 343/43
Culmhead	12779/41, 343/43	Ludham	12779/41, 343/43,
Dalcross	WA1599/43	Maghaberry	12779/41, 343/43
Dallachy	12779/41, 343/43	Market Harborough	12779/41, 343/43
Davidstow Moor	12779/41, 343/43	Martlesham Heath	343/43
Debach	12779/41, 343/43	Matching Green	12779/41, 15371/41
Deenethorpe	12779/41, 343/43	Matlask	12779/41, 343/43
Deopham Green	12779/41, 343/43	Melton Mowbray	12779/41, 343/43
Docking	12779/41, 343/43	Membury	12779/41
Dounreay	12779/41, 343/43	Mepal	12779/41, 343/43
Down Ampney	343/43	Merryfield	343/43
Dumfries		Metheringham	12779/41, 343/43
Dunsfold	12779/41, 343/43	Mill Isle	343/43
Dunkeswell	12779/41, 343/43	Millom	12779/41, 343/43
Duxford	12779/41	Milltown	12779/41
Earls Colne	12779/41, 343/43	Mona	12779/41
East Kirkby	12779/41, 343/43	Mullaghmore	12779/41, 343/43
Errol		Nuthampstead	12779/41, 343/43
Eshott	12779/41, 343/43	North Creake	12779/41, 343/43
Eye	12779/41, 343/43	North Killingholme	12779/41, 343/43
Fairford	343/43	North Pickenham	12779/41, 343/43
Fersfield	12779/41, 343/43	North Witham	12779/41, 343/43
Findo Gask	12779/41, FG 272	Northolt	12779/41
Folkingham	12779/41, 343/43	Old Buckenham	12779/41, 343/43
Fowlmere	343/43, 5966/43	Oulton	12779/41, 343/43

Airfield	Drawing Numbers	Airfield	Drawing Numbers
Perton	12779/41, 15371/41	Sudbury	12779/41, 343/43
Pocklington	343/43	Sumburgh	343/43
Predannack	12779/41, 343/43	Swannington	12779/41, 343/43
Rackheath	12779/41, 343/43	Talbenny	12779/41, 343/43
Raydon	12779/41, 343/43	Tarrant Rushton	12779/41, 343/43
Ridgewell	12779/41, 343/43	Tholthorpe	343/43
Rivenhall	12779/41, 15371/41	Tilstock	12779/41, 343/43
Rougham	12779/41, 15371/41	Toome	12779/41, 343/43
Sandtoft	12779/41, 343/43	Tuddenham	12779/41, 343/43
Saltby	12779/41, 15371/41	Turnberry	12779/41, 343/43
Sawbridgeworth	12779/41, 343/43	Upottery	343/43
Shepherds Grove	12779/41	Upwood	343/43
Silverstone	12779/41, 343/43	Warmwell	12779/41, 343/43
Snailwell	12779/41, 343/43	Watton	12779/41, 343/43, 5871c/55
Snetterton Heath	12779/41, 343/43	West Freugh	12779/41, 3957/58
Snitterfield	12779/41	Weston Zoyland	12779/41, 343/43, 4097/43
Spanhoe	12779/41, 343/43	Wheaton Aston	12779/41, 343/43
St. Angelo	12779/41	Wigtown	12779/41
St. Davids	12779/41, 343/43	Witchford	12779/41, 343/43
Stansted	12779/41	Wombleton	12779/41, 343/43
Stanton Harcourt	343/43	Woodbridge	343/43
Stoney Cross	12779/41, 343/43	Wormingford	12779/41, 343/43
Stretton	12779/41, 10302/42, 1915/43	Worksop	12779/41, 343/43
Strubby	12779/41, 343/43	Wratting Common	12779/41, 343/43
Sturgate	12779/41, 343/43	York	12779/41, 343/43

Drawing No.	Date	Comments
12779/41	10.41	General arrangement – large windows
14741/41		Details unknown
15371/41		Deviation, reduction of window size (small)
ME 16148/41	12.2.42	Internal wiring
W451/42		Details unknown
ME 749/42		Internal wiring
10302/42		Details unknown
10413/42		Additional control room
343/43	3.43	Superseding 12779/41. Reduction in window size (medium)
1915/43		Details unknown
5966/43		Addition of Seco control room
4097/43		Details unknown
ME 2506/44	14.7.43	Superseding ME 749/42
1357/8/44		Addition of QDM boards
5966/43	24.1.44	Additional Seco control room
ME 8265/43	25.1.44	Internal wiring to new Seco control room
5871c/55		VCR General arrangement
3957/58		Addition of VCR (Kinloss)

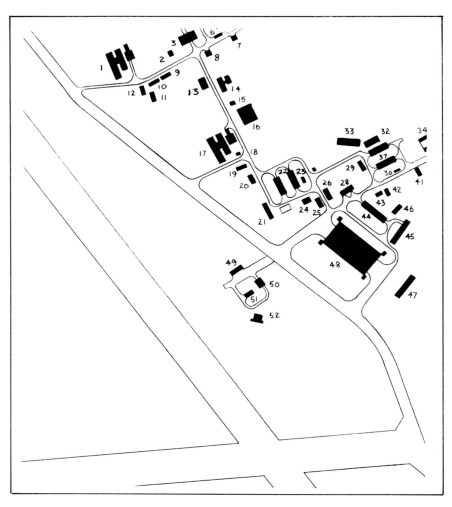

1. Crew rest room 15657/41, Nissen
2. Sub station 1324/41
3. Fuel compound 9108/41
6. MT petrol installation 4619/40
7. Gas chamber 12411/41
8. AM bombing teacher 6301/42
9–11. Flight office 4785/42, Nissen
12. Squadron office 4785/42, Nissen
13. Link trainer 4188/42
14. Photographic block 4781/42
15. Speech broadcasting building 10786/41
16. Free gunnery trainer (EO blister) 4096/43
17. Crew rest room 15657/41, Nissen
18. Transformer compound
19–20. Flight office 4785/42, Nissen
21. Radar workshop 7352/42
22. Main workshops 5851/42, Nissen
23. Technical latrine 9026/41
24. Dinghy hut 2901/43

25. Parachute store 10825/42
26. Main stores office 5852/42, Nissen
27. Bulk oil installation
28. Armoury 12778/41
29. Lubricant store 12406/41
30. Technical latrine
31–32 Main stores 5852/42, Nissen
33. Gas clothing store 13730/41
34. Works services/yard 4914/42
41. Hut
42–43. Gas defence centre 12408/41, Nissen
44–46. Maintenance and armoury 12777/41, Nissen
47. Squadron armoury 3929/43, Nissen
48. T2 hangar 3653/42
49. NFE store 12411/42
50. Flood light trailer tractor shed
51. Fire tender shelter
52. Control tower (watch office) 12779/41

Andrewsfield Technical site (part)

Typically this watch office was built with the technical site behind, with usually one or more T2 type hangars close by. Nearby were NFE store, Fire Tender shelter and Flood Light trailer tractor shed.

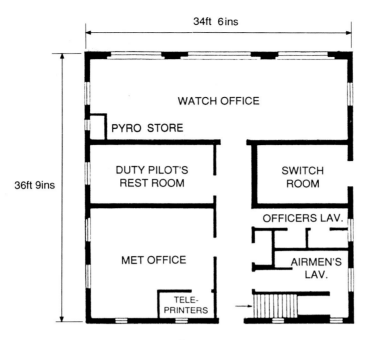

34ft 6ins

36ft 9ins

WATCH OFFICE

PYRO STORE

DUTY PILOT'S REST ROOM

SWITCH ROOM

MET OFFICE

OFFICERS LAV.

AIRMEN'S LAV.

TELE-PRINTERS

Ground Floor Plan
temporary brick construction

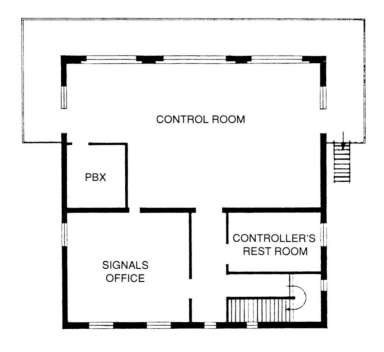

CONTROL ROOM

PBX

CONTROLLER'S REST ROOM

SIGNALS OFFICE

First Floor Plan

Watch Office (all Commands) 12779/41 and 343/43

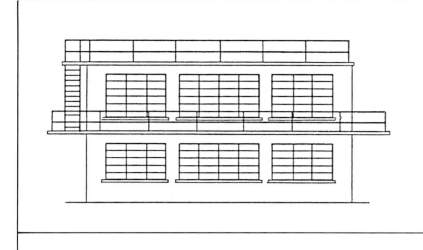

Watch Office 12779/41
Original design.
Temporary brick construction

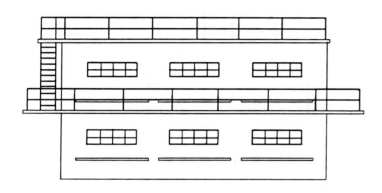

Watch Office 12779/41 and 15371/41
– original window frames removed
and replaced with narrow frames.

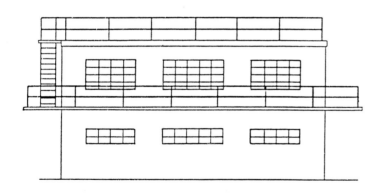

Watch Office 343/43
Standard Type Design
for all Commands. Earlier
12779/41 buildings modified
to this standard after 1943.

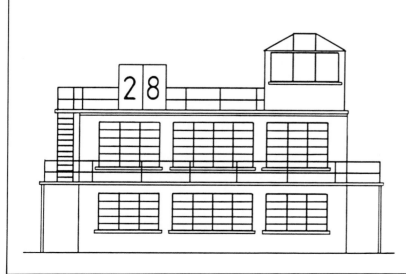

Watch Office 12779/41
with signalling penthouse, Stretton.
(Replaced earlier 3156/41 Watch
Office.

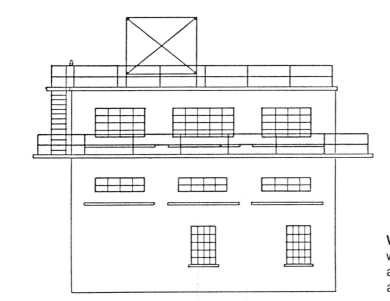

Watch Office 12779/41
with additional floor
and QDM boards
as existing Findo Gask 1991.

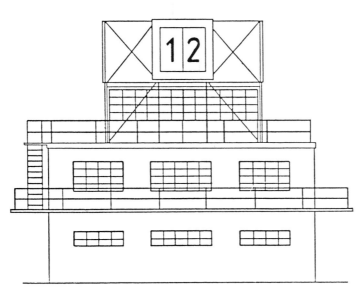

**Watch Office 343/43,
10413/42 and 1358/44**
with additional control room
and QDM boards

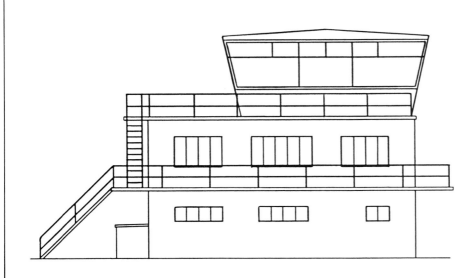

Watch Office 12779/41
with visual control room
as existing Strubby 1991.

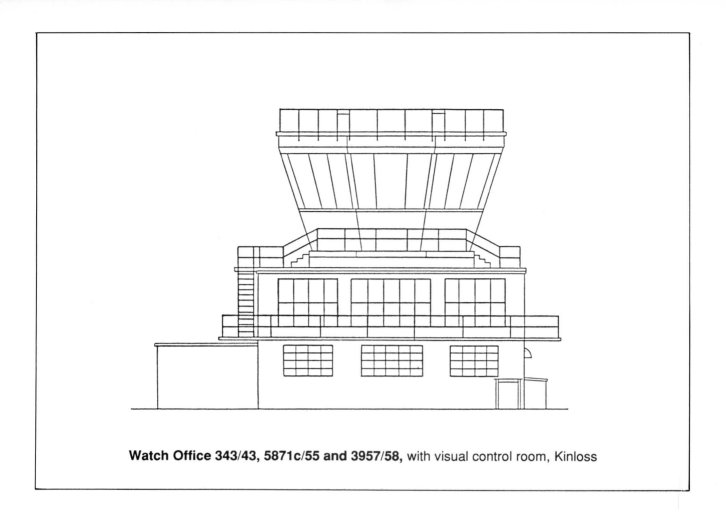

Watch Office 343/43, 5871c/55 and 3957/58, with visual control room, Kinloss

Watch Office for all Commands 12779/41, 343/43, 5871c/55, Watton 1980, showing octagonal extension and modern VCR supported by cased steel concrete columns.

New control room above 343/43 tower, Alconbury 10.5.1945.   Photo: D. Scanlon via John Hamlin

Interior view of old control room 343/43, control tower, Alconbury 10.5.1945. Note large aerodrome map on wall. Photo: D. Scanlon via John Hamlin.

Watch Office for all Commands 12779/41 and 15371/41, Burtonwood 1982.

Watch Office for all Commands 343/43, Kingston Bagpuize. Photo: Dave Smith

Watch Office for all Commands, Strubby 1981.

Watch Office for Bomber Satellite and OTU Satellite Stations

Type Design 13726/41 superseded the watch office with operations room, etc. designs and were built on new stations commencing September 1941. This new detached building without an operations block and crew briefing room was designed on modern lines, similar to but smaller than the building design 12779/41. The operations block was in fact built to drawing No. 13023/41 on a separate administration site on similar lines to the original operations and crew briefing room of 7344/41 and 7345/41 watch office designs. Examples include Bardney, Cottam and Nuneaton. After 1943 at some stations such as Thorpe Abbotts that became re-classified as Class "A" airfields, the operations and crew briefing room was replaced by the latest Type Design 228/43. The original building then became the interrogation centre.

The new watch office was built of 13.5ins brick on the front elevation with the remaining walls in 9ins brick. Roof, floors and balcony were reinforced concrete and the control room floor was clad with timber floor boards attached to the sub-floor below. A cased steel beam ran along the centre of the building and supported the concrete floor above. The large windows of the watch office and control room of the original design were removed at some stations and narrow frames fitted instead to drawing number 15683/41. Furthermore, after 1943 a number of buildings were modified by having the original large window frames removed from both these rooms and replaced with smaller frames. As with the earlier drawing 15683/41, the remaining gap was bricked up with 9in straight joint panel work, evidence of which can be seen today in the form of the original window sills still in situ or inside the control room or watch office where the replacement brick panel work can be seen.

Internal arrangements were the same as the Night Fighter superseding design 15684/41. The main entrance was at the rear with a corridor running towards the front. Immediately on the right was a pre-cast concrete staircase leading up to the first floor. Opposite here were two separate lavatories, the first for airmen and the next for officers. Close to the officers' lavatory was the Met. Office containing a teleprinter kiosk. Next came the switch room complete with underfloor ducting and electric distribution board "A" for watch office lighting and distribution board "B" for airfield lighting, with access from outside only. Opposite was a rest room with a built in flag cupboard having access from the corridor. Spanning the front elevation was the watch office containing a pyro cupboard in one corner.

Up the concrete stairs to the first floor landing and small "L" shape corridor, the first room was a store room, the next the signals office, and opposite was the Controller's rest room. The front half of the first floor was the control room and balcony with access from either side through steel doors. On the balcony on the right-hand side was a steel stair connecting with the flat roof.

Where built, an additional control room of Seco construction to drawing number 5966/43 was simply anchored to the front half of the flat roof, requiring no structural modifications to the building. Modifications to the existing structure were in fact rare, although at Wethersfield an additional floor was provided complete with balcony. It is not known when this was constructed, although it may have originally been so built, similar to that at Gaydon. A visual control room was built in 1952 when the main runway was extended, and the extra floor then became the approach control room for radar monitoring.

Blackbushe also had a visual control room for a short time, until it was removed in late 1961 and repositioned above the old control room of the control tower at Edinburgh Turnhouse. It had to be supported by a steel girder frame. The total cost was £5,000 and it came into use in its new position on 1st February 1962.

Today (1991), the following buildings are still extant:

Bardney	Little Staughton
Barford St. John	Long Newnton
Castle Combe	Newmarket
Chipping Norton	Nuneaton
Condover	Podington?
Enstone	Seething
Finmere	Thorpe Abbotts
Gamston	Turweston
Gransden Lodge	Westhampnett
Lasham	Windrush

The following are still used for air traffic control purposes:

Filton
Lasham
Sleap
Wethersfield (until recently).

Watch Office for Bomber Satellite and OTU Satellite Stations
Known Drawing Numbers

Airfield	Drawing Numbers	Airfield	Drawing Numbers
Bardney	13726/41	Mendlesham	13726/41, 5966/43
Barford St. John	13726/41	Metfield	13726/41
Bibury	13726/41, 14742/41, 15370/41	Milltown	13726/41
Bitteswell	13726/41	Montrose	13726/41
Blackbushe	13726/41	Newmarket	13726/41
Brawdy	13726/41	Nuneaton	13726/41
Castle Combe	13726/41	Peplow	13726/41
Chipping Norton	13726/41	Podington	13726/41, 15683/41
Church Broughton	13726/41	Poulton	13726/41
Condover	13726/41	Sculthorpe	13726/41
Cottam	13726/41, 15683/41	Seething	13726/41
Dalton	13726/41	Sleap	13726/41
Desborough	13726/41	Sibson	13726/41
Enstone	13726/41	Southam	13726/41
Filton	13726/41	Southrop	13726/41
Finmere	13726/41, 15683/41	Steeple Morden	13726/41
Fulbeck	13276/41, 4332/43	Tatenhill	13726/41, 15683/41
Gamston	13726/41, 15683/41	Thorpe Abbotts	13726/41, 15683/41, 5966/43
Gransden Lodge	13726/41	Turweston	13726/41
Great Ashfield	13726/41	Wethersfield	13726/41
Lasham	13726/41	Westhampnett	13726/41 (shown on site plan as 12779/41)
Little Staughton	13726/41		
Long Newnton	13726/41, 15370/41	Windrush	13726/41, 694/41
Longtown	13726/41		

Drawing Number	Date	Comments
13726/41		General Arrangement
14742/41		Details unknown
15370/41		Details unknown
15683/41		Reduction in window size
ME 16148/41		Internal wiring details
5966/43		Addition of Seco control room
ME 8265/43		Addition of Seco control room

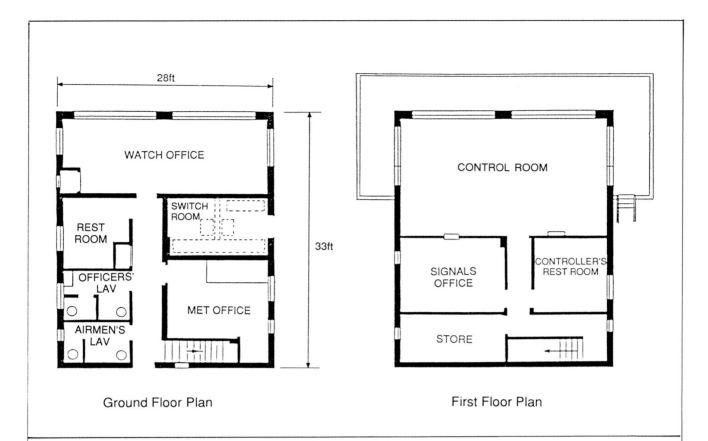

Ground Floor Plan   First Floor Plan

Watch Office for Bomber Satellite and OTU Satellite Stations 13726/41

Watch Office 13726/41 for Bomber Satellite Stations
With additional floor – Gaydon

Watch Office for Bomber Satellite Stations
with additional floor and visual control room
As existing – Wethersfield.

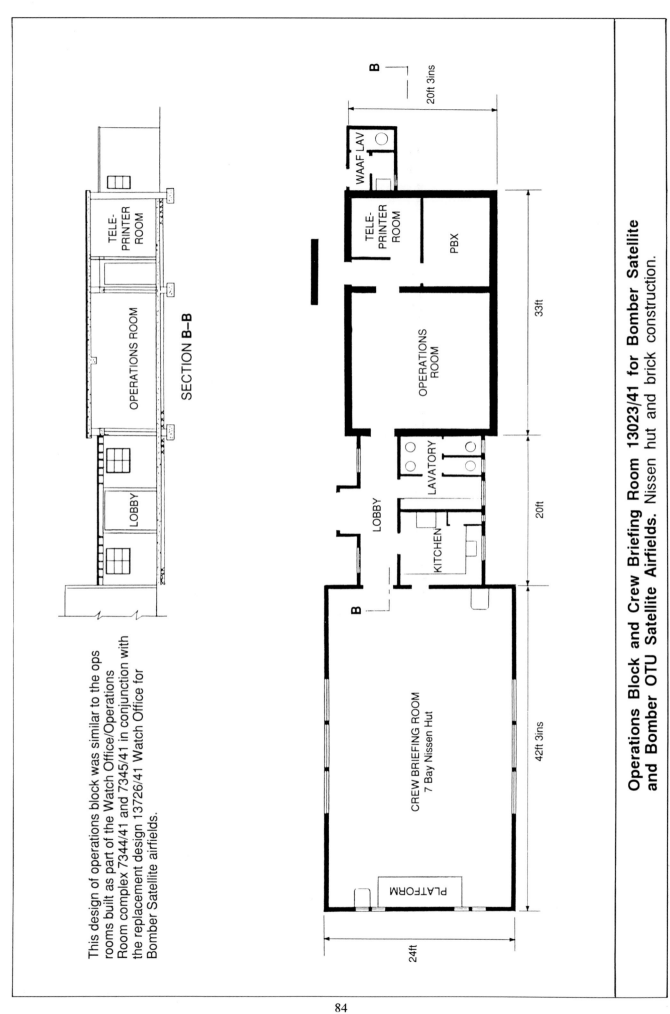

This design of operations block was similar to the ops rooms built as part of the Watch Office/Operations Room complex 7344/41 and 7345/41 in conjunction with the replacement design 13726/41 Watch Office for Bomber Satellite airfields.

SECTION B-B

TELE-PRINTER ROOM

OPERATIONS ROOM

LOBBY

B

WAAF LAV

TELE-PRINTER ROOM

PBX

20ft 3ins

33ft

OPERATIONS ROOM

LOBBY

LAVATORY

KITCHEN

20ft

B

CREW BRIEFING ROOM
7 Bay Nissen Hut

PLATFORM

42ft 3ins

24ft

Operations Block and Crew Briefing Room 13023/41 for Bomber Satellite and Bomber OTU Satellite Airfields. Nissen hut and brick construction.

84

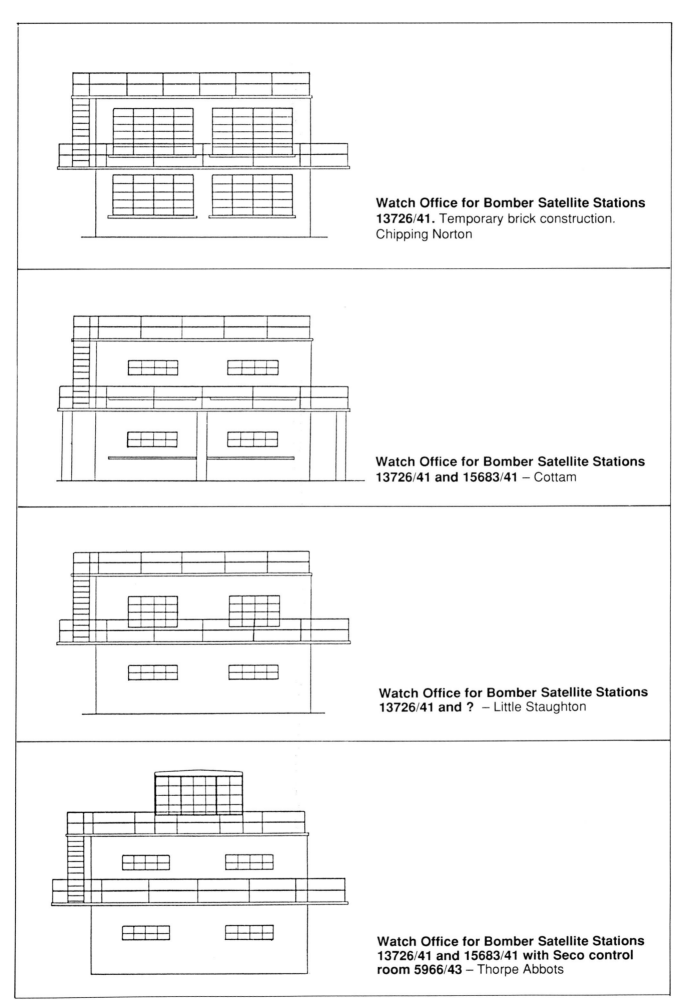

Watch Office for Bomber Satellite Stations 13726/41. Temporary brick construction. Chipping Norton

Watch Office for Bomber Satellite Stations 13726/41 and 15683/41 – Cottam

Watch Office for Bomber Satellite Stations 13726/41 and ? – Little Staughton

Watch Office for Bomber Satellite Stations 13726/41 and 15683/41 with Seco control room 5966/43 – Thorpe Abbots

Watch Office for Bomber Satellite and Bomber OTU Satellite airfields 13726/41. Enstone, 1978

Watch Office, Bomber Satellite and Bomber OTU Satellite airfields 13726/41, Turweston, 1982. Note the original sills below the windows.

Watch Office for Bomber Satellite airfields 13726/41, Wethersfield 1991, showing additional floor expansion and early 1950s VCR.

Associated Buildings

NFE Store

30ft

GOOSE FLARE TROLLEY

GLIM LAMP TROLLEY

ILLUMINATED TEE

18ft

Walls 10ft 6ins high

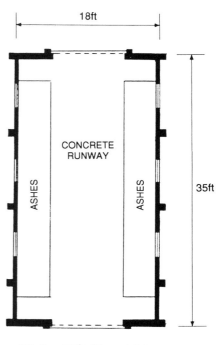

18ft

CONCRETE RUNWAY

ASHES

ASHES

35ft

Walls 13ft 6ins high

Night Flying Equipment Store and Floodlight Trailer and Tractor Shed 12411/41

These two buildings together with a gas chamber/practice bomb store and a gas chamber, are all part of drawing number 12411/41. Construction was in 4.5ins cement rendered brick in 10ft bays with steel roof trusses and corrugated asbestos roof. This drawing design represents the most common wartime buildings of their type.

Night flying equipment store at Turweston, 1982.

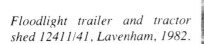

Floodlight trailer and tractor shed 12411/41, Lavenham, 1982.

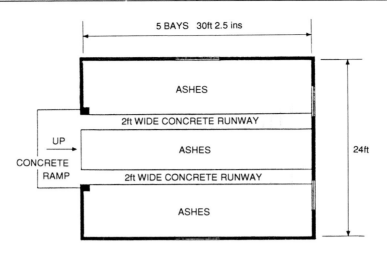

Fire Tender Shelter 12410/41 (24ft span Nissen Hutting)

Drawing 12410/41 was for a fire tender house and fire tender shelter both in 24ft span Nissen hutting. The fire tender house was similar but had a flat concrete floor and a bench at the rear. This building was located next to the guard room. The fire tender shelter was built near to the watch office, normally 12779/41 and 13726/41 designs but is now quite rare.

Fire tender shelter Nissen Hut 12410/41 at Swannington, 1979.

RU pyro store, Goxhill, 1981.

RU Pyro Store (Ready Use)

Usually found in pairs. It is quite common to find a different drawing number for each, 5488/42 for one and 2847/38 for the other; an example is Twinwood Farm. The building was constructed of rendered brickwork with a felt covered reinforced concrete roof. Inside were two compartments with up to five shelves and two air vents. The building measured 11ft 10ins x 8ft 10ins and was 7ft 6ins high.

Control Tower for Very Heavy Bomber Stations 294/45

RAF Sculthorpe was closed for modernisation in 1945, when its runways were lengthened to 3,000 yards x 100 yards with subsidiaries of 2,000 yards. It was designated a Very Heavy Bomber station and reopened in December 1948. As part of the improved facilities, a new control tower 294/45 was built to replace the original 13726/41 building which then became a salt store.

Other airfields with this building type were Lakenheath, Marham and West Raynham. The new building was a three storey structure with an airfield control room on the roof. A single storey wing leading off from a side elevation contained the airfield services. Construction was of a steel frame with unrendered red brick cavity walls. Floors and sub-floors were of precast concrete of the Seigwart type with tongued and grooved timber boarding supported on RSJs and cased steel beams.

The main entrance consisted of a single storey lobby which led into a hallway and corridor connected to the front of the building and gave access to all rooms on this floor of the main building. The stairs connecting with the other floors were located in a stairwell at the rear of the hall and to the left of the stairs were the toilets. A hydrogen cylinder store room was next to the toilets with access only from the outside. The first room along the corridor on the left was the GPO apparatus room and opposite was a large rest room for visiting crews and a kitchen. Next to the GPO room was the signals apparatus room which had under floor ducting in a grid pattern for GPO cables that entered the building underground. After the visiting crew room was the Met. rest room. At the front of the building was the battery and power room and on the right was the compressor and switch room. The corridor terminated at the front of the control tower where there was an exit. The airfield services wing viewed from the front contained the following – fire party office, ambulance garage, crash tender garage and a three bay night flying equipment store (NFE) containing goose (neck) flare trolley and paraffin drums, glim lamp trolley and in the last bay the illuminated landing "T". All garages and NFE bays had large metal doors, the garages being able to open at either end.

First Floor

Here there was a similar arrangement of hall and corridor with toilet above those on the ground floor. Immediately in front of the hall was the operations and planning room containing a large plotting table and map wall. On the right was a small Met. store, next to the forecast room containing charting bench, wind speed and direction indicators and barometer. Access from here led to the teleprinter room at the side of the met store. At the front

of the building the corridor branched out either side where there were offices for the CO, the Navigation Officer, WC plans and the Met. Officer.

Second Floor

A small landing contained a balloon filling room which was supplied with hydrogen gas from the store room on the ground floor. The whole of the second floor was taken up by the approach control room. Above the toilets on the floors below was the senior Flying Control Officer's office. In an area partitioned off at the rear of the ACR were five R/T monitor cubicles. At the front of this large room was the airfield lighting mimic display board and a plotting table large enough to cover 100 square miles. Pneumatic tubes connected with the forecast room and airfield control room. Steel doors, one on either side wall, led to a concrete balcony. Timber stairs gave access to the airfield control room and the main staircase connected with the roof.

Airfield Control Room

Visual control rooms, or airfield control rooms as they were originally called, were required to provide a large space with a 360 degree view. They had to be large enough to accommodate the control desk and airfield lighting control panel and allow plenty of room for the continuing development of this equipment. The design of airfield control room used on this building was not repeated on any other control tower type. It was, in fact, the first of its kind, being octagonal in plan and having angled windows. The internal measurement is 20ft 6ins across flats, and height 8ft 6ins. It is framed with RSJs, clad on the outside with mild steel sheeting and steel framed double glazing units. The centre upper windows are top hung opening sashes, so heavy that they require two people to open them. The roof is also glazed, each section consisting of seven sheets of glass, and is in fact quite crude, not unlike a greenhouse. At West Raynham this window glazing has been painted over and inside a false ceiling of acoustic tiles has been added. Access to the roof of the tower is via a steel framed sliding door which is frequently very difficult to open. Steel tubular railings are fixed to the roof edge.

Today the control tower at West Raynham is looking rather neglected, the VCR is rusting away and most of its equipment has been removed, although the airfield lighting control panel is still in situ. The approach control room is now sub-divided into offices and some of the second floor is unsafe due to fire damage. The NFE store, crash tender and ambulance station have been bricked up and used as offices for the fire section who, with security, occupy the ground floor. A new fire station adjacent to the control tower was built some time ago. A new control tower has been built recently at Lakenheath, and at Sculthorpe the building has been boarded up.

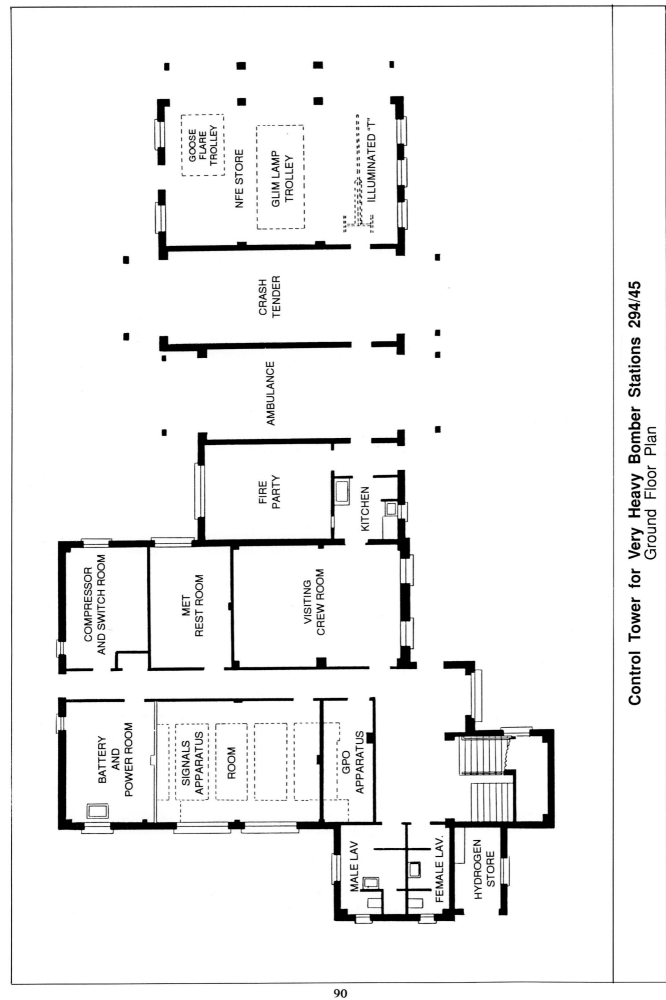

Control Tower for Very Very Heavy Bomber Stations 294/45
Ground Floor Plan

GOOSE FLARE TROLLEY

NFE STORE

GLIM LAMP TROLLEY

ILLUMINATED "T"

CRASH TENDER

AMBULANCE

COMPRESSOR AND SWITCH ROOM

MET REST ROOM

FIRE PARTY

VISITING CREW ROOM

KITCHEN

BATTERY AND POWER ROOM

SIGNALS APPARATUS ROOM

GPO APPARATUS

MALE LAV.

FEMALE LAV.

HYDROGEN STORE

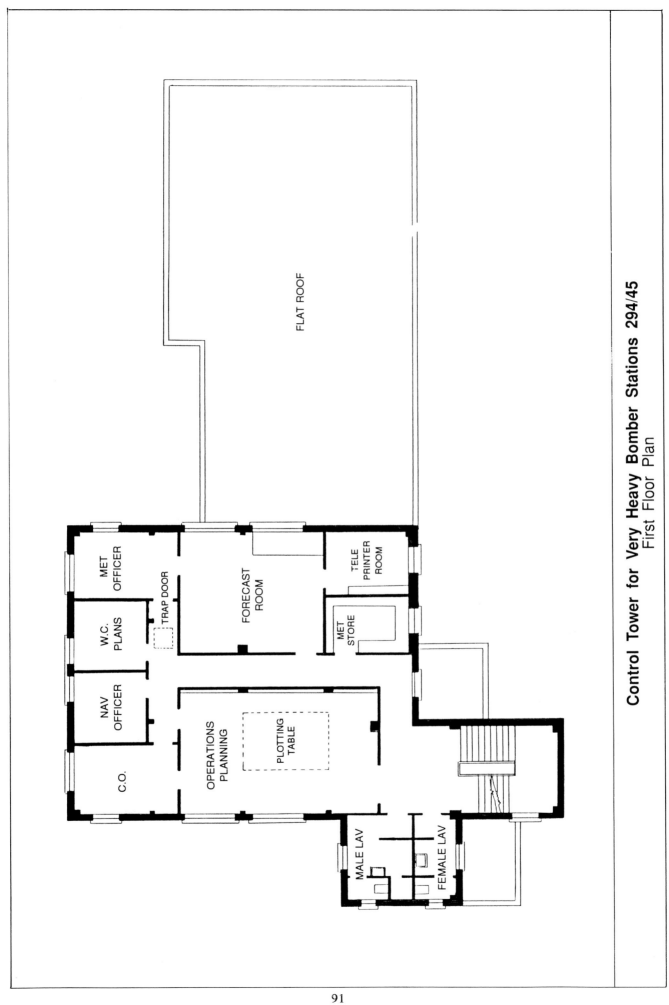

Control Tower for Very Heavy Bomber Stations 294/45
First Floor Plan

FLAT ROOF

MET OFFICER

W.C. PLANS

TRAP DOOR

FORECAST ROOM

TELE PRINTER ROOM

MET STORE

NAV OFFICER

C.O.

OPERATIONS PLANNING

PLOTTING TABLE

MALE LAV

FEMALE LAV

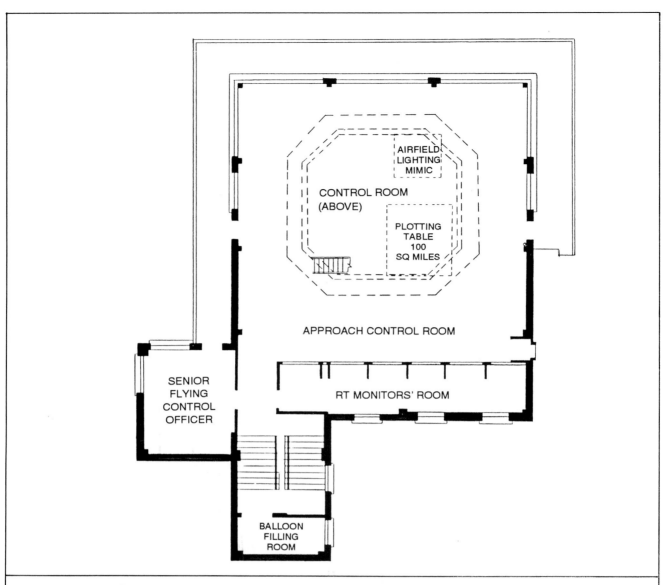

Control Tower for Very Heavy Bomber Stations 294/45
Second Floor Plan showing position of control room above

Labels within plan:
- AIRFIELD LIGHTING MIMIC
- CONTROL ROOM (ABOVE)
- PLOTTING TABLE 100 SQ MILES
- APPROACH CONTROL ROOM
- SENIOR FLYING CONTROL OFFICER
- RT MONITORS' ROOM
- BALLOON FILLING ROOM

VHB type control tower 294/45, West Raynham, 1993.

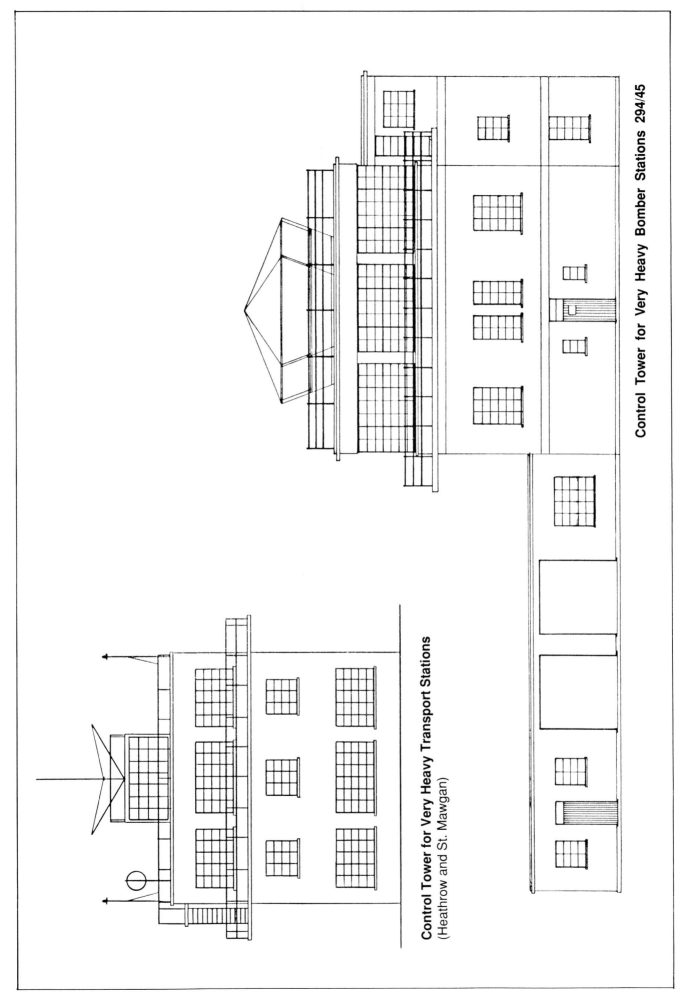

Control Tower for Very Heavy Transport Stations
(Heathrow and St. Mawgan)

Control Tower for Very Heavy Bomber Stations 294/45

Exterior view of VCR at West Raynham, 1993.

Interior view of VCR at West Raynham showing control desk, 1993.

VHT type control tower, Heathrow 1945. Photo: British Airways via Ron Wilson

Control tower 5223a/51 (Revised type)

With the outbreak of the Korean war in 1950 and the knowledge that the Russians were developing jet and turboprop bomber aircraft, it was realized that there was a real possibility of a conventional invasion of Western Europe by the USSR. As part of a large scale rearmament programme the decision was taken for a further deployment of Strategic Air Command bombers and tanker aircraft in Britain. Four airfields were scheduled for redevelopment between 1950 and 1952 to Very Heavy Bomber stations – those at Brize Norton, Fairford, Greenham Common and Upper Heyford, with Mildenhall for tanker aircraft. The reconstruction of Greenham Common for example, started in April 1951 when the 804th Engineering Aviation Battalion demolished the wartime buildings, including the 12096/41 control tower to make way for a new 10,000ft runway. This work was not completed until September 1953.

Also about this time the fighter stations at Biggin Hill and North Weald were modernized. All these stations had in common a new control tower to drawing number 5223a/51. This design consisted of a central two storey tower 33ft 6ins x 32ft 6ins, with a visual control room mounted on the roof. Both side walls had a single storey wing 25ft x 23ft, and at the rear of the building was a small ventilating plant room and pyro store annexe. Construction was of sand faced bricks with cavity walls 15ins wide for the tower and 11ins wide for the two wings. All floors were concrete, and the first floor had a concrete sub-floor with brick dwarf walls supporting deal floorboards, the void containing the mains electrical cables. The front elevation had six metal windows and each of the wings had three.

The main entrance was at the rear of the right-hand wing. Opposite here was the pyro store. Two sets of double doors led into the corridor running the width of the building. The right-hand wing contained at the front two rooms, one for the GPO equipment, identified by the under floor ducting and the other the monitor room. At the rear of this wing was a rest room and female toilets. The front half of the main control tower was the radio equipment room, the rear half containing officers' toilets, the staircase and signals workshop. At the end of the corridor was a small store cupboard. The left-hand wing contained the ancillary rooms, access to which was from outside the building. The rear contained the main medium voltage switchgear room with steel door, and a roofless transformer enclosure containing switchgear and transformer, access being through steel gates. The front half contained the battery room and the "A" Centre equipment, with access from the side elevation through double steel doors. The ventilating plant room was located at the rear, next to the pyro store, access being from the left-hand side.

In the control tower the stairs led to the first floor, the main part of this floor being taken up by the radar control room. From here through double doors it was possible to gain access to the flat roof of either of the wings. Around the edge was a brick parapet wall and railings. The only other rooms on this floor were the SATCO's office and a rest room. A stairwell containing a steel ladder at the rear of the VCR gave access to the visual control room via a trapdoor. This was octagonal shaped and constructed of a steel frame clad with single glazing. Heating ducts were arranged around the walls to demist the glass. All incoming and outgoing cables to the plywood control desk were located in ducts underneath the deal floor. The remaining walls and ceiling were clad with sound proof tiles. Outside the walls were of rendered brick. An escape hatch at the rear of the stairwell gave access to the roof, while a vertical escape ladder was located on the side elevation and led down to the roof of the ventilating plant room. Tubular steel railings were fitted along the edge of the roof.

The building at North Weald is semi-derelict although I understand it may be renovated in the near future and again used for Air Traffic Control.

Control Tower 5223a/51, Biggin Hill 1980. Photo: Aldon Ferguson

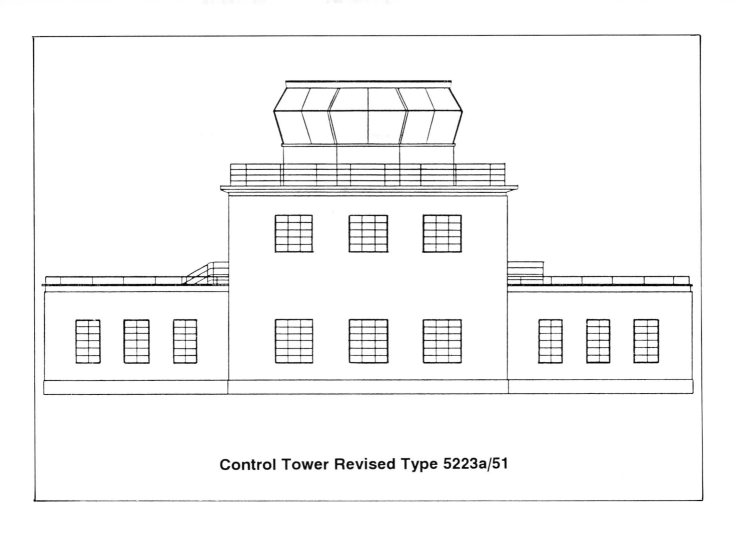

Control Tower Revised Type 5223a/51

Control Tower 5223a/51 North Weald, rear view

Control Tower "V" Bomber Stations

The original contract for the construction of a new "V" Bomber Operational Conversion Unit airfield at Gaydon was awarded in 1952 to John Laing and Son. Gaydon had closed in August 1946 and was under Care and Maintenance. In 1953 a further contract was awarded to the same company for the construction of new technical and domestic accommodation. The first contract was for the construction of a single runway, nearly 1.75 miles in length and 200 ft wide, a taxi-track of roughly the same length, and two access tracks connecting it to the runway. Excavation included the removal of half a million cubic yards of earth, 80,000 cubic yards of concrete from the original runways, taxi-track and 13 dispersal hard standings. This all had to be crushed for use as hard-core for the new runway. The runway and taxi-track was constructed of 8ins of hard core, a working course of 4ins of concrete followed by a 12ins layer of high-grade concrete, 2.5ins of tarmacadam and finally, 1.5ins of bituminous macadum.

The 1953 contract for buildings involved the construction of more than 100 buildings in Laing "Easiform" (concrete cast in situ) construction. There were in fact 30 different shapes of Easiform buildings with heights varying from 12ft to 16ft, all constructed using ten sets of steel shuttering, most buildings being 20ft span but barrack huts for example being 84ft long. Additional accommodation of standard Air Ministry design using more traditional building materials such as brick were the control tower, fire station, stand-by-set house, and the boiler house. Finally Gaydon type aircraft hangars of all steel construction were built. The airfield reopened in March 1954 and in January 1955 138 Squadron re-formed there with eight Valiant aircraft.

The control tower at Gaydon was similar to that built at Wittering, the first operational "V" bomber station, and consisted of a two storey, roughly square shape structure (39ft x 37ft) complete with plant and equipment located in a single storey annexe at the rear and a VCR on the roof of the main building. Construction was in cavity brick walls, external brickwork being sand faced facing bricks. The floor, stairs and roof were of reinforced concrete and all windows were metal framed. There were six windows on the front elevation.

The main entrance, on the right elevation (NE side), led via two sets of double doors into a lobby area with a staircase to the upper floors. To the left of the lobby were the toilets (in the centre of the annexe). A turn to the right and the first room on the right was the GPO equipment room, the only other room on the ground floor with access from inside being the radio equipment room, which spanned the entire width at the front of the building. The air conditioning plant room with flat concrete roof was one side of the toilets and on the other side was the transformer enclosure without roof. On the southwest elevation was the medium voltage switchgear room and the "A" centre.

Halfway up the stairs on the landing was an emergency access to the roof of the annexe below. At the top of the stairs was a large hallway with SATCO's office and female rest room on the right, while on the left was the filter room. Opposite here was the R/T monitors room and opposite the hallway was the extended control room. A further set of stairs connected with the VCR, and access to the flat roof was by one of two doors on the second floor landing. The VCR was the standard type built before 1955.

It is interesting to note that although it seems that only those towers at Gaydon and Wittering were built, the basic design was retained and modified for all new towers until the late 1960s when construction ceased.

At Gaydon, the airfield was leased to British Leyland Ltd for use as a vehicle proving ground. In 1978 the control tower was refurbished for use as an observation tower and office accommodation. The building still serves this purpose for the Rover Group.

Control Tower, Gaydon, 1992. Photo: Rover Group

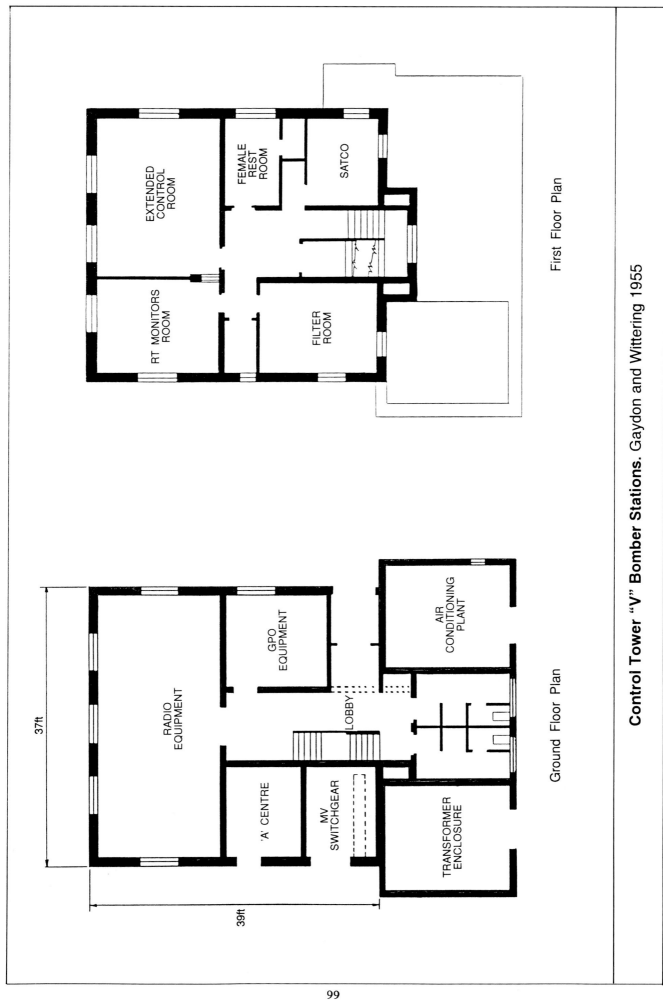

RT MONITORS ROOM

EXTENDED CONTROL ROOM

FEMALE REST ROOM

SATCO

FILTER ROOM

First Floor Plan

RADIO EQUIPMENT

GPO EQUIPMENT

'A' CENTRE

MV SWITCHGEAR

LOBBY

AIR CONDITIONING PLANT

TRANSFORMER ENCLOSURE

37ft

39ft

Ground Floor Plan

Control Tower "V" Bomber Stations. Gaydon and Wittering 1955

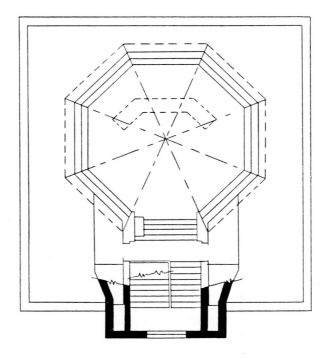

Second Floor Plan
Visual Control Room

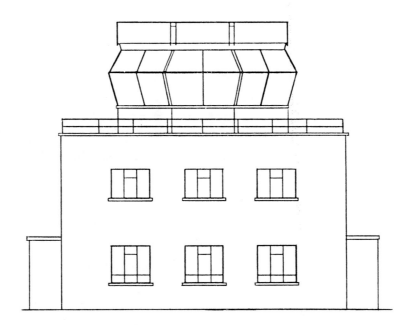

Front Elevation

Control Tower "V" Bomber Stations
Gaydon and Wittering 1955

Basic Flying Training Schools and Reserve Flying Training Schools

By 1951 a number of civilian operated Flying Training Schools were set up as a result of the Korean war. Like the wartime EFTS stations they were established to provide aircrew with their initial training.

At those airfields where flying control facilities were inadequate, a new control tower was constructed in addition to the existing watch office. Examples include Booker, Wolverhampton and Sywell. They were built with either a Seco control room, e.g. Sywell, or a new style (type unknown) as seen at Booker and Wolverhampton. All the schools were disbanded at the end of the Korean war.

Wolverhampton was square (in plan), built of 9ins brick walls 15ft high. RSJs supported a concrete platform onto which was anchored the steel framed VCR. Booker survives in excellent condition, but is now surrounded by other buildings.

Control Tower Wolverhampton Airport 1980.

Control Tower Booker 1982. Built at the time of the Korean war and similar to Wolverhampton.

Seco Control Tower (WA15/213/53)

Seco hutting was used in the construction of the control towers at Edzell and Kirkbride. They consisted of a brick tower built of 9ins walls with brick corner piers supporting, with the aid of RSJs, a precast concrete floor and balcony and a Seco control room anchored to the floor. A standard five bay Seco hut attached to the rear of the tower with walls 7ft 4ins high contained the offices. The entrance was on the right-hand elevation which led into a corridor, and on the left were toilets and five rooms of function unknown. At the front was a switch room, identified by its underground cable duct, and the watch office room which was part Seco and part brick construction. Here an iron ladder (Edzell) or spiral stair (Kirkbride) gave access to the control room. On the front elevation at Edzell was a pyro store, but this was omitted at Kirkbride. The building at Edzell has been demolished, while the one at Kirkbride still stands, although the Seco control room has been removed.

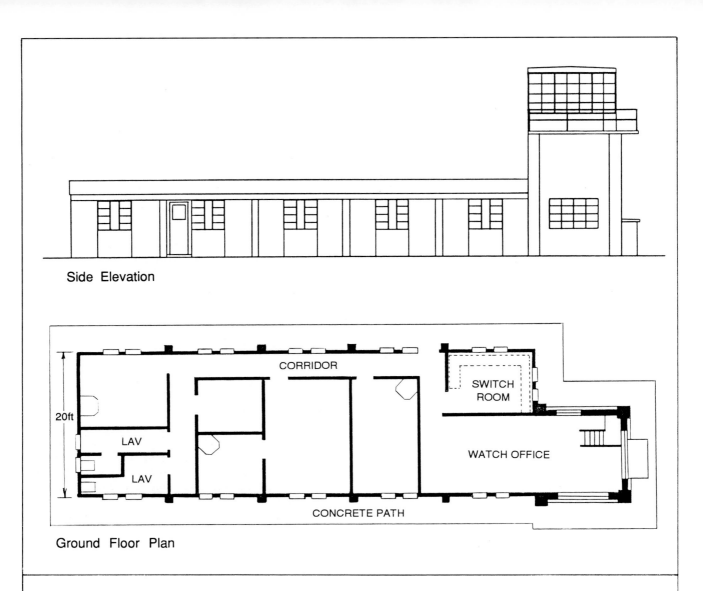

Side Elevation

CORRIDOR

SWITCH ROOM

20ft

LAV

LAV

WATCH OFFICE

CONCRETE PATH

Ground Floor Plan

Uni Seco Control Tower, WA15/213/53, Edzell. Seco hutting and brick

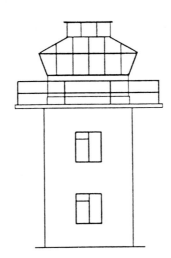

New design of Control Tower for Reserve Flying Training Schools
with small visual control room to supplement existing watch office.
Drawing number unknown. Wolverhampton

Control Tower Designs after 1955

Introduction

Characteristics of the Gaydon control tower building can be found in two different modern designs. The most common structure, to drawing number 2548c/55, is in fact the same size as Gaydon (39ft x 37ft) but had eight windows on the front elevation instead of six.

The other building type (drawing number unknown) as seen at Valley had six windows on the front elevation but was marginally larger at 41ft x 36ft. Both these designs were classed as Vertical Split Control types, i.e. local control is a function carried out in the visual control room and approach control is dealt with in the approach control room on the floor below.

In contrast, at Swinderby the modern tower which consists of a ground floor building and a VCR only, is a Side-by-Side type where local and approach control can be carried out together in the VCR.

All three designs have in common the latest style of VCR to drawing 5871c/55.

Control Tower Vertical Split Control Type (drawing number unknown)

This building type briefly replaced the Gaydon design, and although the basic brick structure was similar, it also has some characteristics of a typical wartime building. At Valley it appears that the building is rendered, unlike other airfields with towers belonging to this group. Valley became a Master Diversion Station and was also a "V" Bomber Dispersal airfield with a single Gaydon hangar. It is quite likely therefore that the control tower was built when the main runway was extended from 6000ft to 7500ft and coincided with the construction of the Gaydon hangar in 1956.

The features of this design are as follows. The latest style of VCR was used; the transformer enclosure was omitted and repositioned inside a detached compound nearby; the AC plant room was moved into the main building; and the main entrance was moved from a side elevation to the rear elevation annexe, not unlike wartime buildings. As a result of these modifications it was necessary to have a small annexe at the rear consisting of entrance and toilets only. Inside the main building there were only two rooms on the ground floor with access from inside the building. These were both located at the front and consisted of a large radio room and smaller GPO room. The switch room, "A" Centre on the left-hand elevation and air conditioning plant room on the right were all entered from outside the building.

Up the stairs there was a central landing area with access to the filter, teleprinter rooms, and offices for SATCO and FIS. A further set of stairs gave access to the VCR and roof. At the front was the approach control room and monitor room. One other feature is the lack of a parapet wall around the edge of the roof; instead there were just tubular steel railings (again similar to wartime designs).

Today, at Valley the building has been extended several times, making identification difficult, and many rooms described have had a change of function. Other buildings similar to this style, although I am not sure whether they belong to this type, are found at Northolt and Odiham. Both these are similar in size and style but are not completely cement rendered, just the panels above the window openings.

Local Control Building 7378a/55 Side-by-Side Type

This small building consisted of a single storey brick structure 34ft x 35ft 4ins with the standard modern VCR anchored to the roof. This design was built on only two locations in the UK, at Swinderby and Waddington. It was designed for both local and approach control Side-by-Side, or for local control only as at Waddington. Here approach control is carried out in the original watch office (2328/39) which has been suitably modified for this purpose.

Construction was of 11ins cavity brick walls using facing bricks of a colour typical of the local area and flush pointed. Internal walls were 9ins wide to support the reinforced concrete roof and visual control room.

An internal porch gives access to the AC plant room containing condenser, air cooler, refrigerant compressor fan and control panel. It is also possible to gain access to the GPO and technical apparatus rooms and, from either of these to get into the main lobby. The main entrance is in fact from a side elevation which also gives access to both of these rooms and toilets as well as stairs connecting with the VCR. The "A" Centre is reached from outside the building. At Swinderby, in the mid 1980s a single storey radio room and workshop was built onto the front elevation.

The VCR (5871-2/55) was similar to those built on all modern RAF control towers and built above many existing wartime buildings when they were modernised as a cheaper alternative to the construction of a modern building on a vacant site. It was octagonal shaped in plan view with an internal measurement of 20ft (across flats). The room was framed in angled RSJs, the outside wall being clad with expanded metal and cement rendered with metal framed double glazed windows above. Inner glazing panels could slide open, and around the walls were heating ducts to prevent the glass from misting up and to provide a heat source. Interior walls were insulated with fibre-glass and clad with sound insulation boarding. The timber floor was raised above the flat concrete roof and the void contained the incoming and outgoing electric cables to the control desk and air conditioning inlet and outlet ducts. Normally the VCR was positioned in the centre and to the front of modern control towers, but on the local control building it was positioned directly in the centre of the roof.

Control Tower Vertical Split Control Type 2548c/55

By far the most common design of modern control tower on RAF stations is built to drawing No 2548c/55. The basic building is 39ft long and 37ft wide (excluding the rear annexe) and therefore similar in size to the previous modern designs. Construction was in brick cavity walls, the external skin being of local facing bricks with common bricks behind. Normally there were eight window openings on the front elevation, but Manby had the approach control room window openings bricked up and replaced with two extra ventilation fans. Manby was built in 1967 and was only in operation for six years as the station closed in 1974. In contrast Shawbury was built in 1958 and is still in use.

The main entrance was on the right hand side, which allowed access to to an "L" shape corridor and staircase. On the right at the front was the GPO room and opposite here was another room of function unknown. The main room on the ground floor was the radio equipment room; a turn to the left past the stairs were the toilets which were in fact in the centre of the annexe at the rear. Outside on the left hand side were two doors which give access to the "A" centre and switchgear rooms. A third door was for the ventilation plant room which was part of the annexe. On the other side of the toilets in the annexe was the transformer room.

Halfway up the stairs on a landing was the emergency access to the roof of the annexe. Further up the stairs was a corridor and rooms which included filter, and teleprinter rooms that were both on the left, and SATCO and another office on the right. At the front was the approach control room, complete with a section partitioned off as a radio monitor room. The staircase continued up to the VCR (5871c/55), through which was access to the roof. A brick parapet wall and steel tubular railings ran around the edge of the roof.

Today, most control towers of this type have been altered, with a number of rooms having a change of function, and most have been extended at ground floor level. These all appear to be local modifications rather than a standard addition as construction varies from Seco hutting (Scampton) to brick. At Manby the main entrance lobby and a further room were built against the entrance elevation. On the opposite side wall is another extension consisting of a corridor and three rooms, all of unknown function.

This control tower type was built at the following airfields:

Abingdon	Honington?
Bassingbourn	Kemble
(soon to be demolished)	Leuchars
Benson	Little Rissington
Colerne	Lyneham
Cottesmore?	Manby
Cranwell	Scampton
Dishforth	Shawbury
Finningley	Thorney Island

Control Tower 2548c/55, Finningley, 1978. Photo: Aldon Ferguson.

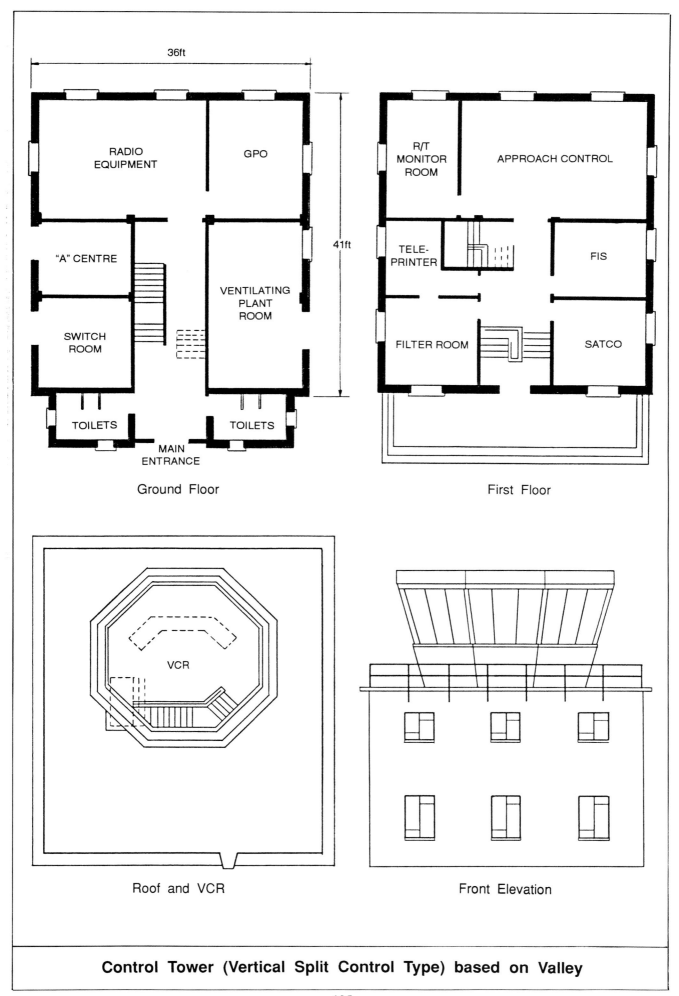

36ft

41ft

RADIO EQUIPMENT

GPO

"A" CENTRE

SWITCH ROOM

VENTILATING PLANT ROOM

TOILETS

TOILETS

MAIN ENTRANCE

Ground Floor

R/T MONITOR ROOM

APPROACH CONTROL

TELE-PRINTER

FIS

FILTER ROOM

SATCO

First Floor

VCR

Roof and VCR

Front Elevation

Control Tower (Vertical Split Control Type) based on Valley

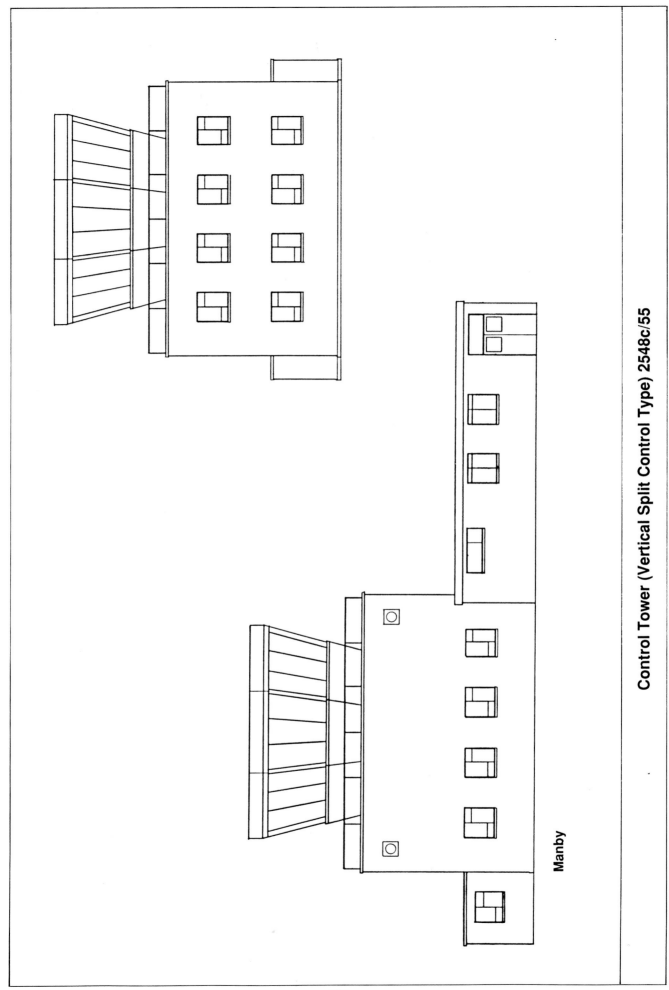

Manby

Control Tower (Vertical Split Control Type) 2548c/55

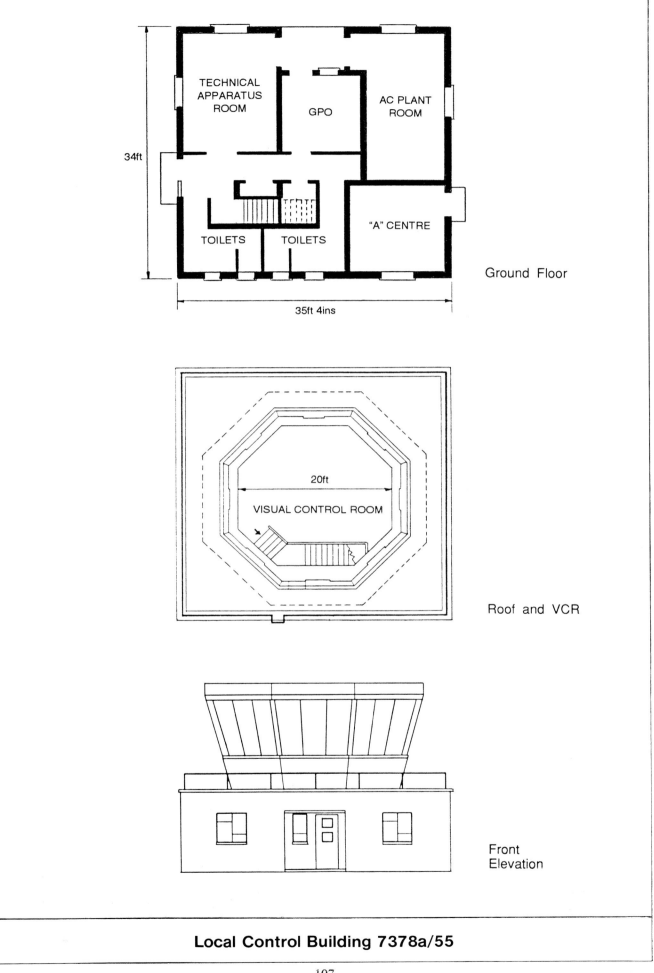

TECHNICAL APPARATUS ROOM

GPO

AC PLANT ROOM

34ft

35ft 4ins

TOILETS

TOILETS

"A" CENTRE

Ground Floor

20ft

VISUAL CONTROL ROOM

Roof and VCR

Front Elevation

Local Control Building 7378a/55

107

Colerne Control Tower, Vertical Split Control type, 2548c/55. Photo: Julian Temple

Thorney Island Control Tower, 1977. Vertical Split Control Type, 2548c/55. Photo: Aldon Ferguson

Local Control Tower, 7378a/55, Swinderby 1993.

Interior view of VCR, Swinderby 1993

Watch Office, Thorney Island, located at West Thorney, 1951. Photo: Jim Anderson

Control Tower built onto WW1 hut. Andover 1977. Photo: Aldon Ferguson

Watch Office at Wroughton, 1991.

Watch Office/Control Tower, Chivenor 1990. This is understood to be a Watch Office without Meteorological Section type as opposed to the Meteorological Section (518/40). The Meteorological Section was housed in an adjacent building. Lyneham and East Fortune are similar.

Control Tower 5589/58 at Chelveston, 1974. Similar to Elvington. Photographer unknown

Early 1950s Control Tower at Alconbury. Photo: John Hamlin

Control tower Burtonwood 1982. Note VCR similar to Chelveston.

Early Radar Beacons and Poor Visibility Landing Systems

Standard Beam Approach (SBA)

The first really new aid to blind approach landing aids for RAF airfields was an adaptation of the Lorenz system to operate on VHF radio frequencies. This was known as Standard Beam Approach (SBA) and was manufactured by Standard Telephones & Cables Ltd.

On 23rd September 1936 when the Lorenz system was under evaluation for possible use on RAF stations, F/Lt. R.S. Blucke flew from Farnborough to Abingdon in a Monospar aircraft. Visibility was 150-200 yards and the cloud base was 100 ft. His conclusion was that the Lorenz system was satisfactory for fog landings. It was not until early 1939 that the RAF began to train pilots in its use. R.S. Blucke (now Squadron Leader) then trained RAF pilots at Mildenhall using Anson Mk. I L9155.

In July 1939 Boscombe Down became one of the first stations to have the new equipment when blind approach T1122 and T1123 transmitters were installed, aligned and in operation, but it is doubtful whether the Battle Squadrons of 75 Wing were able to benefit much by it. However, it was possible to form and operate the Blind Approach Training and Development Unit, thus continuing on an established basis the early work carried out by Sq\Ldr. Blucke at Mildenhall.

One of the first operational aircraft to be fitted with the Lorenz receiving sets was the Armstrong Whitworth Whitley, and Linton-on-Ouse was one of the first bomber airfields to be fitted with the Lorenz beacons. In the mid expansion period (early 1938) the requirements of the Lorenz system and the safeguarding of flying gaps and approaches necessitated the laying down of flying lanes for every airfield and the "Aerodrome Improvement Board" was set up for this purpose.

In October 1940 Lorenz equipment removed from Holland was installed at Watchfield for the Beam Approach School. It was decided to equip every Operational Training Unit airfield and SFTS airfield with the Lorenz equipment. However, it would have taken three and a half years to equip all 130 stations with contact lights, due to manufacturing problems. (It had been decided that it was essential to have contact lighting in addition to SBA.)

By October 1941 only 35 stations had been equipped with SBA, these being:

Abingdon	Honington	Sealand
Ballykelly	Horsham St. Faith	Silloth
Bassingbourn	Leuchars	Swanton Morley
Boscombe Down	Linton-on-Ouse	Tangmere
Bramcote	Manston	Thornaby
Chivenor	Marham	Upavon
Coningsby	Middleton St. George	Upwood
Cranfield	Mildenhall	Waddington
Driffield	Pembroke Dock	Wattisham
Dyce	Prestwick	Wick
Finningley	St. Eval	Wyton
Harwell		

It was intended to add a further 14 stations by the end of the year.

Only 80% of Bomber Command airfields were suitable for SBA systems. The requirement was for a ten mile straight approach to the main runway which did not cross another SBA beam. (Some airfields had an outer marker at 10 miles from the runway with a middle marker at two miles and an inner marker at 250 yards from the runway.) Quite often, due to poor visibility, it was decided not to use the normal NE approach as there was little wind and therefore stations such as Thornaby and Middleton St. George had beams pointing SW to avoid the industrial conurbation of Teeside.

SBA was not suitable for fighter aircraft as there was no room for the receivers in the cockpit. Some other aircraft also had problems, notably the Blenheim, Beaufort, Hudson and Liberator.

IFF and Radar Beacons

IFF equipment was invented by scientists at Bawdsey Manor and its primary function was to enable radar operators to recognise friendly aircraft. First introduced at the beginning of the war, the older types of IFF used a system of direct interrogation. The transmitter and receiver of the IFF set worked on the same frequency and this swept periodically through a wide frequency band. Radar equipment working within this wide band received a response from the IFF responder for a fraction of a second each time the responder tuning swept through the radar frequency. Therefore, for most of the time the radar display tube showed a normal echo, but every few seconds this echo increased in amplitude for an instant. Echoes showing this periodic increase were identified as friendly.

Later equipment used the indirect interrogation system, in which radar equipment that needed to interrogate IFF was provided with a subsidiary set, called the "interrogator". This was of a relatively low power so it could only "see" the relatively strong pulses from the IFF set and not the normal aircraft echo.

Radar Beacons

Radar beacons (transponders) of the IFF type could also be used as navigational aids in aircraft. They were first introduced into service in 1940 and fall into two main categories – homing beacons and beam approach beacons (BABS).

Homing beacons situated on airfields worked on the IFF principle and aircraft wishing to use them were fitted with interrogators with specially designed aerial systems. These worked on the beacon frequency and received responses back from the beacons in the form of "flashes" which could be coded to give morse letters.

The receiving aerials, one on each wing, pointed away from line of flight by a few degrees and the horizontal polar diagram of the aerials overlapped so that when the aircraft was flying directly towards the beacon the signals received by the two aerials were equal, or if the aircraft's course did not coincide exactly with the direction of the beacon one aerial would receive a signal of slightly greater amplitude than the other. The signal from the starboard aerial appeared on the scope as a deflection to the right and the port signal appeared as a deflection to the left. Therefore, an indication of the beacon's bearing was shown by the relative lengths of the deflections and, by altering course until the signals were equal from both aerials, the pilot was able to find the airfield beacon.

The first beacons were used by Coastal Command and were modified IFF sets which responded to ASV Mk II. Fighter Command then followed suit and installed beacons on their airfields. These were also modified IFF sets and could be interrogated by AI Mks IV, V and VI. Transport Command also used ASV Mk II beacons whereas Bomber Command used GEE for homing purposes.

BABS Mk I

The beacon was situated at the further end of the runway so the pilot approached it when landing. A receiving aerial array (two receiving aerials) was mounted so that its line-of-shoot lay along the runway. The beacon responded to about 1.3 seconds on one of the aerials and about 1.6 seconds on the other, changing over at the rate of approximately 30-40 cycles per minute. The beacon was interrogated by ASV MkII (as used by Coastal Command, Transport Command and Fleet Air Arm), AI Mks IV, V, VI (Airborne Intercepter and used by fighter aircraft) or by Lucero. Bomber Command BABS was interrogated by a bomber version of Lucero which worked on a frequency in the Rebecca band, used in conjunction with H2S equipment.

The aircraft approached within a few miles of the airfield by using the airfield homing beacon. The navigator switched his interrogator over to BABS and detuned his receiver to the BABS response frequency. If the aircraft was approaching the airfield from the correct direction it received equal responses from the two transmitting beacon aerials, and the navigator would see steady, wide pulses on the display tube. If, however, the aircraft was approaching from slightly the wrong direction the signals received would be unequal and the echo display changed in amplitude as the aerials switched. The navigator could tell whether he was to port or to starboard of the BABS beam by noting whether the length of the echo increased for a short time and fell for a longer time, or vice versa, and could therefore correct his course. The range was limited to 20 miles to avoid interference between neighbouring airfields.

BABS Mk II

The slotted aerials switched over more quickly than before and they operated at equal lengths of time. One aerial transmitted narrow pulses and the other wide pulses. When the aircraft was making the correct approach, both pulses had the same amplitude. If, however, the aircraft was to one side of the beacon, one of the pulses appeared longer than the other, which made it easier for the navigator to judge whether he was making the correct approach.

The disadvantage of the Rebecca equipment (airborne BABS set) was that it was bulky and required operation outside the cockpit from where the information displayed was interpreted by the pilot over the inter-phone system. This demanded implicit confidence in his navigator.

The RAF system in 1946 of a controlled landing for aircraft in poor visibility had the advantage of being mobile. The system required a Eureka beacon, a BABS van and an aircraft carrying the necessary Rebecca apparatus and orbit meter. The aircraft was handed over from area control to approach control at about 50 miles from the airfield when the pilot identified himself. Approach control passed the usual weather and airfield condition in "Q" code while the aircraft maintained a constant height and passed on its true airspeed to control. The direction from which the aircraft was approaching was indicated on the cathode ray direction finder and was checked by the pilot's own estimate of his magnetic track.

As the aircraft homed on the Eureka beacon at 2,000 ft, the Controller applied the airspeed and wind velocity to the computer and from the data the Controller was able to plan the landing to fit in with other aircraft. If a delay was necessary the aircraft was ordered to orbit the airfield at a given radius. The pilot then joined the orbit, flying on his indicator at 1,500 ft (this dashboard instrument told the pilot whether the aircraft was inside or outside the selected orbit, and also showed the distance in miles to the Eureka beacon) until he was within the BABS zone. He was then transferred to the beam approach.

GEE

GEE was a system of radio position-finding which could be used by an unlimited number of aircraft simultaneously. Two ground stations were required for a position line and three for a "fix"; each one was separated by 70 miles and radiated a steady succession of pulses which were received in the aircraft and displayed on a cathode ray tube as a "blip" on a scale. The range was 200 miles at 5,000 ft. For direction of approach two master lattice lines were selected to cross eight miles down wind of the runway. This position was called the "gate".

When about 70 miles from the airfield the pilot sent an R/T message with his position and the time he expected to leave area control and to enter approach control. The Controller then decided with his knowledge of other aircraft movements and wind speed, etc., the course which would be flown by the aircraft to reach the gate. If no other aircraft was approaching the gate, a direct line could be ordered, but if there was a delay to allow another aircraft through, a computed course was ordered to bring the aircraft on to one of the master lattice lines at a height of 2,000 ft. On reaching the master lattice line, the aircraft homed in on it to the gate and here the aircraft became dependent on the approach system.

SCS 51

This was an instrument landing system used in conjunction with GEE. The "localizer" told the pilot whether he was to the left or right of the runway centre line. The "glidepath" indicated any error in elevation from the correct approach path and a series of marker beacons, normally two, gave warning that the aircraft was passing over specified points on the approach. A double needle indicator receiver was used to show necessary corrections as follows:

(a) a vertical needle indicated that a turn to the left or right was required and

(b) a horizontal needle indicated the necessary corrections in height.

A red light flashed on the pilot's dashboard to indicate that he was passing over a marker beacon.

GCA

GCA (ground controlled approach) system of blind approach as a radar navigational aid was originally developed by the Massachusetts Institute of Technology in 1940. This system was introduced into this country in 1944 and by 1945 nine airfields were equipped with it, including Lyneham, Heathrow, Manston, Prestwick, St. Eval and Waddington.

It differed from most other contemporary approach systems in that it required no special equipment in the aircraft cockpit apart from normal HF or VHF R/T. It was therefore possible for pilots who had no previous training to land an aircraft in conditions of low visibility.

GCA equipment was fully mobile (it was possible to change runways in 30 minutes) and consisted of a large trailer towed by a six-wheeled truck which contained the generating plant The trailer housed the radar gear and its operators and was normally sited about a mile from the touch down point on the left side and 375 ft from the runway centre line.

GCA landings were made in two stages. An aircraft could arrive from any direction and so it was necessary to put it in the correct position relative to the runway before the approach could begin. To do this the GCA equipment had a "search" radar system to give a 360 degree picture of everything within 30 miles of the airfield. When an aircraft asked for assistance, its echo was identified on the plan position indicator (PPI) tube and was directed by the PPI Director using R/T into a circuit which would bring it to the correct position on approach. Two PPIs were provided so that large numbers of aircraft (such as bomber aircraft returning from a raid) could be handled. One aircraft could, for example, be making an approach while another one was brought into position and others were orbiting the airfield awaiting their turn. Up to 15 aircraft could be handled in this way to be landed at the rate of one every three to four minutes.

The PPI Director finished with the aircraft when it was about seven miles downwind from the airfield, within 2,000 ft of the approach track and heading towards the runway at the correct height (1,500 ft). At this stage the aircraft became visible on the radar screens of the "precision" system.

In addition to the PPI aerial, which scanned continuously through 360 degrees, the GCA had two further radar aerials which produced extremely narrow beams. One scanned the vertical plane at an angle of seven degrees, exploring a narrow triangle of space ten miles long and seven degrees high. Any echoes picked up were displayed on a pair of "elevation" scopes on which the ground was shown as a horizontal line with the aircraft blip above it.

The vertical scope was exaggerated so that any small change in height could be seen at once. The operator was known as the "Elevation Tracker" and by means of a hand wheel kept an illuminated cursor centred on the aircraft echo. This fed elevation information to the controller, who had a large meter showing him the aircraft's distance above or below the glide path.

Azimuth information was obtained in a similar manner by the second "precision" beam which scanned horizontally through a sector 20 degrees wide and ten miles long. The resultant echoes were displayed on a pair of azimuth scopes which showed this triangular section expanded three times in width, and gave the impression of "looking down" on the approach from above, showing any slight movement of the aircraft to the right or left. The azimuth tracker kept his cursor on the moving echo as it flew towards the runway. This information was given via the cursor to the Controller whose azimuth meter showed any deviation of the aircraft from the required track.

Both meters therefore gave the Controller a continuous record of the aircraft's position and its movements. Once the two trackers had the aircraft on their screens, the approach began and the pilot switched his radio to "receive" while the Controller "talked him down".

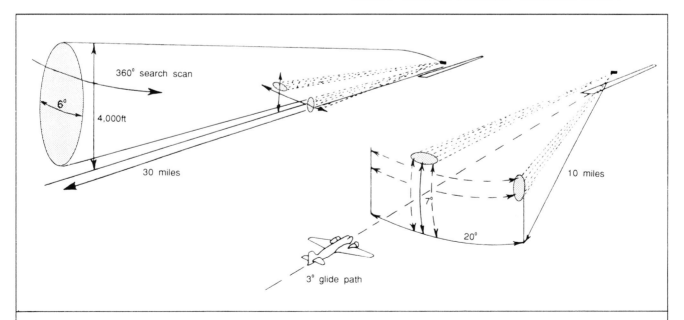

Diagrammatic representation of the sections of the radar beams used in the GCA system. On the left is the search "lobe" for which two plan position indicator tubes were used to give a 360 degree picture of the area within 30 miles of the airfield. On the right is a diagram showing the "precision" part of the system to bring the aircraft in on to the runway.

Equipment

Unit Control System

The "A" Centre equipment translated the requirements which the FCO had selected from the control desk into coded signals which were sent out via underground cables to the selected "B" Centre (electrical power substations) located near the ends of the runways and then on to the runway lighting served by the selected "B" Centre. This allowed the economical distribution of electric current and was called the Unit Control System.

This system was originally designed by Standard Telephones and Cables Ltd. of New Southgate, London who, working in conjunction with the Air Ministry Works Directorate, installed the first system at Heathrow in 1946.

Heathrow then consisted of only three runways and the requirement was that each was capable of being used in both directions. The control desk was designed with detachable switch units so that if any unit failed it could be removed easily without disturbing any other. Furthermore airfield lighting control could be provided for any future runways simply by adding new switch units and extra sub stations where necessary. The control desk at Heathrow in 1946 had a mimic display showing the three runways and corresponding lighting; any fault could be seen at a glance as it was an exact reproduction of the airfield lighting. On the control panel was a large knurled knob for runway selection, wind direction and speed indicators and an emergency blackout button was also provided. Approximately 50 switches enabled the setting up of whichever combination of lights was required. A master pulse key operated a series of telephone relay units rather like the branches of a tree, each branch spreading out to further branches and capable of infinite extension. The pulse signal took a path down a particular branch (12 telephone wires in a ring main cable) that had been decided by setting up the switches and lit up the various landing lights and corresponding airfield mimic display lamps.

Defence Teleprinter Network (DTN) 1939-1945

The Post Office and Standard Telephones and Cables Ltd. installed the first RAF multi-channel telegraph system of DTN for Fighter Command on 31st March 1939 for operation between Uxbridge, HQ of 11 Group and the Faraday Building, London.

The system was known as "Stop-Start Telegraphy" using coded 7-hole ticker tape sent and received at 80 volts positive and 80 volts negative (up and down). They ran off the 250-volt mains supply with a 110-volt motor which had a governor preventing the speed exceeding 3,000 RPM. Most stations were issued with the following:

Teleprinter type 7b
Equipment table DTN 2000
Rectifier 22 (for 110v motor)
Rectifier 26a (for signalling power)
Bell type 546a

The day-to-day maintenance was carried out by RAF personnel on the station but major faults were repaired by the local GPO engineer. Most control towers had two teleprinters, one for Met. reports and one for communications. At other locations such as Group HQ there could be any number up to twenty. At these locations there were facilities for major repairs and overhauls by GPO engineers.

Working Procedure

Starting procedure was manual, an operator at one end pressing a 110v motor start button located on the right-hand side of the table. He would then press the "space bar" which in turn operated an electro magnet at the receiving station to start the teleprinter there. With a conventional typewriter set of keys in front of him he would then press "figs D". "D" indicated the code "who are you?", and this he held down until a code returned, which could be, for example:

Q BIN (Binbrook) or Q NCT (North Coates)

This ensured that the receiving station was operative. Should a reply be required he would press "figs J" which operated the bell 56a under the table. This brought the attention of the operator who would then reply. When the messages had been passed, he would again press "figs D" and wait for the return "Q BIN", thus confirming that the line had been connected all the time and that both teleprinters had been working at the same speed. Occasionally the line may have become disconnected, thus breaking the transmission. Although the operator at each end had to manually start the teleprinters, the actual signalling power was never switched off.

The Met. teleprinters in control towers were only operated "on broadcast" which meant that once a code had been sent to the machine it would switch on and receive information and did not have the capability to transmit back any code to the originator. If the Met. broadcast had not been received by a certain time the Met. Officer would telephone the originator and state so. It might have been that the broadcast had not yet been sent through, or that the machine was faulty, in which case the local GPO engineer would be called out.

En Route Code 1964

The en route code is used to designate all ATC facilities – four letters identify the airfield. For example, Hatfield is EGTH. The first letter E signifies Europe, G = Great Britain and TH = Hatfield. Letters can also be added to designate a particular facility at the airfield, e.g. 2T = ATC. This code was used for teleprinters and other signals.

Station	En Route Code
Abingdon	EGUD
Acklington	EGQA
Alconbury	EGWZ
Andover	EGWA
Arbroath	EQQR
Aston Down	EGDW
Ballykelly	EGQB
Barkston Heath	EGYE
Bassingbourn	EGUJ
Benson	EGUB
Bentwaters	EGVJ
Binbrook	EGXB
Bitteswell	EGBC

Station	En Route Code		Station	En Route Code
Bovingdon	EGWX		Oakington	EGUO
Brawdy	EGDA		Old Sarum	EGVK
Burtonwood	EGOB		North Coates	EGYO
Chelveston	EGWC		Pershore	EGDO
Christchurch	EGXG		Radlett	EGTL
Colerne	EGYC		Renfrew	EGPF
Dishforth	EGXD		Rufforth	EGYJ
Elvington	EGYK		Sculthorpe	EGUP
Gaydon	EGWG		South Marston	EGLF
Halton	EGWN		South Cerney	EGDF
Hullavington	EGDV		Tangmere	EGOE
Langar	EGYL		Thorney Island	EGUV
Leconfield	EGXV		Watton	EGYR
Lee-on-Solent	EGQL		Wethersfield	EGVT
Little Rissington	EGVL		Wick	EGPC
Lindholme	EGXQ		Wisley	EGTN
Manby	EGXA		West Raynham	EGYV
Mona	EGOO		Wymeswold	EGYZ

Teleprinter machines inside the restored tower at Elvington, 1991.

Mimic Diagram ME4358/42

The mimic diagram either in the form of an attachment to the control panel or for wall mounting was generally a panel about 2ft to 2ft 6ins square showing the layout of the runways and taxi-tracks, with a mimic representation of all lighting on and surrounding the airfield. As each circuit was energised the corresponding lamps on the mimic lit up, confirming that the correct switching sequence had been carried out. This enabled the Flying Control Officer to see at a glance the set up of the lighting. The illumination was provided by 50-watt miniature Edison screw lamps mounted at the back of the panel. These lit up coloured translucent plastic buttons set in the front of the mimic diagram in positions corresponding approximately with the runway and surrounding lighting.

Broadcasting Installation

The broadcasting system was first introduced at RAF Stations in the early part of 1940. Its purpose was to pass operational instructions rapidly, clearly and simultaneously to personnel stationed at aircraft dispersal points, etc. Essentially the system comprised microphones placed at the main operational centres including the operations block, control tower and battle headquarters. The microphones were connected to the speech broadcasting room or building which housed the amplifying equipment and from here cables ran to the loudspeaker units around the airfield. There were two common drawing numbers for this building, 10786/41 (Bardney) and 5648/41 (Castle Camps) and the building measured 14ft 3ins x 10ft 4ins.

The Development of Airfield Lighting

The history of the development of airfield lighting is not an easy subject to relate to non-technical readers. The aim of this section is to provide a narrative overview without too much detail. A more thorough technical appraisal of each of the systems described, together with the specifications of the various lighting units involved, is contained in the next two sections.

To date one book has been instrumental in relating the history: *Works* – (AP 3236), published by the Air Ministry in 1956, and subject to the 30 year rule. The primary source of the information regarding airfield lighting in that book was a paper by Watson & Hyde entitled *Ground Lighting Aids for Operation of Aircraft by the Royal Air Force*. This appeared in a book *The Engineer at War,* which was published in 1948. Not all the information in the paper was correct. Some had been corrected in *Works,* but further errors, often purely in transcription, had crept in. More importantly, many new developments took place during the years 1946 – 1950 which clearly were omitted.

The other chief sources have been AP 3024, *The RAF Manual of Air Traffic Control* – (1951), and official papers from the RAE found in the PRO. There is however an unacceptable degree of non-conformity not only between documents, but within some of the documents themselves! In addition many aeronautical magazines were consulted, and again many more discrepancies were noticed.

The frequent, rapid and comprehensive changes which occurred with regularity throughout the war period meant that all too often mistakes were made both in installation and documentation. Hindsight reveals that pilots in particular were not aware of the latest "standards". Confirmation of the variance and lack of understanding of AFL systems is demonstrated in the 1942 "census" of airfields and facilities. The following replies were received from airfields when asked what night landing facilities they supported.

Gransden Lodge	Yes
Holme	Full
Drem	Modified Drem
Polebrook	Unmodified Drem
Cluntoe	Airfield Lighting
Cranage	All facilities
Winthorpe	Full, when station completed
Fulbeck	Flarepath laid every night when suitable

In contrast East Moor provided what could only be described as a model answer:

"Drem Mark 2; glims, goosenecks, money flares; contact lighting on long runway."

Finally *Military Airfields in the British Isles,* using information from AIR 10/4039 describes the airfield

lighting available in December 1944. No attempt was made to include Contact or High lighting, both of which in many respects would have been superior to Drem for any pilot attempting to land in inclement weather. Furthermore, information regarding the actual Drem systems installed is frequently incorrect.

Pre WW2

Night flying was first attempted in the UK shortly before WW1, when it was realised by the military that such operations would be desirable in times of war. The primary source of light throughout the Great War was the paraffin flare, most of which were custom built.

At Brafferton, for example, gravel filled pits were installed on the landing ground. Paraffin was then poured over the gravel and ignited. Portable flares consisted of paraffin filled cans attached to poles which could be stuck into the ground at strategic points.

Prior to WW2 two commercially manufactured flares had been introduced – the Money flare and the Gooseneck. Both were used during the early years of the war, especially the latter which, of the two, was far more convenient to use.

In the 'thirties a standard procedure for landing and taking-off was adopted using a minimum of six flares laid out in the shape of a "T". The long arm was a minimum of 250 yards, and the top was 200 yards. Red obstruction lights were placed at the top and bottom of the "T". The pilot would land alongside the "upright" of the "T" towards the bar.

The obstruction lights were so placed such that a pilot attempted to touch down at the first flare, and aimed to complete his landing before the last one. In the event of the landing ground becoming obstructed, one flare would be removed from the top, thus converting the "T" into an "L". The pilot would then use only that part of the airfield inside the "L". Interestingly enough there was already a degree of discrepancy regarding what actually constituted the "Standard Flarepath" in the various official publications available at the time.

Civil aerodromes

By the mid 1930s the convenience of powerful electric lighting had already become available and an increasing number of civil airports were using a variety of commercial devices designed to improve landing in poor visibility:

    a)   A flashing beacon unique to the aerodrome.

    b)   A system of electric lights marking the airfield boundary.

    c)   High powered floodlights to illuminate the landing area.

    d)   An improved form of wind direction indicator.

    e)   Obstruction lights.

The neon beacon, typically 3 kW in power, was often sited on the top of a hangar and flashed the aerodrome identification in morse. This neon red characteristic was found to be the ideal colour for observation in bad visibility.

A number of fixed floodlight units were installed on the larger airfields. Most airports possessed at least three; Croydon had nine. The smaller landing grounds tended to use two or three self powered portable units.

Wind sleeves, later called sleeve streamers, were supplemented at many airports by illuminated wind direction indicators, usually in the form of a "T". As well as being usable in low visibility conditions, these provided reliable information even at very low wind speeds.

In brief, night landings prior to WW2 presented few problems considering the style and availability of equipment. Aircraft numbers were low and speeds were slow. Before 1938 all airfields were grass surfaced and presented a large area on which aircraft could land and take-off. By 1938 the majority of aircraft were being fitted with landing lights. The use of the electric floodlight literally turned night into day. The pilot could see images of buildings and possibly hedges which gave him the essential height and perspective information. In addition the flickering effects of the paraffin flare provided further feedback regarding height and perspective. At the time this latter feature was of unknown value and was to cause criticism when they were eventually withdrawn from service.

Navigational Aids

Before and during WW2 there were only two standard forms of visual aid to navigation - Landmark Beacons and Aerial Lighthouses.

In 1937 all aerodromes which theoretically supported full night flying facilities were equipped with a Landmark Beacon, commonly known as the Pundit. This utilised eight neon tubes and flashed a red two letter morse identification with the aid of interchangeable cams. It would be located between two and five miles from the airfield, and its position and flashing characteristic would be changed periodically, though care had to be taken that there was no duplication of the characteristic within a 1,000 mile radius. It was visible over 360 degrees in azimuth.

The Aerial Lighthouse was mounted on a standard RAF trailer and consisted of a powerful filament lamp surrounded by a customised rotating venetian blind. It emitted a single white letter in morse (unique within a 150 mile radius) which could be seen for around 60 miles. A number of these were in operation in the UK as part of the Occult system. They were used to indicate particular geographical features, points of entry or exit to air routes, and turning points and were generally not associated with airfields.

The Electric Flarepath.

In 1937 the RAE low intensity flare, universally known as the Glim Lamp, superseded the Goosenecks. These were small self contained electric units, twenty of which were supplied to each airfield. Since the units were effectively invisible above some 1,500 feet they could theoretically be left illuminated during operations.

Owing to the number of accidents resulting from attempts to land in bad visibility, six RAF stations were designated Regional Control Aerodromes in late 1938. They were equipped with a complete system of boundary lights, an illuminated landing "T", a runway of 1300 x 400 yards complete with SBA, and obstruction lights. Any aircraft in difficulty would be diverted to the nearest Regional Control Airfield.

Shortly before WW2, permanent "Electric Contact Lighting" was being installed at a number of airports in Britain, Manchester (Ringway) being the first. This took the form of a single row of lights embedded in a concrete line, called the Contact Strip which ran down the centre of the grass landing area. One important bonus of the system was discovered one winter when it was noticed that snow melted from the lamps.

Developments between 1940 and 1945

During the Second World War, the types of electric lighting installed on airfields in the UK fell into the following categories:

a) **Contact Lighting**, Marks 1, 1a and 2, (1939 - 45). This was a high visibility system intended for use with the Standard Beam Approach, or similar landing aid. It assisted the pilot in landing his aircraft in low visibility conditions.

b) **Airfield Lighting**, Marks 1, 2 and 3, (1940 - 45). Commonly described as "Drem", it was a low intensity system designed for use in blackout conditions with good visibility when enemy air activity might be prevalent.

c) **High Intensity, Low Visibility Lighting**, supplied in 1944/5 by the American Army, principally to their airfields in the UK.

d) **Specialised or hybrid systems**, including those installed on flying boat bases, Fleet Air Arm airfields, Emergency Landing Grounds and the new Very Heavy Bomber stations.

In the mid 1940s, Contact Lighting Marks 1, 1a and 2 were reputedly renamed Airfield Lighting Marks 4, 5 and 6. This was not correct and to avoid confusion, the original airfield lighting systems are described as DREM Marks 1, 2 and 3 throughout this document. Contact Lighting descriptions use the original numbers - 1, 1a and 2.

The cost of providing "permanent" electric lighting during WW2 was of the order of eleven million pounds. It has been stated that the installation cost at a single station was less than the material cost of a single large aircraft write-off due to lack of lighting facilities.

The requirements

The overall objective of an airfield lighting system is to assist the pilot in landing his aircraft at night, or during periods of low visibility. (Take-off is by comparison a much simpler operation). Ideally it should provide:

1. An **approach** system to guide the pilot to the threshold of the runway on which he intends to land.

2. A **flarepath** (runway) delineating system and the associated **taxi-track** lights to guide the pilot from touchdown to dispersal.

3. An **orbiting aid** to allow a pilot to circle his airfield if he is unable to land immediately.

4. A **horizon aid**, desirable for taking off at night, especially in low visibility conditions, situated at the upwind end of the runway.

In conditions of daylight or poor visibility at night High Intensity lighting is ideally used. In clear conditions at night Low Intensity lighting will suffice. In some instances simply reducing the brightness of the former will be acceptable.

In times of war Low Visibility lighting may be desirable, otherwise High Visibility lighting is used.

Standardised lighting for war

By the autumn of 1940 it became obvious that some form of specialised permanent airfield lighting was required in order to meet the ever increasing demands of Bomber Command in particular.

The chief requirements were for:

a) A versatile lighting system in which all or parts of the system could be switched on or off at immediate notice, either in the event of a returning aircraft, or during enemy attack. This was likely to be a discrete low visibility system.

b) A means by which a returning squadron could locate, orbit and then be guided to the runway threshold of their airfield when it was safe for individual aircraft to land. Ideally a high visibility system would prove effective in this case.

Many airfields realising the need for their aircraft to land and take off in blackout conditions had already produced their own systems. There was a great deal of variance in the ideas adopted; however, certain of the features in use at RAF Drem in October 1940 showed great promise. One aspect of particular interest was the provision of an "approach" system, this being probably the first time this important feature had ever been used. After analysis and modification by the Air Ministry a standard system of airfield lighting was defined.

Commonly known as Drem Mark 1, it consisted of:

1. An "Outer Circle" of lights, slightly more than 1 mile in radius from the centre of the airfield.

2. An approach "Funnel" of six lights in a "V" shape which directed the pilot towards the runway in use. There was a separate funnel for each runway, and clearly only one was lit at any time.

3. Two pairs of Totem Poles per runway, delineating the overrun areas at each end.

4. A "Glide Path Indicator", plus a "Floodlight" at the touch-down point.

5. A "Flarepath" of electric lights spaced at 100 yard intervals down the left hand side of each runway.

Two extras were considered essential at fighter stations:

1. Four groups of "Outer Lights" which effectively increased the radius of the outer circle for faster aircraft.

2. A pair of "Taxi-ing Post" lights for each flarepath. These marked the holding or marshalling point for the runway in use.

A returning aircraft would orbit the station using either the outer lights, or the circle until it was given the clear to land. A mobile floodlight outside the airfield could assist the pilot in locating the funnel in use. He would then turn and enter through the funnel. The threshold floodlight would then be switched on and with the aid of the totem poles, the pilot would be able to judge the touch down point on the runway. As soon as he had landed, the floodlight would be extinguished, and he would continue down the runway using the flarepath on his left hand side as a guide.

Within a very short time experienced pilots were suggesting that if the runway had the flarepath on both sides, it would give a much better appreciation of height and distance than could be obtained at present using the floodlight and totems. This was tried and proved to be such a substantial improvement that it was then suggested that the totems and floodlight were possibly superfluous!

Drem Mark 2

Around 80 airfields had been equipped, either fully or partially, with the system by the end of 1941. Unfortunately flarepath lighting on grass surfaced airfields caused many problems in that it concentrated the landing area, rapidly making it unusable in wet weather. The system was much more successful when combined with hard runways.

Feedback from the pilots, plus increased speeds of aircraft soon meant that an upgrade was required, and the Mark 2 system was designed. Drem Mark 1 was modified accordingly:

a) The outer circle was increased in diameter, and a series of lights – the "Lead-in String" bridged the gap between the circle and the funnel.

b) A second funnel was installed between the original funnel (now called the Outer or Main Funnel) and the runway. This was to assist the pilot in conditions of poor visibility, and was appropriately named the Fog Funnel. (Unfortunately many documents refer to the Fog Funnel as the Lead-in lights, which conflicts with the Lead-in string mentioned above.) However, the fog funnel at the opposite end of the runway was known as the "Lead-out" Funnel (or lights) as it provided the horizon on take-off .

c) As pilots were unconvinced as to the effectiveness of the angle of approach indicator on the Mark 1 system a second AAI was now added to improve the resolution. All units were also modified to emit a flickering light to obviate possible confusion with other lights near the threshold.

d) A "cautionary zone" or bar was added, consisting of a line of blue lights crossing each runway 800 yards from the upwind end.

e) The taxi-track was illuminated, and taxi-ing point lights were installed as standard.

f) The power of all lights in the approach and outer circle was doubled in intensity. Wiring external to the airfield was now performed as far as possible above ground, with the aid of support poles. This not only saved on rubber insulation, a valuable resource, but made it quicker to install, and easier to inspect and repair.

g) The size of the runway fittings was reduced by a factor of five, providing a substantial saving in cast iron requirements.

h) The control panel, now far more complex and therefore liable to error, was made "user friendly".

Drem Mark 2 became the chief landing aid during WW2. However, despite the substantial improvements over Drem Mark 1 it still suffered from two major disadvantages. It became less and less effective as visibility reduced, and it still took too long for a returning squadron to land. Intervals of two minutes between landings meant that many aircraft were forced to circle for up to an hour before being given the clear to land. This practice was universally disliked, and resulted in many non-standard additions being made to speed up landings. Other unofficial modifications were also tried in an effort to improve the system, often resulting from local features unique to a particular station.

Improvements

In March 1943 at Langar the taxi-track lights on the outside edge had their blue filters replaced by amber ones. By delineating the track this dramatically improved the pilots' chances of negotiating the tighter curves on the perimeter without running the risk of ending up with one tyre bogged down on the grass. Within a few weeks all Bomber Command airfields were using two-colour taxi-track lights. This was a very worthwhile improvement and substantially reduced the number of cases of aircraft leaving the paved areas.

In December 1943 Silverstone installed cats'-eyes in the taxi-track and dispersal lanes. They were of particular value when taxi-ing to dispersals as they were illuminated by the nose light of Wellingtons. They were also used at airfields with "bottleneck" runways, such as Cark and Millom to mark the centre line of the narrow section.

93 OTU produced a bizarre scheme to warn the pilot of short runways when landing. All runways less than 1400 feet would have a red warning lamp system on the approach funnels, the actual system used depending on the length of the runway. This was abandoned as being too complex.

Another experiment tried during this period was the provision of illuminated dumbbells to indicate that the grass strips were unusable and the hard runway had to be used. These were discontinued in May 1943 as they caused an obstruction on landing.

Several airfields adapted old petrol tins as dispersal markers. These had the dispersal number cut into the side and contained a 15-watt pygmy lamp powered from the taxi-track lights. Syerston introduced an extensive system of coloured Glim lamps to enable aircraft to taxi to their correct dispersals.

Usually when the airfield was situated adjacent to the coast, that part of the outer circle over water was omitted. Searchlights were sometimes used to indicate the start and finish of the break in the circle. In certain cases this was far from desirable and lights were mounted on buoys, or even installed under the water. Kinloss had its outer circle extended across Findhorn Bay by the use of steel tripods.

The Crossbar

Across each runway, 800 yards from the downwind end, was a line of blue screened lights which denoted the last safe touch down point. Initially this was known as the crossbar - later it became the cautionary zone.

Pilots' opinions on the usefulness and functionality of this crossbar varied in the extreme: 91 Group stated that the crossbar served no useful purpose whatsoever. Another Bomber Group was of the opinion that though the bar was of assistance when landing, it should be extinguished during take-off as it spoilt the pilots' perspective. A report dated December 1942 revealed that many pilots thought that the crossbar was the optimum point of touchdown – with obvious consequences (though it did dramatically speed up the rate at which a squadron could land!).

Despite the blue screening, which theoretically reduced the light output by a factor of fifty in comparison with the runway lights, many pilots insisted that the crossbar was still too bright. At airfields where the intensity of these lights was deemed unacceptable, local dimmers were provided by the side of each runway alongside the bar. Again 8 Group was of the opinion that this was simply not necessary. In general however, most pilots preferred to have a dim line of lights across the runway, as they always appeared noticeably brighter than the runway markers, causing glare when they were passed.

Sodium

Though the Mark 2 Drem was perfectly adequate in conditions of down to what was technically described as "poor visibility", it was far from satisfactory in adverse conditions. Even the most experienced pilot had great difficulty in interpreting the approach funnels when visibility was one mile or less, since he could not see all twelve lights simultaneously. By the time the funnels made sense he would be too close to the runway to effect a safe landing. Unfortunately he was unlikely to improve on the situation if he then made a second circuit. Consequently there were many occasions when returning bombers were unable to land at their home station following a raid. This usually meant that these aircraft would not be able to take part in the following night's operation, thus making "Maximum Effort" a difficult target to achieve.

Late in 1942 many pilots had reported that when attempting to find their home base in poor visibility in daylight, certain airfields were easy to locate. These stations were those which were using the Day/Night Flarepath, a blind landing training device which used powerful sodium vapour lamps on the runway.

Tilstock experimented with a group of three sodium lights arranged in a triangle on the roof of the control tower after claims that pupil pilots often lost the airfield in daylight conditions due to industrial smoke haze. Though at first disapproved of as non-standard they were eventually allowed to use the facility at this base and a few others in the vicinity, particularly as they were used mainly under daylight conditions.

Early in 1943 modifications were made to the Drem systems at two Bomber Command airfields in areas noted for poor visibility, the aim being to produce a standardised system which would render airfields operational in bad weather conditions.

Syerston installed 140-watt sodium "street lamps" in the funnels, and fitted similar units in place of some of the flarepath fittings. Bottesford added a centre line of eight mercury vapour lamps through the funnels. As at Syerston a number of sodium lamps were also used as flarepath lamps. Both types of lamp were tried in various positions on the approach funnels and on the flarepath. These lamps proved very superior to their tungsten counterparts, giving a light increase of some 800 times over the flarepath, and 50 times over the funnel fittings.

At Bottesford a 20-foot-high illuminated airfield identification panel, "AQ", was installed near the approach to the funnels. The spacing, number and intensity of the tungsten light fittings were varied to provide optimum clarity. The pilots agreed that it was a very useful accessory but were unconvinced about readability, unanimously stating that it looked more like an "AO". On inspection it was found that cattle had damaged the bottom of the "Q"!

The eventual outcome was that the mercury vapour lamps were inferior to the sodiums due to dazzle, and the system at Syerston was as good as could be expected at the time. The sodium flarepath allowed landings in visibility down to 400 yards, and in March 1943 six aircraft had succeeded in landing with visibility down to 30 yards. It was also felt that the provision of sodiums would make contact lights redundant.

Though the addition of sodium lamps had made landings possible under conditions which previously would have meant diverting to another base, in poor visibility a landing time of roughly 3.5 minutes between aircraft was typical.

Problems of adjacent airfields.

Difficulties experienced when aircraft were attempting to land at airfields in close proximity to each other were resolved after twin trials at Woodhall Spa/Coningsby, and Scampton/Dunholme Lodge. The two circles were combined into a single elongated outer "circle" with overriding control at one station. This facility greatly reduced the danger of collision, yet had no effect on the landing time. The feature was then extended to Mildenhall/Tuddenham, Witchford/Mepal, Skipton-on-Swale/Topcliffe, Wyton/Warboys, and West Raynham/Great Massingham. If adjacent stations had differing functions, the outer circles were allowed to overlap as at Croughton and Weston-on-the-Green.

A further proposal in 1943 called for certain systems to be extended into "Great Circles" of three overlapping airfields. However this proposal was not adopted and where there was a problem when all three bases were available for flying, one station became a training airfield, e.g. Ingham became the BDTF when Scampton reopened, and Warboys became the Pathfinder Training Unit to avoid possible problems which would have resulted when Upwood became operational again following runway construction. The wiring diagram for the latter, however, reveals a pair of cables heading off in a south easterly direction described as the "Warboys Alarm".

Pilots would typically orbit their airfields some 300 – 400 yards outside the outer circle. Hence there were also many cases where two systems came unacceptably close, yet did not warrant a combined circle. In these cases a bar of occulting lights 1,000 yards in length was placed tangentially between the two circles where they were closest. (An occulting light is a flashing light in which the "on" duration is noticeably greater than the "off" period.)

Drem Mark 3

As a result of the above work, and numerous other trials in the Summer of 1943, a third generation of airfield lighting was specified, named Drem Mark 3. The requirements of this standard have been stated in several articles and official documents. Not only is there a conflict, but analysis and hindsight reveals that in the majority of cases these standards were not adhered to. Probably due to the pressure of war and lack of resources, many of the so called Mark 3 systems simply did not possess the essentials, whereas other stations were heavily modified, yet remained as "Modified Mark 2" systems.

The new system was to consist of Drem Mark 2 with the following alterations, the first four considered essential.

1. Marshalling post indicators. These illuminated signs indicated the point on the taxi-track where an aircraft would halt and await the Controller's "green" before proceeding onto the runway. (See page 14.)

2. Improved taxi-track lighting with closer spacing on bends.

3. Improved lighting of dispersal tracks and closer spacing if the dispersal lane was bent.

4. Dispersal point indicators. Illuminated signs bearing the number of the dispersal were situated at the junction of the dispersal lane and the taxi-track, thus speeding up the process of dispersing bombers following an operation.

5. Sodium Lighting in funnels, as at Syerston. This was the first use of high/low intensity approach lights. By the beginning of 1944 all 1, 4 and 5 Group stations had sodium funnels and work was progressing on the rest.

6. Portable Sodium Flarepath (type F) available for the runway. By November 1943 all Bomber Command operational Stations and the majority of HCUs and OTUs were in possession of this equipment. It was intended that all eight fittings should be laid out alongside the runway, but 93 OTU preferred to fit four of the lamps on the roof of the control tower to act as an orbiting aid.

7. Airfield Identification Panel, as at Bottesford.

8. Illuminated "C" at control tower – installed at a few airfields to enable pilots to locate the tower at night. The sign was invisible from above.

9. Threshold fittings across the runway to replace the portable glims often used.

10. Traffic Lights – installed at airfields generally where vehicular traffic across runways was heavy.

11. Treatment of orbiting aid for adjacent airfields – the provision of the "Thousand yard occulting bar".

12. Sectionalisation of taxi-track lighting, if there was a choice of routes. This was desirable when older airfields had been upgraded to Class A standards by lengthening the runways. Usually there would be an old and a new taxi-track leading to the runway, with the resulting complications of routing aircraft at night. It was important that the sections were never illuminated simultaneously.

13. Remote control of crossbar lights. The saga over the intensity of the crossbar lights described earlier had now reached such proportions that at certain stations they were fed separately from the flarepath, via a dimmer in the control tower. Individual pilots had their own preference for brightness on landing which they would request by radio!

The advent of sodium lighting had produced a marked improvement on the tungsten funnels, but it had been realised for some time that there was no substitute for a long straight approach, as in the beam approach and contact lighting system. However, given the constraints of wartime, i.e. large numbers of aircraft returning to airfields in close proximity, there was probably no alternative to the outer circle arrangement.

Contact Lighting

The aim of this generic form of runway lighting was to illuminate the landing strip, the pilot having been guided to the airfield by a radio aid – usually the Standard Beam Approach. It was installed on the main runway only since poor visibility is usually associated with minimal wind conditions. First installed in late 1938 at Ringway Airport, it was then introduced into the RAF at Regional Control Aerodromes.

Agreement was reached in 1941 to install the equipment at all operational, OTU and SFTS airfields, a total of 130 stations. Largely due to geographical constraints, certain airfields were not suitable for beam approach systems, though it is not known whether Contact Lighting was fitted.

Contact Lighting Mark 1

The civil systems consisted of a single line of contact lights on the grass field, but by 1939 two parallel lines were installed to mark the edges of the landing strip. The lights near the ends of the runway were coloured red at the upwind and green at the downwind ends. Later these colour filters were removed to avoid confusion with a system in use by the USAAF which showed red at the downwind end.

In 1941 manufacturing problems, principally concerning the toughened glass lens, resulted in delays in completing the blind landing systems. Trials were conducted to see if contact lighting could be dispensed with in order to speed up the programme, which at the present rate of progress would take well over three years to complete. Unfortunately they were found to be an essential component of the blind landing system. During the testing goosenecks were also tried, and some pilots reported that these were preferable to the contact lights, and it seems likely that at some stations they were used as an interim measure. The advantage of paraffin flares was that they flickered, which gave the pilot an extraordinary degree of perspective that electric lighting simply could not match.

Two basic types of runway light were used on the Mark 1 installations. During the early years of the war a star shaped fitting known as the C2 was used. This fitted into a large diameter studded seating ring which was set into the runway, or adjoining concrete pit. In 1942 a more compact design, the C3, appeared, which required a much narrower seating ring, thus saving valuable cast iron.

Four, or occasionally five, approach floodlights completed the lighting installation. These were installed a short distance from the SBA inner marker.

It is interesting to note that in 1945 more than 300 stations were operating with at least one form of blind landing system, and yet there were only 175 stations equipped with contact lighting. The provision of sodium lamps on many bomber bases had obviated the need for contact lights. However, Full Sutton, one of the last stations to be built, still had contact lighting installed on its main runway, despite the provision of sodium lighting as standard equipment.

Contact Lighting Mark 1a

The runway fittings described above were proving less and less satisfactory as the war progressed. Aircraft speeds had increased and glide slopes now tended to be lower, as a result of which in bad visibility conditions the lights were simply not powerful enough. There were now over 40,000 contact lights lining Britain's runways and there was clearly no question of their being replaced en masse. Fortunately the RAE at Farnborough devised a simple internal modification to the optical system of the present units which focused the light output towards the pilot, increasing its intensity by a factor of six. The upgrade, costing around £4, could be carried out in situ.

Contact Lighting Mark 2

As a result of the problems experienced above, work had already begun on a redesigned system of lighting for use in bad visibility. A new contact fitting was produced which provided substantially more light output than the previous types and was also able to take the weight of heavier aircraft.

Longer and more comprehensive approach systems were also specified, again using completely new designs of lighting units. These were a medium power omni-directional fitting for use in clear visibility at night, and a high power directional unit intended for bad visibility in daylight. The actual shape of the approach, a very narrow "V", was a compromise between the Drem funnels and the desired straight line approach.

The first airfields to use these fittings were the Very Heavy Bomber stations at Lakenheath, Marham and Sculthorpe.

USAAF HILV system.

A large percentage of the airfields used by the 8th Air Force had been equipped with Drem Mark 2, actually 30 stations by November 1943, but since the Americans operated mainly by day the system was of little use.

Station 111, Thurleigh, reported that in good visibility an average spacing of 25 seconds on take-off, and 30 on landing could be achieved for a group of 50 aircraft. In practice this meant that during landing there were always two aircraft on the runway and a third about to touch down. Unfortunately visibility was very often far from good with the obvious consequence of greatly increased times, particularly on landing.

What was needed was a high intensity system which would make landings possible in poor visibility. Short take-off times were equally essential so that the Bomber Groups could assemble quickly. Sodium lighting was an obvious possibility, but an unacceptably large number of units would have been required at a time when the RAF was having to use converted street lights on bomber stations.

In 1943 in the USA a new form of airfield lighting had been pioneered by J.B. Bartow. Later that year it was installed and used successfully for the first time at an airfield in Newfoundland noted for bad visibility. It permitted landings to be made in daylight with visibility down to 2 miles. In the summer of 1944 the system became available to the USAAF in Britain. Its official name was High Intensity, Low Visibility, but it soon became known as "High Lighting". (In North America it has always been known as Bartow). Seventy systems were installed on the main runways of most USAAF airfields from the summer of 1944 onwards. It was also tried at several "permanent" RAF stations such as Aldergrove, Driffield, Leuchars and Hemswell as a comparison with the contact system. The flarepath used elevated lighting units along both edges of the runway. The approach was a continuation of the flarepath, using red screened lamps for a distance of 800 yards.

As the units projected a beam of light along the line of approach only, the pilot aimed to land his aircraft on the relatively dark strip between two sheets of controlled light. Elevated units, apart from being usable in over a foot of snow, had the immediate advantage of being very much brighter than the flush lights previously used. This is due to the fact that the bulb filament is around fifteen inches above ground level and is therefore easily focused to areas where the light is most useful.

However, the ease at which they could be struck and damaged by aircraft was one of unprecedented magnitude – a very high percentage of lights were written off on USAAF bases and obtaining replacements proved to be a major headache. No further systems were installed in the UK after the war, though it was used extensively throughout the USA, and was the major system at New York's Idlewild Airport. The flarepath can be seen in operation at Hemswell in the film "Night Bombers".

Flying Boat stations

Principally due to geographical difficulties and the small number involved, serious development did not take place until 1944. The system at Alness used buoys to mark the "flarepath", but all seven approach funnels were on land (only the main funnel was installed). Traffic lights were essential to prevent boats and other aircraft from crossing an active flarepath! An excellent description of these

systems is given in chapters 11 and 16 of *Britain's Military Airfields* by D.J. Smith.

Emergency Landing Grounds

The so called "Crash Strips" used a combination of Drem Mark 2 and Contact lighting. The enormous runway was divided electrically into nine panels of 80 x 1000 yards, any combination of which could be selected via the comprehensive lighting control desk in the tower.

Whilst it is understandable that lighting facilities differed to some degree on normal airfields, it could reasonably be assumed that the three emergency runways would at least be standardised. This was not to be the case. The Air Ministry clearly believed that the pilot of a badly damaged plane needed one last challenge!

The northernmost strip (three panels) was delineated by amber lights the centre strip was coloured white and the southernmost was green. Some reports have stated that the southern strip was illuminated white by day, but no evidence of this has been found. Aircraft in distress, possibly without radio, would land unconfirmed on the green lane. A complex sodium approach system was installed and Sandra was provided.

Portable Flarepaths

Early in 1943 the need arose for cheap portable electric flarepaths to cater for three requirements:

1) As a reserve for operational stations.

2) For stations not equipped with Drem

3) For advanced and temporary sites.

Three systems – the Mobile "Q", the Upavon, and the Controllable Glim were tested at Hartford Bridge in

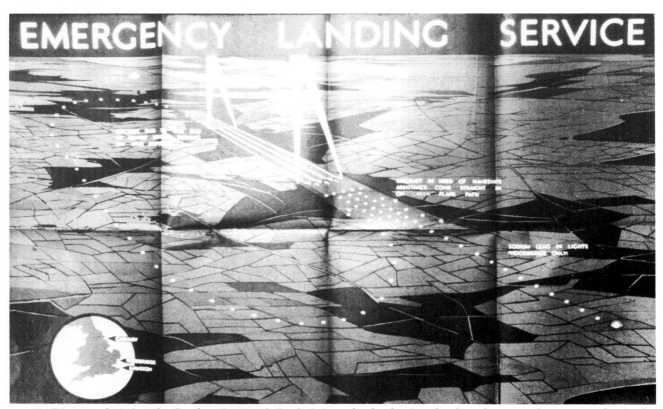

An Air Diagram depicting the Bomber Command Crash Strips, clearly showing the three lanes on the runway, the Sandra searchlights, the "half" outer circle joining the funnels at both ends of the runway, the long "distant" approach and the three "local" straight approaches. The diagram incorrectly states that sodium lead in lights were only found at Woodbridge. Photo: G. Crisp

February 1943. The conclusions were that the "Q" was the most satisfactory in that it provided many of the facilities offered by Drem Mark 2. The Upavon could be produced in the shortest time, and could be easily modified to rival the "Q". However, owing to its availability, the Glim would be used as a back-up system at operational airfields.

Portable electric flarepaths were also used extensively in overseas Commands. Unfortunately there were severe problems in the Middle East due to frequent wholesale theft of the cabling by the locals!

Obstruction Lighting

Flying obstructions fell into four categories:

1) Obstructions on the airfield, e.g. hangars, masts.
2) Outfield obstructions within approx. two miles of the airfield boundary, e.g. tall farmhouses, churches.
3) Runway approach and circuit obstructions, as above.
4) Navigational hazards, e.g. broadcast transmitter masts.

All these were lit at night, though in the case of (3) only the group relating to the active flarepath was energised.

Sandra

By late 1941 some airfields had already discovered that a single searchlight, situated in the middle of the airfield and pointing vertically provided a useful orbiting aid, especially when the Drem circle was probably invisible due to bad weather. Early in 1942, experiments were conducted at a number of Bomber Command stations, the objective being to make airfields easier to find in poor visibility, and especially in conditions of low cloud. The tests used small calibre searchlights which were unsuitable for aerodrome defence, such as the Projectors, Mark 6 & 7.

Up to four lights were used at various points on and close to the airfield. It was found that the cloud penetration of three lights forming an equilateral triangle around the airfield was very much more effective than two. As an example the Woodhall Spa "cone" was clearly visible from aircraft approaching the coast over the Wash.

In the Spring of 1943 it was proposed to equip all Bomber Command airfields with three Sandra lights. Parent stations would also carry a fourth as a spare, and despite a shortage of personnel it was hoped to man at least two lights every night.

When only two lights were available they would normally be located at the left hand side of both ends of the runway in use. The light at the upwind end would project its beam almost vertically, whilst that at the downwind end would project towards it at an angle of 45 degrees to the ground.

FIDO

The problems in enabling aircraft to land in conditions of fog had been investigated as early as 1921. It was realised that the generation of heat was likely to be the most successful method of dispersing fog, although the heat source would have to be smoke free, otherwise it would have been self defeating. Alcohol was an ideal fuel, but totally out of the question due to the quantities required. Petrol was another obvious choice but initial tests produced an unacceptable amount of smoke. Coke proved to be reasonably successful when burned in continuous lines of braziers but due to the extraordinarily long time

required to make the system functional, and then to shut it down it was not progressed. Tests with petrol and petrol mixtures continued, and in 1942 it was found that by using vaporised petrol in special burners, fog clearance was a definite possibility.

The project was originally named from Fog Investigation & Dispersal Operation, but by 1944 Fog, Intensive Dispersal Of became the more commonly accepted acronym.

The Air Diagram showing FIDO in operation. Note the "box" at the downwind end which prevened fog from entering the open end of the runway. Photo: G. Crisp

FIDO was tried at a Pathfinder airfield, Graveley, in January 1943. The early experiments were successful and it was then installed on a second 8 Group airfield – Downham Market. Eventually thirteen more installations were constructed on the following UK airfields:

Blackbushe	Melbourne
Bradwell Bay	Metheringham
Carnaby	St. Eval
Fiskerton	Sturgate
Foulsham	Tuddenham
Ludford Magna	Woodbridge
Manston	

More systems were installed at Wright Field in Ohio, and in the Aleutian Islands, and in addition a portable FIDO was constructed for use in France during the invasion.

After the war Manston continued as the only operational FIDO equipped airfield, though Blackbushe was reinstated for a short period in 1948. The increasing cost of petrol, and the effectiveness of ILS systems resulted in the installation at Manston being eventually decommissioned in 1959.

A detailed account of the development of Fido can be found in chapter 12 of *Britain's Military Airfields* by D.J. Smith.

Post-War Developments

The lifting of the blackout immediately made the Drem system virtually useless, and on many airfields it fell rapidly into a state of disrepair, largely due to damage in the cabling. The outer circles were therefore now redundant and were dismantled in most cases, relieving the need for the Air Ministry to pay wayleave to landowners. Totem poles too were removed from airfields unless the runway was considered excessively "humped".

Three concurrent programs began shortly after WW2 as airfields required updating.

1) Existing stations which were to be retained required changes to their lighting aids to make them usable in non-blackout conditions.

2) Three VHB and one VHT stations were under construction, and their lighting systems had already been specified.

3) An Airfield Lighting Committee was set up, principally involving the Air Ministry and the RAE. A Working Party was also formed and many new ideas were tried and incorporated on selected stations whilst (1) and (2) above were taking place.

Modifications to existing stations

As mentioned earlier, aircraft speeds had been steadily increasing throughout WW2, but the appearance of jet aircraft now confirmed the requirements of the long straight approach. In 1948 about 20 airfields which would be retained had the funnels feeding the main runway reconfigured to form a 1500 yard straight line approach, the lights being spaced at 100 yard intervals. This was technically known as the "Interim" approach. These airfields were:

Aldergrove	Manston
Bassingbourn	Middleton St. George
Brize Norton	Mildenhall
Coltishall	St. Eval
Coningsby	Scampton
Dishforth	Shawbury
Hemswell	Tangmere
Hullavington	Valley
Kinloss	Waddington
Leuchars	West Malling
Linton-on-Ouse	

Once more records show that there were several variations on this theme, using different numbers of lights, different spacing, and at least one installation had a couple of crossbars! Twelve other airfields were later recommended for this upgrade, but it is possible that these were left unmodified at this stage. They were:

Abingdon	North Luffenham
Binbrook	Syerston
Cottesmore	Ternhill
Fairford	Topcliffe
Feltwell	Upwood
Lindholme	Wyton

Three new systems of airfield lighting were specified by the Air Ministry in the late 1940s. These were Airfield Lighting, Marks 4, 5 & 6, (AFL 1 – 3 being retained as the official name for Drem 1 – 3). Some documents stated that AFL 4 – 6 were actually the WW2 Contact lighting systems 1, 1a and 2, although in the case of the last two this is definitely not so.

Airfield Lighting Mark 4

Contact Lighting Mark 1 was renamed AFL Mark 4 shortly after WW2. It appears that the only change to the system was the provision of red filters for the approach lights to conform to current practice, pending future international agreement.

Airfield Lighting Mark 5

This apparently used the old Mark 1 runway contact fittings, but at a spacing of 80 feet instead of the original 50 feet centres, which suggests that the system had to be a new installation. A totally new approach was specified, consisting of a narrow "V" of omni-directional lights. The "V" extended from the main runway for a distance of 2000 yards, and 1500 yards on subsidiaries.

AP3024 stated that Mark 5 was added to existing Drem Mark 3 systems to overcome the problems caused by the lifting of the blackout, i.e. the lack of an orbiting facility and the low visibility of the approach system. It was to be used only in good weather conditions.

Airfield Lighting Mark 6

This was a high intensity system that was intended to be added to the main runways of certain stations which had been already equipped with Mark 5. It effectively converted that strip into an "All-weather" runway.

The low intensity contact lights on the runway were replaced by high intensity lights which could be dimmed. High intensity uni-directional approach lights were added to each omni-directional approach fitting. Finally a "horizon bar" was added to the approach system.

Though AFL 6 is akin to Contact Lighting Mark 2 in many respects it differs in certain others. These post war numbering systems are largely academic, since hindsight reveals that many of these systems were only partly installed. By the mid fifties the descriptions "Drem Mark X" and "AFL Mark Y" were being omitted from ICAO landing charts, probably due to the confusion they were causing.

VHB Stations

A major construction programme had begun in 1944 on four airfields, three of which were to become bomber airfields for the Vickers Windsor and the American B-29. These demanded a new lighting system, one reason being that the runway lights would be incapable of withstanding the weight of the new aircraft. The original intention was that all three runways would be fully equipped with Contact Lighting Mark 2, plus Drem Mark 3.

In the event Drem Mark 2 was fitted to the runways and the rest of the system was described as "Modified Mark 5 AFL". This used the long "V" approach (up to 3,000 yards in cases) with a Mark 6 style horizon bar for each runway. However, for some unknown reason the siting and construction of the bars differed between the three stations.

New ideas

Between 1947 and 1950 a number of experimental lighting systems were tested at several airfields in the UK, notably Great Massingham and Lakenheath - the latter being one of the new Very Heavy Bomber stations.

In addition a simulator christened the "Cyclorama" was constructed at RAE Farnborough, the aim being to appraise prototype approach systems without having to install them. Several hundred experienced pilots used this device from October 1947 onwards.

As climate and weather conditions varied throughout the world and since there was a desire to standardise lighting, following the confusing variations, chiefly of colour schemes during WW2, a number of other airfields were also equipped with British experimental landing aids - Gatow and Gutersloh in Germany, and Arcata, California being of significance.

Apart from the systems described elsewhere, some of the more bizarre devices tested included the "Olympic Torch" low intensity light, and the Westinghouse Flash Discharge system. The latter produced a series of intense flashes each of 3,300 million candles - just what a tired pilot needed on returning to base no doubt! As well as the obvious effectiveness of each system tested, other factors evaluated were cost, effects of obstruction, ruggedness, ease of adjustment and light spread.

In 1948 four separate approach systems were installed at Heathrow for evaluation purposes. They were:

1. A single 1170 yard line of lights mounted on 16 foot poles, similar to the RAF Interim approach.

2. Omni-directional 250-watt red lamps forming a narrow "V" approach to the runway. The angle of the "V" was 4 degrees, and the length was 4,000 feet, similar to AFL Mark 5.

3. An identical layout using high intensity 250 and 500-watt uni-directional lamps similar to car spot-lamps beamed towards an approaching aircraft. This was similar to AFL Mark 6.

4. A new system known as the Calvert approach, after Mr E.S. Calvert of the RAE. This was the now familiar "line and bar" system which had been installed at Lakenheath in 1948 as an addition to part of its AFL Mark 5 lighting.

Most pilots agreed that the Calvert system was undoubtedly the best to date and versions of this have been installed at airfields and airports all over the world for over 40 years. It had the advantage over the others in that it provided the pilot with additional information, apart from the fact that he was on the runway centre line. Provided that each bar appeared to subtend the same angle at the pilot's eye on approach then his angle of approach was correct. It also made the pilot aware of any wing droop. One bar of the installation at the upwind end of the runway would be illuminated as a horizon aid.

Great Massingham and Lakenheath were the first military airfields in the UK to be fitted with the Calvert system. The Admiralty too were keen to try it and an installation commenced in 1950 at Ford.

Progress in the 'fifties.

The objective now was to equip one runway with a variety of radio and lighting aids to suit varying conditions. The concept of the WW2 "Main runway" had already become the "Instrument runway". This now became the "All-weather runway".

Despite the advantages proved by the Calvert approach at Lakenheath in 1949, it was not immediately adopted. The 1955 ICAO landing chart for that station depicts only the "V" approaches for each runway, suggesting that the Calvert was not used. It was not until the end of the decade that the system became the standard and most airfields were eventually modified to have one. A "cut down" version was usually installed at the "wrong" end of the runway.

Generally two sets of approach lights would be provided, a day and a night set. The latter would consist of red, low intensity, omni-directional fittings which could be dimmed. The day set would use uni-directional high intensity lights, typically of the sodium or "car spot-lamp" variety. These would also be used in fog at night.

Whereas light intensities of 120 candles in the approach, and 10 for runway fittings had proved satisfactory for clear blackout conditions, a minimum of 5000 per fitting was found to be essential for daylight operations in poor visibility. Sodium lights had an output of 8000 candles and were therefore most suitable for the immediate requirements.

The long approach of 3000 yards specified for the VHB stations was proving unnecessary. Provided that the light output was sufficient, a shorter approach as provided by the 1200 yard Calvert was suitable and, importantly, did not sterilise as much land. As a comparison the Calvert had a light output of 1.5 million candles, whereas the Drem Mark 1 approach was less than 400 candles.

Runway lighting

During WW2 it was found that illuminating both edges of the runway was preferable to a centre line, or a single edge line owing to the perspective provided. In 1950, with runways of 200 feet in width there was the likelihood that in bad visibility a pilot would not be able to see the edges of the runway, so centre line illumination appeared to be preferable. However the cost and inconvenience of having to dig up recently laid runways was a prohibitive factor, and so centre lighting was only fitted to a limited number of new constructions. The VHB station solution of having the lights 25 yards in from the runway edge was a very good compromise.

Later the "elevated" style of runway light, as used in the High Lighting system was reintroduced. The useful light output from these was very much greater than that from a comparable flush fitting. The WW2 problem of large numbers of lights being destroyed during landings would hopefully not occur as that problem had been caused principally by aircraft which had suffered serious battle damage.

Since runways were no longer camouflaged it was found advantageous to mark them in a bold manner with a one foot wide broken centre line in white. Taxi tracks were similarly marked with a narrower yellow line.

Glide Path/Angle of Approach Indicators

The original AAI developed as part of the Drem system, though effective during the war years, was virtually useless except at night or at short range in dull daylight conditions. The Visual Approach Slope Indicator (VASI) was designed post-war and was basically an improved AAI with much increased power, such that it could be seen from about three miles from the runway, giving the pilot ample time to correct his angle of descent. By the mid 1970s VASIs were in use at most military and civil airfields of importance throughout the world.

Although the VASI was a vast improvement on the AAI, it had two shortcomings. It did not provide accurate information below 200 feet – the decision height, and in poor visibility conditions its range was insufficient, bearing in mind that aircraft speeds had increased significantly in the last 20 years. To overcome this a third type of device, the Precision Approach Path Indicator, (PAPI) was developed by RAE Bedford in the mid 1970s and aimed to provide a range in excess of 7 miles, together with improved resolution. The actual colour change point is so sharp that at a distance of two miles, the pilot has only to descend 3 feet to notice a colour change.

Colour standards

The blue filters used in many WW2 applications were really too dense in that they only transmitted 2% of the available light, whereas the amber transmitted 40%. In practice this meant that the amber appeared twenty times brighter that the blue, so the decision was made to abandon blue and replace it with green. The three colours in use were now standardised world-wide and described as "Aviation Red" etc. Many years later with the advent of small powerful lamps, "Aviation Blue" returned to the scene.

Developments in airfield lighting since the mid 'fifties have been minor in comparison with the progress made over the previous twenty years, and have largely been confined to improvements as a result of the introduction of more efficient light sources, such as halogen bulbs.

Description of Airfield Lighting Schemes

The dimensions given below are for the ideal airfield. In practice there was probably no such thing, and in most cases dimensions for the precise siting of individual lights will be found to vary slightly from the recommendations. The Air Ministry drawing for the Drem Mark 2 layout, (ME 14119/41) contains the following statement:

"The diagram shown is typical for the general run of station layouts, but may be **freely adapted** for non-standard layouts."

Contact Systems

Contact lighting system installed at Manchester (Ringway) Airport in 1938.

A 2ft wide x 1400 yard concrete strip was installed down the centre of longest (grass) runway. Contact Lights, type C1 were installed every 50 feet along this strip. Five cross bars were located at 0, 350, 700, 1050 and 1400 yards. Additional contact lights were installed in these cross bars such that:

The first bar contained green lights

The second bar used no filters

The third bar (centre) had two rows of unfiltered lights

The fourth bar had red lights, as did the centre lights in the last quarter of the line.

Contact Lighting Mark 1 (AFL Mark 4)

Type C1, C2 or C3 fittings were installed at 50-foot intervals down the main runway. Six fittings spaced at 50-foot centres formed a bar across each end of the runway (Fig. 1). When added to an existing runway they were installed in concrete blocks in the grass verges alongside the runway, making a separation of 162 feet. When supplied during construction of the runway they became part of it, as can be seen today at Silloth where the separation is 136 feet. Each lighting unit required an isolating transformer to maintain the series circuit if the filament failed. This was suspended beneath the unit when fitted in the runway, and in a separate concrete pit when installed alongside a runway.

Four approach floodlights type A1 were located at the touchdown end, close to the SBA inner marker (Fig. 2). The actual siting and spacing appears to have been "standardised" several times throughout the life of this system. AP 3024 shows the first pair as being located 750 yards downwind from the threshold, and the second pair 300 yards further downwind. The spacing was 25 yards and 75 yards respectively off the extended runway centre line.

Control Unit

This consisted of a very simple control box providing separate "On" and "Off" switches for the runway, and approach lighting. The lamps were not switched directly from this box but via relays and contactors in the ME enclosures out on the airfield.

Contact Lighting Mark 1a

The runway used modified contact lights type C2A or C3A, with yellow threshold lights at the upwind end and green lights at the downwind end. It is believed that no other changes were made to the system as a whole.

Contact Lighting Mark 2

The flarepath fittings were type C7, spaced at 80-foot centres, with provision for intermediate units at 40-foot spacing to be added later if desired. They were located 25 yards in from the edge of the VHB runway, i.e. at 50 yards separation.

The approach consisted of a narrow "V" of two lines of lights 3000 yards in length measured from the runway (Fig. 3). The angle of the "V" was 4 degrees and it theoretically came to a point 400 yards down the runway. Twin fittings were installed every 100 yards back from the threshold, one being a low intensity type A5 and the other a high intensity type A6.

Distance markers were provided at 500, 1000, 1500 and 2000 yards from the threshold. These markers consisted of four, three, two and one extra fitting respectively. The markers, spaced at 100 feet, were also angled back at 45 degrees, giving the appearance of barbs along the approach. (These were never actually installed.)

At the widest point of the "V" were two high intensity beacons, with a station identification panel located between them.

Airfield Lighting Mark 5

This consisted of Drem Mark 3 with the addition of extra omni-directional flarepath fittings (low intensity) installed at 80-foot centres. The blue filters of the 800 yard crossbar were replaced by yellow ones.

The approach was reconfigured in the form of a narrow "V" (as described above), of 1200 yards in length. Red type A5 fittings were used.

Airfield Lighting Mark 6.

AP 3024 suggests that this is not the same as Contact Lighting Mark 2, but consists of AFL Mark 5 with the following changes:

The low intensity flarepath fittings were changed for high intensity ones. Intermediate units at 40-foot spacing could be added if required. High Intensity approach fittings type A6 were added to each pole already carrying a type A5 low intensity fitting. The length of the approach was increased to 2000 yards, with the possibility of a further 1000 yards at a later date if deemed necessary.

An horizon bar, 500 yards in width, consisting of sixteen type A6 fittings was located 1200 yards from the runway threshold.

The Drem systems

Drem Mark 1 (Airfield Lighting Mark 1)

This comprised:

Outer circle – a circle of radius 2,000 yards from the geometrical centre of the runways. 23 light fittings type A2 were used.

Outer Lights (fighter stations only) – four groups each located three miles from centre of airfield at 90 degree intervals. Each group consisted of three A2 fittings in a triangle, 100 x 100 x 25 yards.

Funnels – for each runway there were six type A2 fittings in a right angled triangle with two sides of 350 yards. The centre lights of each side were located on the outer circle (Fig. 3).

Totem Poles – two units at each end of runway, 460 feet apart, sited as close to the airfield boundary as possible, thus marking the safe overshoot area.

Flarepath – type C4 fittings down both sides of the runway, 100 yard spacing. (Initial installations used the left hand side of the runway only). Units were unscreened except for the last 400 yards of each runway which were amber screened.

Approach Indicator – a single Glide Path Indicator was installed 5 feet from the left hand side close to the upwind end of each runway.

Floodlights – a Chance light was situated 25 feet out from the above indicator, and 75 feet down the runway. A humped runway would probably use a second unit part way down the landing area. There was usually an additional self powered device located just outside the outer circle and aimed into the approach funnel.

Taxi-ing Post Lights (fighter stations only) – Two fittings were installed at the end of each runway, one in line with the first C4 runway lamp, and a second 250 yards back around the taxi-track. (The fitting is unnumbered, but described later.)

Drem Mark 2 (Airfield Lighting Mark 2) – see figures 1 & 2.

This comprised:

Outer circle – an asymmetric "circle" joining the six points, each of which lies some 2000 yards along an extended centre line from a runway threshold. Alterna-tively for "obscure" shapes, the circle is produced from a smooth curve which meets the lead-in strings tangentially from each runway. The perimeter is roughly 12 miles and some 50 – 60 fittings, type A3 were used at a nominal spacing of 400 yards.

Lead-in string – a curve of A3 fittings, usually between six and ten in number, provided a smooth approach from the outer circle to the main funnel. The distance between lights was 200 yards (Fig. 1).

Funnels:

Outer main – Six A3 fittings arranged as a 90 degree triangle.

Centre – Four A3 fittings arranged as a 60 degree triangle. Occasionally this was known as the Outer Fog, or Intermediate funnel.

Inner – Two A3 fittings.

The ideal spacing between funnels was 500 yards (Fig 1). If space did not permit the outer funnel to be located at 1500 yards from the runway, it could be located within the range 1200 – 2000 yards. This would then affect the spacing of the other two funnels which would ideally be at one third and two thirds of the outer funnel distance.

Where space did not permit the installation of the main funnel at the 1200 yard minimum range, as might be the case at coastal airfields, the fog funnel would be enclosed within a separate narrow "V" using twelve additional fittings.

Fighter stations had the funnels replaced by a "Spitfire" lead in approach as shown on Fig. 3. This had a radius of 800 yards.

Totem Poles – two fittings each end of runway, 150 yards apart, sited as close to the airfield boundary as possible, thus marking the safe over/undershoot area. The poles were often staggered, but a maximum displacement of 18 degrees from the normal to the extended runway centre line was allowed for (Fig 2).

Flarepath – type C6 fittings down both sides of the runway, nominally 100 yard spacing. Closer spacing was essential on humped runways, where a pilot on take-off should be always able to see a minimum of 4 fittings. The lights were white except for the last 400 yards which were blue screened.

Crossbar (cautionary Zone) – a line of seven type C5 fittings, at 25-foot intervals across each runway 800 yards from the downwind end (five in the runway, two in the prepared grass surface alongside the runway). These were blue screened, and when installations permitted, two were combined with the flarepath fitting.

Angle of Approach Indicator – two units installed 6 feet from the edge and 75 yards from the end of each runway. A Flicker mechanism was incorporated.

Floodlight – one Chance light would be installed 25 yards from the edge of the runway in use, and 75 yards from the upwind end. An extra light might be situated part way down the runway if it was humped.

Taxi-track – type T1 fittings, blue screened on the inside of track, amber on the outside. Spacing on straights was 150 yards, but much closer on bends - typically one quarter of the radius.

Two fittings were used at the "taxi-ing point" for each runway. This second lamp was, however, connected to the

flarepath and was therefore only illuminated when that particular runway was energised.

Drem Mark 3 (Airfield Lighting Mark 3)

This comprised Drem Mark 2, plus:

1. Marshalling post lights. These consisted of a two foot square steel plate, bearing the QDM number of the runway in black on a yellow background. Each was illuminated by three blue screened pygmy fittings energised from the flarepath. Two plates were installed per runway end, mounted one foot off the ground at a point 75 yards from the runway and 25 yards from the taxi-track edges.

2. Improved taxi-track lighting. The existing "quarter radius on bend" rule was found to be inadequate and was amended by a somewhat complex set of rules which are well beyond the scope of this section. Twin blue lights were also provided at the ends of "splayed" runways.

3. Improved dispersal lane lighting. The situation described above also applied to curved lanes in excess of 150 yards.

4. Dispersal point indicators. These were usually made up from discarded four-gallon petrol cans. Holes were punched in the side to display the number of the dispersal, which was illuminated by a 15-watt pygmy fitting. Two indicators were each situated 75 feet from the junction of the dispersal lane and the taxi-track.

5. Sodium Lighting in funnels. A 140-watt type A4 fitting was attached to each of the twelve poles supporting the funnel lights. Only the "normal" end of the main runway was modified in this way.

From a practical point of view the Drem 2 wiring was just capable of running the normal funnel lamps, and hence problems were experienced when 12 sodiums were added to the system. Often in cold weather the lamps would fail to "strike" when energised. The solution was to operate the funnels on a changeover principal. Either the sodiums or the original tungsten lamps could be operated at any one time, via contactors at the funnels. This switching was controlled from the watch office.

6. Portable Sodium Flarepath (type F). The flarepath was set up alongside the runway in use and plugged into the existing Chance Floodlight socket, which was being rarely used at this time.

7. Airfield Identification Panel. Two wooden "letters", each 20 feet high by 12 feet wide were installed near the lead in string. The boards were mounted at an angle of 60 degrees to the ground and faced a pilot about to enter the funnels. Each letter was illuminated by up to 22 screened pygmy fittings at one foot intervals, as used on the totem poles.

8. Control Tower sign. A wooden "C" measuring 12 feet by 6 feet was illuminated by 30 lamps mounted at 9 inch centres. Each 40-watt lamp was enclosed within a blue filter and was screened from the sides and from above. The unit was mounted vertically, adjacent to the control tower and power was obtained from a separate switched supply inside the building.

9. Threshold fittings across the runway. A line of C6 fittings with green screens was installed across the ends of the runways.

10. Traffic Lights. If traffic lights were installed they would normally be situated at the ends of runways, and where the taxi-track crossed a runway. They would normally show green, but would change to red whenever the associated flarepath was energised. At some stations it was possible to set all lights to red in the event of an emergency landing.

11. Treatment of orbiting aid for adjacent airfields. The "Thousand yard Occulting Bar" which marked the safe limit where two outer circles were in close proximity consisted of 6 type A3 fittings on poles, spaced at 200 yard intervals. Each contained two 75-watt lamps with amber screens. The bar was powered only when both outer circles were illuminated.

12. Switched taxi-track lighting when a choice of routes existed. The taxi-track feeding the end of the runway would be energised if the flarepath was live, otherwise an existing track which crossed the runway would be illuminated. This prevented aircraft from inadvertently entering a "short" runway for take off in bad visibility. When the flarepath was dead the shortened route was illuminated.

13. Remote control of crossbar lights. The watch office was provided with a separate box attached to the lighting control panel, containing a calibrated dimmer for the seven lights which formed the 800 yard crossbar on each runway.

Drem Control Panels

The Mark 1 system used two separate wall mounted panels of a very primitive nature. Each consisted of a teak baseboard, 34 inches in height, on which was mounted the attachments described below.

Panel 1 was 18 inches wide and contained the switches and associated indicator lamps for the Outer Circle, the Outer Lights (where appropriate) and the Floodlight. Two large dimmers were also provided for the outer circle and lights calibrated from 25% to 100% brightness. Eighteen fuses completed the panel.

Panel 2 was 28 inches wide and contained the switches for the Flarepaths and Funnels. Occasionally these were combined, but in most cases separate switches (usually 12 in total) were used, making operation of the system far from foolproof. Indicator lamps and two dimmers were fitted, one for the flarepath and one for the funnels. Twenty eight fuses completed the panel.

The Mark 2 system used a single panel as shown in Fig. 4, though this is just one example of a number of variations. It consisted of:

On/off switches and associated indicator lights for:

1. The Outer Circle
2. The Main Funnel and associated Lead-in string
3. The Fog Funnel
4. The Flarepath, together with the Crossbar, Taxi-ing point lights, Totem Poles and AAIs
5. The Lead-out lights (the Fog Funnel at the upwind end of the selected runway)
6. The Chance Floodlight for the selected flarepath
7. The Obstruction lights on any Chance Lights which were plugged in around the airfield
8. The Taxi-track lighting

A Master Flarepath Switch automatically selected the correct circuits for items 2 – 6, thereby making the system foolproof.

Obstruction Lighting

A complex system was responsible for the control and monitoring of this critical part of an airfield lighting system, which is outside the scope of this book. The explanation below is a much simplified version.

Most obstruction lights were switched indirectly from a local relay or contactor energised from 50 volts transmitted over telephone cables. Some local lights could be energised directly from 230 volts obtained from the tower.

Lighting remote from the airfield received its 230-volt mains supply from the nearest local source, via a contactor energised from the control unit. A third wire from the remote box sent confirmation back to the tower that the circuit was operational.

Originally the approach obstruction lights were linked via the appropriate flarepath feeds, thus making the system foolproof to set up. This had an unfortunate disadvantage in that a failure in the Drem system would also extinguish the associated obstruction lights.

The actual control system consisted of two units in the control tower, the "A" and "B" boxes, and a number of remote type "D" boxes.

The "A" box supplied the 50 volt control voltage to all obstruction lights, plus the control voltage for the "B" unit. It incorporated a lamp failure detector, and could switch one group of local obstruction lights.

There were two types of "B" box. The "B1" provided individual control of six remote units, and the "B2" controlled six groups via one switch.

There were several types of "D" box, the particular choice depending on the supply voltage and the number of lights to be fed. Basically it received the incoming 50-volt control signal from the tower via a telephone cable, and energised contactors to power the lights. Back indication was provided to confirm that the circuitry was operational, and a separate switch energised the lamps directly in the event of a failure in the remote control circuitry.

Hybrid Control Units

Some airfields were fitted with a customised control desk which contained all the equipment necessary for the control of both obstruction and contact lighting. A smaller number still had one comprehensive desk which controlled the Drem system as well. They were often complex units with multiple lamp failure detection circuitry and separate control of obstruction lights associated with the Station, together with an elaborate mimic display.

American HILV System

Flarepath: Barlow lights were installed 15 feet from the edge of the main runway, spaced at 200-foot intervals. Twin units five feet apart were located at the four corners of the runway and were green screened. All other flarepath units were unscreened except for the final 1500 feet of runway in both directions which was screened yellow/white. Thus on landing the major part of the runway was illuminated white, except for the cautionary zone (the last 500 yards) which was yellow.

Approach: see Fig. 3. Two parallel lines of Barlow lights continued on the same tracks as the flarepath, i.e. 180 feet wide nominally. Spacing was 200 feet as before and a red/red filter was used. The total length of each approach was 800 yards, and ideally all units were pole mounted at the same height – a few feet clear of the ground.

The control box had two separate switches for the two approach systems and the two runway directions. A five stage dimmer was available for both circuits providing

---

Four Dimmers were provided to vary the brightness of:

a) The Outer Circle
b) All Funnel Light
c) The Flarepath, Crossbars, Totems and AAIs
d) The Taxi-track

Owing to the much greater loads experienced with the Mark 2 system in comparison with its predecessor, infinitely variable dimmers were impractical. Instead each dimmer consisted of a four position switch which selected voltage tappings from the main transformers located in the control tower switch room, thus giving preselected levels of intensity.

It was normal practice to inspect the lights within the airfield boundary at regular intervals and replace where necessary. Inspection of the remote lights however, was a different matter, since the distances involved most of these fittings contained two lamps, making it extremely difficult to obtain accurate estimations of serviceability. To overcome this four Lamp Failure Meters were fitted to the control panel. These were used in a very ingenious "balanced bridge" circuit and were "zero" calibrated with all external lamps working. They therefore indicated the number of lamps which were not working in:

a) The Outer Circle
b) The Main Funnel and Lead-in String
c) The Fog Funnel
d) The Lead-out Funnel

Since the circuit operated as a bridge, the instruments still gave the correct response no matter what brilliance had been selected for the circuit in question.

If the airfield lighting was later upgraded to Mark 3 the extra controls, if any, were usually mounted on a separate panel attached to the main desk. In a few cases a new comprehensive lighting desk was installed.

Other Systems

The Portable Sodium Flarepath, type 'F'

Commonly known as the "Day/night" flarepath, this system consisted of six units, connected by suitable cabling to enable it to be laid out alongside the runway in use. In most cases this would be the main runway, since it was the only one to be equipped with sodium funnels.

Normally two units were placed either side of the runway at the threshold. The remaining four were then placed at 200 yard intervals down the left hand side of the runway. All units were set out 10 yards from the edge.

In the original tests, each unit consisted of a single type A4 sodium fitting. Photographs taken towards the end of the War, however, frequently show a series of twin fittings mounted on small trolleys positioned at the side of the runway.

In 1945 an upgraded portable flarepath became available and is described later.

100%, 30%, 10%, 2% and 1% brightness. A complex constant current unit was required for this system, since a failure in any one lamp would normally result in an increased current to all the other fittings.

Emergency Landing Grounds

The entire runway was split into three strips, 80 yards in width, by means of four lines of lighting, running due east-west. Each of the above lines was then electrically split into three panels, of 1000 yards in length.

The top (northernmost) line used amber contact lights (type C3) at 50-foot intervals, and amber Drem fittings, type C6 at 300-foot intervals.

The next line used amber contact lights at 50-foot intervals, amber Drem fittings at 300-foot intervals, plus white Drem fittings at 50-foot intervals.

The next line used green contact lights at 50-foot intervals, green Drem fittings at 300-foot intervals, plus white Drem fittings at 50-foot intervals.

The bottom line used green contact lights at 50-foot intervals, and green Drem fittings at 300-foot intervals.

Blue screened crossbars were installed 800 yards from the eastern and western ends of the runway. The overshoot areas were delineated by portable glims, and floodlights were available to illuminate these areas.

A portable sodium flarepath was available for laying out on any section of the runway, as were numerous portable obstruction lights for marking crashed aircraft.

The approach system consisted of:

a) Extra wide Drem funnels at both ends of the runway.

b) Three sodium straight line approaches, one for each strip, starting at 500 yards from the threshold and extending back 1200 yards. These were called the local approaches and the lights were spaced at 200-yard intervals, in line with the left-hand edge of each strip.

c) A single distant approach starting at 200 yards out from the point above and extending eastwards for a further 3.5 miles, using sodium fittings spaced at 440-yard intervals. This line was coincident with the centre line of the runway. At the SBA marker two miles from the threshold there was a "distance" crossbar consisting of two extra fittings spaced 100 yards either side of the centre line.

In addition there was an outer circle – actually a part ellipse. Aircraft overflying the runway would be guided south on a parallel course to re-emerge at the funnels at the easterly end of the runway. Four AAIs were provided at each end of the runway. Originally Totem Poles had been fitted but were later discarded. Sandra was available, comprising a searchlight at each corner of the runway.

The Calvert approach system

The 1948/9 version, shown in Fig. 3, and installed at Lakenheath and Heathrow comprised:

1. A line of white high intensity 500-watt lamps, each of 100,000 candlepower extending from the runway for 3500 feet. For the first 1000 feet (from the runway) a single line of lamps was used. The next 1000 feet used two lamps side by side, and in the final section three lamps were used. The lamps were located every 100 feet along the extended runway centre line.

2. 500 feet from the runway there was a "bar" of ten 140-watt sodium lamps. The ends of the bar subtended an angle of 4 degrees at a point 1000 feet down the runway.

3. Six further bars were installed at intervals of 500 feet from the first bar. The ends of each subtended the same angle from the same point on the runway as described in (2). The number of lamps used in these six bars was 14, 18, 28, 32, 36 and 40.

The total light output from the system was 1,424,000 candle power at a load of 66 kW.

Temporary & Portable Flarepaths

1. (Mobile) "Q" flarepath. This was designed by Colonel Turner's department and comprised a 1400 or 1600 yard x 400 yard "T" flarepath, 1 AAI, 4 totem poles, 2 obstruction lights, a 1.5 kW generator, and field telephone equipment.

2. Controllable Glim Flarepath. The same department was also responsible for this equipment which consisted of: 21 (+4 spare), glim lamps, 4 totem Poles, 2 x 24-volt batteries. Unlike the standard portable glim lamps, this system was controlled from one central point.

3 Upavon flarepath. This used old 5 gallon oil drums, perforated and containing a 60-watt lamp. Each unit plugged into a cable harness which was powered from the system's mobile floodlight. It was somewhat bulky.

4. Sodium Flarepath, types F, FF and G. The type "F" was developed as part of Drem Mark 3, and is described in that section.

It was later replaced by the "FF", which used 26 units, some of which were mounted on trolleys. Ten units were used at the downwind threshold, and four at the upwind end. The remaining twelve were used down both sides of the runway. The actual layout depended on the visibility at the time. For night landings the fittings were generally set out at an angle of 45 degrees to the runway to avoid dazzling the pilot. The fact that much of the light was now directed away from the runway and the high brightness of the units meant that they could be used as an orbiting aid. During the day, and in fog at night, the units were aimed towards an approaching aircraft.

The "G" was a comprehensive Drem mark 2 replacement issued to Commands abroad only. It was intended mainly for temporary sites, or those without lighting. Since it utilised approach lights and AAIs, it took a long time to install and hence was not suited to altering when the wind changed.

Airfield Lighting Equipment

Pre-war equipment

Neon Beacon

The GEC manufactured unit consisted of a square section vertical steel framework sited at least twenty feet above the ground. It contained four neon tubes, each 20 feet in length and 30 mm in diameter. The red light output was around 1400 candles. Power consumption per tube was 300 mA, from three separate 2.25 KVA transformers. A "morse flasher" was incorporated, and the unit was switched from the control tower.

Boundary Lights

These were low voltage orange coloured lights located at 300-foot intervals to indicate the exact shape of the landing area. Their height above ground level varied between two and four feet.

The GEC unit used a six hundred lumen tungsten lamp inside an orange shield supported on a thin tube from its base. The lamps, rated at 6.6 amps - 6.6 volts, were fed from a constant current series circuit, and the base below the ground contained the isolating transformer, which would maintain the series circuit if the unit suffered a fault. A "safety nipple" at ground level ensured that the lamp support tube broke easily if struck by an aircraft, whilst the low voltage used minimised the risk of fire.

The Chance device incorporated a reflector such that the majority of the light was directed onto the airfield surface, illuminating a cone of about 30 degrees surrounding the unit.

Wind indicators

A horizontally mounted "T" was supported at its centre of gravity from a supporting pylon by roller and ball bearings. Slip rings were provided to feed power to the illuminating lamps. The "T" was fitted with a vertical directing vane at the end of the "upright" which ensured that the T' always faced into the wind, providing that the speed was greater than around 3 mph.

The accuracy was typically within 3 degrees, and a damper was fitted to minimise undue oscillation.

The GEC device was supported on a small pylon about 6 feet from the ground. The "upright" of the 'T' measured 20 x 2 feet, and the "top" was 15 x 2 feet. The upward facing surface incorporated 15-watt 220-volt filament lamps at six inch intervals, fed from three slip rings on the support pole. Lamp fittings were coloured green and red alternately, the former group being powered when permission was given for an incoming aircraft to land, the latter indicating that he must not descend.

The Chance device was supported on a larger pylon 14 feet from the ground. The "T" "upright" again measured 20 x 2 feet, but the "top" was 10 x 2 feet. Lighting was provided by double rows of fluorescent tubes, mounted on the yellow painted upper surface, which was of an inverted "V" section to make it impossible for snow to collect. An optional extra was a velocity indicator which showed one bar of light for low wind speed, two for medium and three for high speed. The light bars were of a different colour from the direction "T", and the low/medium/high levels could be pre-set by the user.

Martin Baker manufactured a wind indicator in the form of an elongated "airship", with a large vane on the downwind end. It was unlikely to have been as obvious from the air as the "T" type indicators.

Later, Chance produced an improved "T" which was motor driven from signals derived from a remote miniature sensing unit. The latter possessed negligible inertia which meant that the much larger "T" was now accurate down to wind speeds below 2 mph. Additionally, electronics were added to the control system to ensure that the "T" only moved to a new position when the wind direction had stabilised. When there was no wind the "T" could be moved electrically to the optimum position from the control tower.

Landing floodlight

The Chance unit consisted of a single high power filament lamp located between two mirrors. The smaller curved mirror, square in shape, reflected light into the much larger curved rectangular mirror which faced the airfield. A single installation used three of these devices side by side, allowing the system to be powered directly from a three phase supply. This gave a "balanced load" which saved on cabling and transformers.

GEC then produced an improved floodlight using three tubular tungsten lamps housed in each level of a three tier steel framework. The line filaments of each 1 kW lamp were placed at the foci of reflectors. The use of nine "small" lamps again enabled the system to be powered directly from a three phase supply. In addition it allowed the device to be switched on at full power, saving more control gear. Also the failure of a single lamp reduced its effectiveness by a mere 11%.

The unit, mounted on a cast roller turntable, produced a 170 degree spread of light in the horizontal plane, of about 640,000 candles. The vertical spread was very small, and a single unit would typically illuminate an area of 350,000 square yards. An example of this device was installed at Gravesend airport in the mid 1930s, fitted onto a 22-foot supporting structure, and equipped with an obstruction lamp.

Often a "Shadow Bar" was fitted to the floodlights. This consisted of one or more vertical strips mounted in front of the floodlight. The bar could be moved according to the prevailing wind, thus allowing a pilot to land into a forward, or cross facing floodlight without dazzle.

Obstruction Lights

The pre-war unit consisted of twin electric lamps contained within a red globe. Only one lamp was normally illuminated, the second being switched in automatically if the first failed. This feature was considered essential to guard against what could result in a disaster due to a broken filament.

Aerial Lighthouse/Floodlight Beacon

The common variety consisted of a filament lamp surrounded by a customised rotating venetian blind. The Chance unit utilised a 5 kW, 500 mm floodlight with a dioptric mirror and lens assembly which concentrated the 550,000 candle beam at an angle of about 33 degrees to the ground. The entire unit was mounted together with its generator on a trailer. It emitted a single white letter in morse, (E, J, O, Q, Y, Z excepted) which could be seen for up to 60 miles. They were used extensively abroad and were situated such that at least two would be visible under normal conditions.

Portable Flares

Flare, Type "A", (Money) The first mass produced flare consisted of a metal bucket fitted with a lid containing a burning wick or "flare", usually of cotton waste partially immersed in paraffin. The flare was removed from the bucket with a hook and ignited externally, placing it on a metal tray. To extinguish the unit the flare was dropped back into the bucket with the aid of the hook and the lid was immediately closed. The burning time was around two hours. Modified versions of the unit utilised a drum fitted with a tap to economise on the amount of paraffin used. The Money flare was obsolete by 1937, but two were retained at most aerodromes for emergencies.

Flare, Type "B" (Gooseneck) The requirements for a much lighter and more portable unit resulted in this device, which until recently was still to be found on a significant number of airfields in the UK. It measured 9 inches in diameter, 6.8 inches tall with 10.5 inch neck of diameter 1.8 inches, (see photograph). The wick protruded from the neck and was extinguished by closing the hinged sliding flap at the end of the neck. In use the spout was placed downwind. The typical burning time was six hours.

RAE Low intensity flare (Glim Lamp) This was the first mass produced electric unit which consisted of a vertical cylinder, approximately 12 inches in height by 8 inches diameter. A glass domed top contained a large reflector in the centre of which was a 2-volt, 1.5-watt bulb. A later version had a 12-volt, 2.4-watt lamp. They were equipped with interchangeable white, orange and red globes for marking the flarepath, boundary and obstructions respectively.

Electric Airfield Lighting equipment used during and after WW2 .

Contact Fittings

The term "Contact" originated from "the point at which a landing aircraft makes contact with the runway". The first permanent runway lights were installed in the concrete "Contact Strip". Light units which lay almost flush with runways and taxi-tracks were later universally known as contact fittings.

Unfortunately this leads to a conflict in description in that distinction must be made between the two generic forms of lighting used on WW2 airfields – Contact and Airfield (Drem) lighting.

C1 Contact Light, pre 1939 – Circular casting, extremely rare. Originally manufactured by Chance, this unit did not possess sufficient light output at angles close to ground level.

C2 Contact Light, 1941 – Low intensity fitting, star shaped casting, large seating ring. Manufactured by Chance and GEC.

Though officially described as the "1941 style" on an Air Ministry identification chart and in certain reports, this particular fitting has been seen on photographs in aviation journals dated 1939! It probably should be described as the 1939 unit.

Originally split filters, green/red, were fitted to the last 750 feet of runway, plus the end crossbar (showing green at the touchdown end and red at the far end). In 1944 the screens were removed to conform to the USAAF High lighting system, but were later replaced by green/yellow filters.

Contact lamps were energised at a constant current of 6.6 amps. Either of two bulbs could be fitted – 44 watts/600 lumens, or 64 watts/1000 lumens, the latter being used when colour screens were fitted. This produced a light output of 155 candles at 24 degrees to the horizontal and 360 degrees in azimuth.

C2A As above, but with modified reflector and the addition of a truncated cone refractor giving a concentrated bi-directional beam. The emitted candle power in the optimum direction increased by a factor of six.

C3 Contact Light, 1942 – High intensity, 64-watt 6.6-amp lamp, small seating ring. Manufactured by GEC and Holophane.

C3A As above, but with modified reflector and a 60-watt lamp, to achieve the effect of the C2A (High intensity, bi-directional).

C3B as C3, but modified to achieve the effect of the C12, (Low intensity, omni-directional).

C4 Drem Mark 1 – Flarepath fitting, (often confusingly called Glim lamps as the name conflicts with the RAE low intensity flare described earlier). Uni-directional, 15 watt 24.5 inch diameter dome, projecting 4.375 inches above ground. A single adjustable glassless light aperture was provided 2.5 x 3.5 inches maximum. The 230-volt, 15-watt bulb was housed in a horizontal pygmy well-glass fitting giving a light output of 10 candles.

C5 Drem Mark 2 – Uni-directional (Crossbar) fitting, cast iron, no external glass, 8 inches in diameter. 15-watt 230 volt pygmy lamp with a polished metal reflector. The light was visible through 30 degrees in azimuth and 13 degrees vertically. Used in several other applications, in particular light bars on naval airfields.

C6 Drem Mark 2 – Bi-directional, flarepath fitting. Cast iron, no external glass, 8 x 12 inches housing 2 x 15-watt 230-volt pygmy lamps, with polished metal reflectors, providing an output of 10 candles. The light emitted was visible within an angle of 13 degrees above the ground with a 40 degree spread horizontally and was invisible above 3,000 feet.

C7 Contact Light Mark 2, 1945 – Bi-directional, low visibility. Two 6-amp 36-watt 500 lumen lamps are used. Behind each lamp is a hemispherical reflector which was adjusted to set the beam to intersect the runway centre line at 4000 feet down the flarepath. The light power along this line was 3,000 candles. Used initially on the VHB stations.

C11 Post war runway fitting – Improved high intensity bi-directional unit manufactured by GEC. 13.7in square casting with 13.25in diameter glass ring with 9.25in round cast iron centre. The lamp was normally 6 volt 36 watt. External adjustment of beam elevation and toe-in was possible. Typically found on runways having ORPs, and normally installed at 80-foot intervals. Yellow screened units were used as the cautionary zone distance markers at 25-foot spacing across the runway. Green screens were fitted to the runway threshold markers, spaced at 12.5 feet.

C12 Omni-directional, low intensity flush runway lamp, normally used at a spacing of 400 feet.

In the 1950s the term "Blister" fitting came into use for all "almost flush" runway fittings, though there was still evidently a distinction between flush, semi-flush and blister!

Taxi-track lights

?? Drem Mark 1 – Taxi-ing Post light. Dimensions as C4 fitting. Pygmy well-glass housing was vertically mounted so that the light would emit from eight apertures, 6 inches wide x 2 inches high around the periphery. The light output was 10 candles and unscreened. They were installed at fighter stations only.

T1 Drem Mark 2 – omni-directional 15-watt, 230-volt pygmy lamp. 8 inch diameter cast iron fitting with 6 glassless apertures.

T1a As above, but with the well-glass replaced by a circular "lens" giving improved light output.

Fifteen years development in lighting: Top row – T2 taxi-track light, gooseneck flare, C11 runway light.

Bottom Row – C6 Drem Mark 2 flarepath fitting, C5 crossbar fitting, 15-watt pygmy well-glass housing with its coloured filters and reflector. Photo: G. Crisp

T2 Post war glass encased, replacement for above. 12-volt lamp at either 12, 24 or 36 watts. Manufactured principally by GEC and Revo. 8 inch diameter with 5 inch glass dome. This unit was often fitted with a lens to provide a bi-directional beam and then used as flarepath lights at 100 yard spacing on subsidiary runways of some airfields in the post war period.

Raised/pole mounted (Approach) lights

A1 Approach floodlight, series 1, 2 & 3 – Used for contact lighting systems. 230-volt, 1kW tubular lamp mounted horizontally at the focus of a reflector inside a rectangular casing supported from a pivot mounting.

A2 Bulkhead fitting for Drem Mark 1 – Twin 25-watt lamps, used for funnels and outer circle. These units were mounted on 4 inch diameter poles shining upwards through 360 degrees in azimuth.

A3 Ditto for Drem Mark 2 – Twin 60 (or 75) watt lamps, twelve inch diameter soup bowl shaped housing with curved glass lid. The light output was 185 candles vertically upwards from the ground. In open country they were located 20 feet above the ground, but in many areas poles of up to 60 feet were required.

A4 Sodium Fitting – used on Drem Mark 3 approach, and for the portable flarepaths. The light source was typically the Philips 15J tube rated at 140 watts, enclosed in a 12 by 24 inch housing. The starter, choke and capacitor were housed in a box beneath the tube which formed a base when the unit was used as a flarepath lamp. The light output was 8,000 candles. Principal manufacturers were Revo and Wardle. Often requisitioned street lighting was used.

A5 Approach Fitting, 1945 – low intensity, used in 'V' or centre line applications, consisting of a 250-watt filament lamp inside a 360 degree red domed cover. The optical angle of beam at 5 degrees above horizontal was 1,000 candles.

A6 Approach Fitting, 1945 – high intensity, car spot-lamp type, used in "V" or centre line systems. Two types were produced:

500 watts, 7,250 lumens, 100,000 candles, 15 degree beam width

250 watts, 3,100 lumens, 85,000 candles, 10 degree beam width

The approach line was divided and the wide angle units were used in the half furthest from the runway.

A7 Approach cross bar sodium fitting, 1945 – for VHB stations. 10,000 candles.

Post War Fittings, used until the mid 1950s

Lamps tried in Germany, principally at Gutersloh, were numbered BAFO.49/1028 or similar.

With the exception of the above, all runway and approach lamps were numbered LR or LA. This was an experimental period and many types were tried, most outside the scope of this book. To summarise, LA/9, LA/11, LA/12, LR/14-17 and LR/19 are various fittings all taking the shape of a car spot-lamp. Principal manufacturers were Simplex, Holophane, GEC and Benjamin. These "elevated omni-directional" lamps were installed over concrete pits fitted alongside or into the runway surface. The mounting spigot of the lamp fitted into a cast iron cover plate, type

PC/3, or similar, and large numbers of these can still be found on disused airfields which were active in the 'fifties and 'sixties.

The LA/10 was a low intensity omni-directional approach lamp manufactured by Simplex and Holophane. The LR/18 was an elevated bi-directional runway lamp of 100-watts from GEC.

Miscellaneous WW2 Lighting units

Mobile Floodlight/Chance Light

Self powered mobile floodlights were used until the Drem system was introduced. The most common type was a Chance unit dating back to 1930. This was mounted on a four wheel trailer and had the appearance of the top of a small lighthouse mounted on a steel box. Typically this unit was used as the approach floodlight for Drem Mark 1, but since the light direction could be angled it could also be used as a beacon with a range in excess of 45 miles. The film *Target for Tonight* featured a twin unit, again from Chance Brothers.

The Drem systems provided power for the light at the end of each runway, hence a more basic unit was introduced. This took the form of a box containing the light assembly, supported on a girder frame from a tricycle undercarriage, (Fig. 5). The base measured approximately 8ft by 6ft, whilst the overall height was 10ft. Two cables terminated in plugs for connection to sockets situated at strategic points beside the runways. One plug was for the floodlight itself, the other fed the two red obstruction lights mounted on the top. The light unit itself consisted of a parabolic reflector, 20 x 24 inches, at the focus of which was a 5 kW horizontal burning line-filament lamp, producing an output of one million candles. This assembly was housed in a waterproof case with an armoured glass front.

Totem Poles

The aim of these devices was to mark the extent of the safe overrun for each end of a runway. Two poles situated 75 yards from the extended centre line were installed at the end of each runway, usually as close as possible to the airfield boundary. The height of the pole was a minimum of 10 feet, though RAF Wing required some 40-foot versions to cater for an abnormally humped runway. The maximum height was theoretically 50 feet. Poles well in excess of 10 feet could usually be lowered to the ground during daylight to reduce the chances of being struck. When the poles were fixed, a yellow cross was attached as in Fig. 5.

The poles themselves were constructed from 6 inch square timber. At the top were two sets of pygmy well-glass fittings in a vertical line, six facing the runway, and six the approach. The fittings were located at one foot centres and were screened by metal tubes 2.5 inches in diameter, 8 inches in length.

On installation the lights facing away from the runway were adjusted so that the red lights shone directly towards an aircraft on correct approach through the fog funnel. The fittings facing the runway were adjusted so that the white lights shone towards an aircraft leaving the runway at a predetermined point.

Units installed early in the War had the fittings attached to two boards measuring 6 inches wide by 6 feet high. The boards were hinged to the top of the support pole, such that they could be angled up to 10 degrees from the vertical. The hinges were also slotted so that the board could be swung in the vertical plane by up to 20 degrees. Metal straps were then attached to secure the boards in their respective positions. This was considered far too complex, and later units simply had the lamp fittings screwed directly to chamfered sections of the poles.

Glide Path/Angle of Approach Indicators

The first AAI was designed for use with the Drem Mark 1 lighting system of 1941. The angle from the horizontal was set so that an aircraft on the correct angle of glide, nominally 5 degrees, would see a green light. A red light was seen if the aircraft was too low, and an amber one if too high.

The unit was manufactured by Messrs R.E. Beard Ltd., and was similar to the device already in use by the Fleet Air Arm. It measured approximately 1 foot square by 2 feet in length, and contained a 230-volt, 250-watt optical projector lamp, plus associated spherical reflector, condensers and a 6 inch focal length lens assembly. A 500 watt lamp could be used following an internal adjustment.

Since the width of the green beam was 2 degrees, the single unit used with Drem Mark 1 was unable to resolve glide angles between 4 and 6 degrees, both being too close to the limits for a good landing. Drem Mark 2 used two units mounted either side of the runway, angled at 4.5 and 5.5 degrees to the horizontal, thus giving improved resolution to the pilot; two greens would only be seen with a glide angle between 4.5 and 5.5 degrees. Each unit was also modified by the addition of a rotating shutter which made the light flash, thus distinguishing it from other lamps in the vicinity.

Visual Approach Slope Indicator

One VASI was provided at each side of the runway, and a pilot on correct approach would see one red bar and one white bar. Two reds would be seen if the aircraft was too low, and two whites if too high.

Precision Approach Path Indicator

The system consists of four units, two each side of the runway. Each unit has three high intensity lamps, three red filter glasses, and three lenses to focus the light into an upper white beam and a lower red beam. All four units are set to slightly different angles so that a pilot on correct approach can see two red and two white lights. Too high means four whites, and too low results in four reds. The instrument eliminates the "pink zone" which was often a problem experienced with the VASIS.

HILV (High Lighting) Lamps

The Bartow Beam Controlled Unit was used for both flarepath and approach systems, as well as acting as an orbiting aid. It was manufactured by the Line Material Company of Pennsylvania.

The flarepath fitting took on the general appearance of a large "acorn" usually mounted on a frangible spigot some 6 inches off the ground (Fig. 5). The height of the acorn (actually a metal bowl topped by a hemispherical lens assembly) was about 12 inches. The lamp was enclosed in a fresnel lens and the mounting was adjustable such that toe-in and glide slope could be precisely set. The approach fitting was almost identical, having a longer spigot for attaching to a pole.

The lamp was rated at 6.6 amps, 200 watts and units were connected in series. When the globe was opened to change the lamp the supply leads were shorted to maintain the series circuit. Each fitting also contained a transformer which powered a small 12-volt fan to prevent internal condensation which would obstruct the optics. Spirit levels were attached to the external casing as the unit had to be mounted dead level. The peak light output was 35,000 candles, reducing to 7,000 when filters were added.

A later version rated at 300 watts was introduced, principally to increase visibility when coloured filters were fitted. A paper film cut out maintained the series circuit by shorting the unit in the event of a blown lamp filament.

Obstruction Lights

Two principal types were used throughout the war years, a two lamp globe and a three lamp unit for obstructions deemed extra critical. Unlike the earlier pre-war model which powered only one lamp at any one time in case of failure, these units energised all the lamps as lamp failure indicators were now available in the control tower.

The standard fitting consisted of an aviation red well-glass containing two 75-watt tungsten lamps providing a light output of between 22 and 37 candles. The lamps were screened from above during WW2.

The second unit contained three 100-watt lamps, thus improving the visibility (see Fig 5). It was installed principally on air navigation obstructions found on frequently used routes which were subject to bad visibility.

Graham Crisp, 1993.

Weston-super-Mare control tower and floodlight c1938. The light is a triple 1kW unit from Chance Brothers and features three synchronised shadow bars for the lights. Photo: P. Warrilow via Aeroplane Monthly.

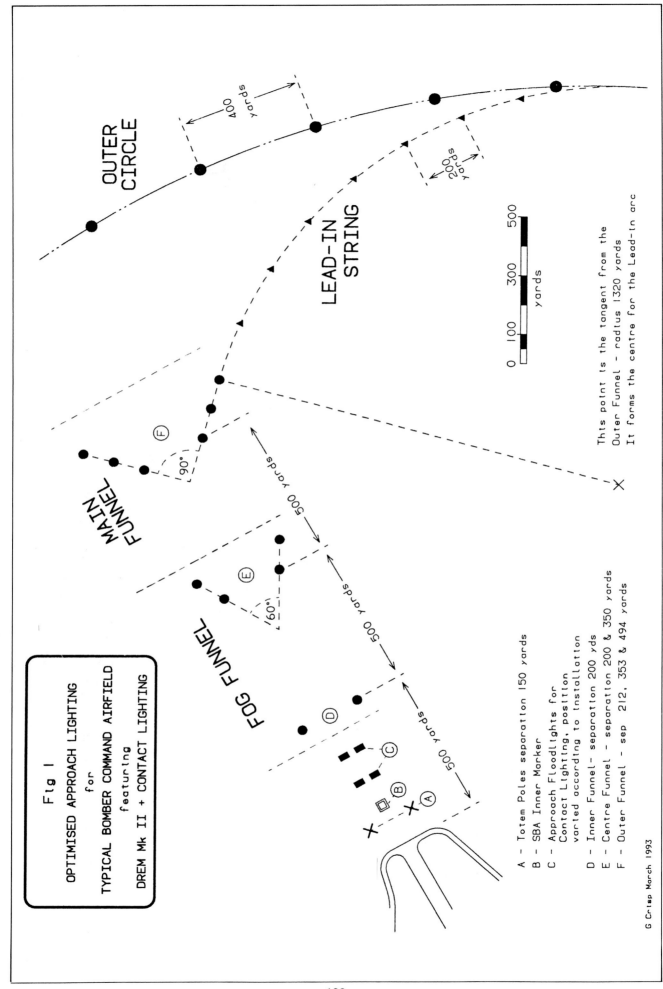

Fig I
OPTIMISED APPROACH LIGHTING
for
TYPICAL BOMBER COMMAND AIRFIELD
featuring
DREM Mk II + CONTACT LIGHTING

OUTER CIRCLE

400 yards

200 yards

LEAD-IN STRING

MAIN FUNNEL

FOG FUNNEL

90°

60°

500 yards

500 yards

500 yards

F

E

D

C

B

A

0   100   300   500

yards

This point is the tangent from the
Outer Funnel - radius 1320 yards
It forms the centre for the Lead-in arc

A - Totem Poles separation 150 yards
B - SBA Inner Marker
C - Approach Floodlights for
      Contact Lighting, position
      varied according to installation

D - Inner Funnel - separation 200 yds
E - Centre Funnel - separation 200 & 350 yards
F - Outer Funnel - sep 212, 353 & 494 yards

G Crisp March 1993

138

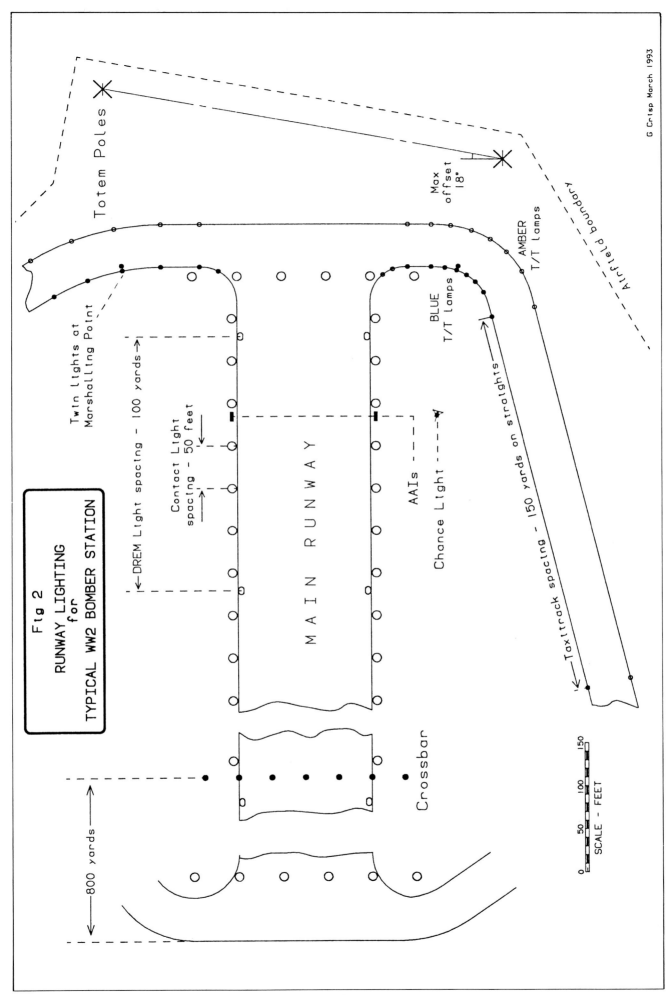

Fig 2
RUNWAY LIGHTING
for
TYPICAL WW2 BOMBER STATION

Totem Poles

Twin lights at Marshalling Point

Max offset 18°

AMBER T/T lamps

BLUE T/T lamps

Airfield boundary

MAIN RUNWAY

DREM Light spacing - 100 yards

Contact Light spacing - 50 feet

AAIs

Chance Light

Taxitrack spacing - 150 yards on straights

800 yards

Crossbar

SCALE - FEET

0   50   100   150

G Crisp March 1993

139

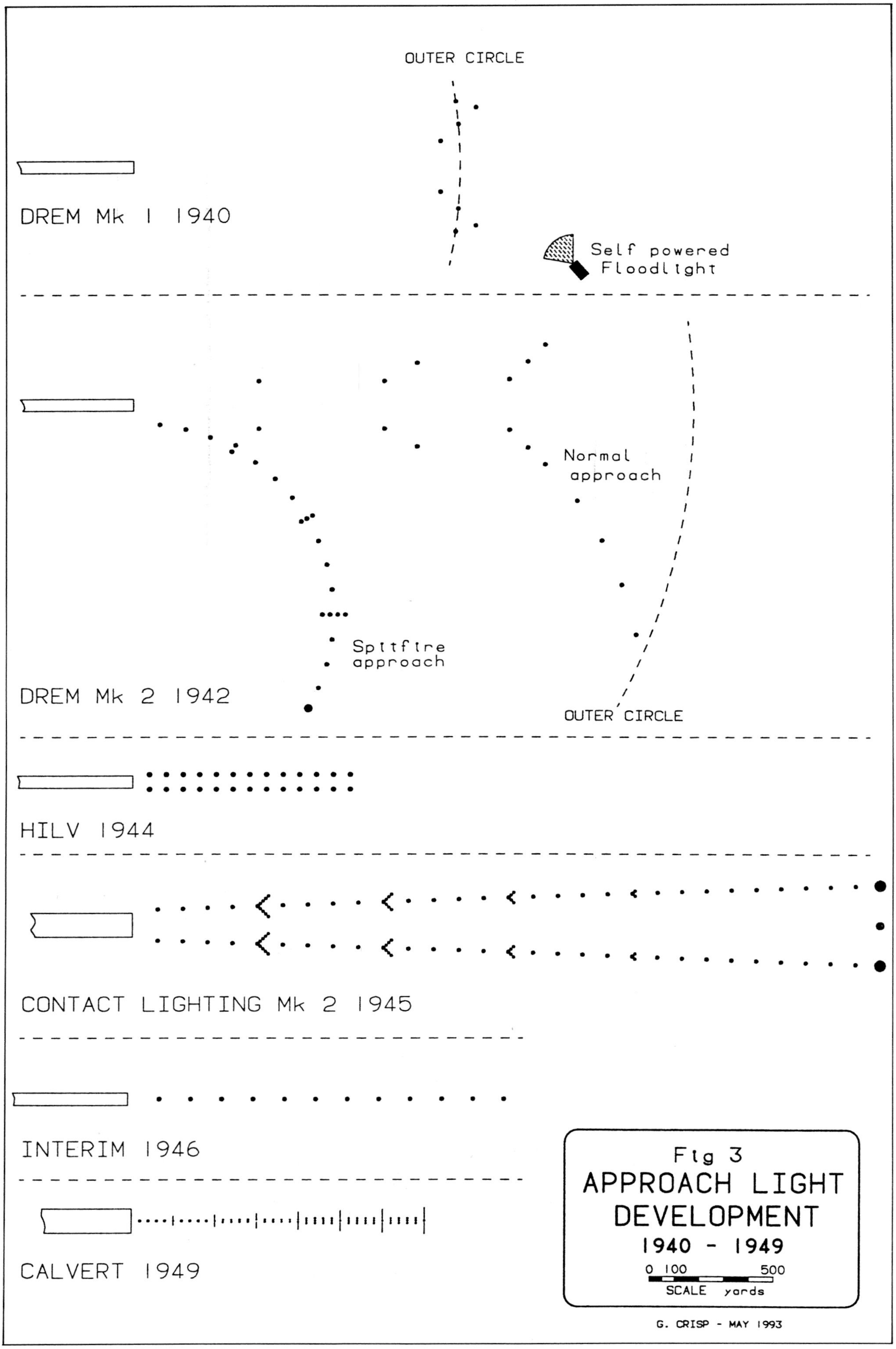

OUTER CIRCLE

DREM Mk I 1940

Self powered
Floodlight

Normal
approach

Spitfire
approach

DREM Mk 2 1942

OUTER CIRCLE

HILV 1944

CONTACT LIGHTING Mk 2 1945

INTERIM 1946

CALVERT 1949

Fig 3
APPROACH LIGHT
DEVELOPMENT
1940 - 1949

0 100   500
SCALE yards

G. CRISP - MAY 1993

140

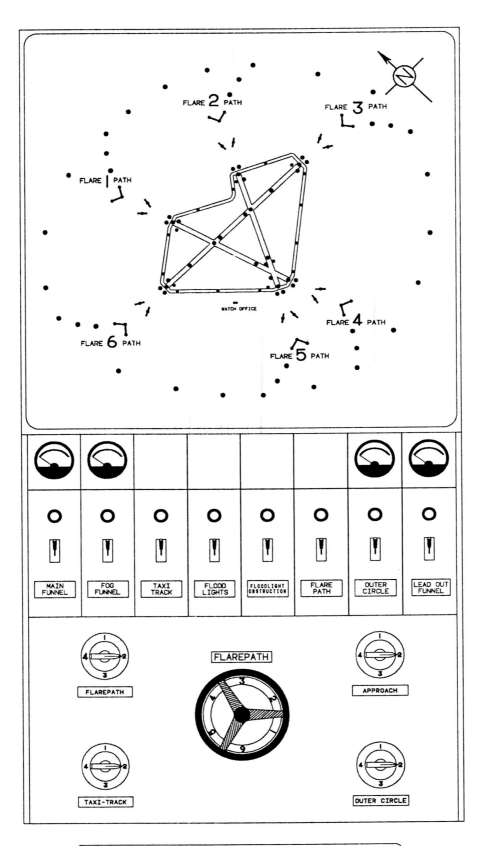

FLARE 2 PATH

FLARE 3 PATH

FLARE 1 PATH

FLARE 6 PATH

WATCH OFFICE

FLARE 4 PATH

FLARE 5 PATH

MAIN FUNNEL	FOG FUNNEL	TAXI TRACK	FLOOD LIGHTS	FLOODLIGHT OBSTRUCTION	FLARE PATH	OUTER CIRCLE	LEAD OUT FUNNEL

FLAREPATH

FLAREPATH

FLAREPATH

APPROACH

TAXI-TRACK

OUTER CIRCLE

Typical DREM Mk 2 Lighting Control Panel and mimic for Barford St. John

Fig 4

G Crisp March 1993

141

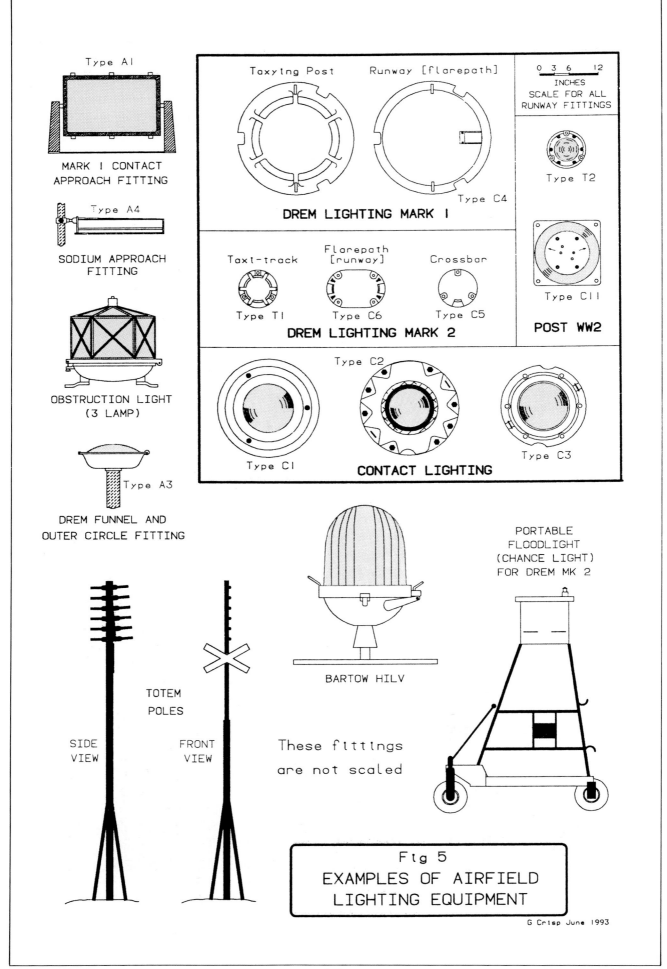

Type A1

MARK 1 CONTACT
APPROACH FITTING

Type A4

SODIUM APPROACH
FITTING

OBSTRUCTION LIGHT
(3 LAMP)

Type A3

DREM FUNNEL AND
OUTER CIRCLE FITTING

Taxying Post   Runway [flarepath]

DREM LIGHTING MARK 1

Type C4

0 3 6   12
INCHES
SCALE FOR ALL
RUNWAY FITTINGS

Type T2

Type C11

Taxi-track   Flarepath
[runway]   Crossbar

Type T1   Type C6   Type C5

DREM LIGHTING MARK 2

POST WW2

Type C2

Type C1   CONTACT LIGHTING   Type C3

TOTEM
POLES

SIDE
VIEW

FRONT
VIEW

These fittings
are not scaled

BARTOW HILV

PORTABLE
FLOODLIGHT
(CHANCE LIGHT)
FOR DREM MK 2

Fig 5
EXAMPLES OF AIRFIELD
LIGHTING EQUIPMENT

G Crisp June 1993

142

APPENDIX
List of Sources and References

Periodicals

Flight

9 May 1930	8 July 1937
11 Sep. 1931	2 Feb. 1939
1 July 1932	12 Nov. 1942
15 July 1932	11 July 1946
1 Feb. 1934	19 Sep. 1946
30 Jan. 1936	20 Mar. 1947
21 May 1936	16 Apr. 1954
21 Jan. 1937	2 July 1954
28 Jan. 1937	10 Dec. 1964

Aeronautics

August 1946
May 1951
February 1952

Aircraft Engineering

December 1936

Aviation News

8–21 Feb. 1985
18–31 Oct. 1985
7–20 Aug. 1987

Books

Air Publications

3236 (Works) 1956
3024/7 1951
3024/7 1962
En-route Document 1964
Radio Facility Charts 1952

The Civil Engineer at War, 1947

Aeronautics – A complete Guide to Civil and Military Flying, Vol. IV

A History of RAF Shawbury – Aldon P. Ferguson

Attack Warning Red – Derek Wood

The Air Pilot, 1937

Practical Flying, 1918

Action Stations 3 and Action Stations 7, D. Smith

Aeroplane Radio Equipment – Institution of Mechanical Engineers, 1940.

The End – Desborough Watch Office 13726/41. Photo: Fred Cubberley